REVELATIONS

By Nick van der Leek

Copyright (c) 2014 by Nick van der Leek

All rights reserved. No part of this book may be used, reproduced or transmitted in any form or by any means, electronic or mechanical, including photocopying, recording, or by any information storage or retrieval system, without the written permission of the author, except where permitted by law, or in the case of brief quotations embodied in critical articles and reviews.

Cover design: Nick van der Leek

Explanations, Rationalisations and Acknowledgements

If some questions are not acknowledged but the state prosecutor, or the court, we must ask, *why not*? Is it because they can't be proven, or is it because by asking these questions it puts counsel (and possibly even the court itself) in a bad light?

The reader is encouraged to check off the '14 Unanswered Questions' as and when they are raised in court. If they are raised, the reader should evaluate whether these are indeed answered (or in some cases, even addressed) to our satisfaction in court. Why to our satisfaction? Isn't that arrogance? Not at all, as society we have an interest in this case, and we need to be satisfied that the standards of the law and the standards of justice meet our standards. The law in fact is based in part on the modern or contemporary consensus of society; on what is sociable acceptable, what are the norms for behaviour, and when these fine lines are crossed.

We're paying attention to this case because we want to understand why this terrible incident took place, and how this can – and does – happen, all too often. We live in a dangerous society. Just how dangerous is one of the key *REVELATIONS* in this narrative.

Just as the three chapters on motive were added at the last moment to complete *RESURRECTION* (following Peet Van Zyl's groundbreaking testimony), so too was *REVELATIONS* fast-tracked to become the fourth narrative in this series, rather than the fifth, as originally planned.

The reader who has been attending to each of these narrative in turn will realise book four was originally going to be *RESTITUTIO*. However a series of eye-opening events scuttled those plans. Sometimes we must let go of the life we have planned, so as to accept the one that is waiting to be lived (or written) to paraphrase Joseph Campbell.

In this vein, Book four has been timed for release just prior to the State's presentation of final argument on August 7.

I would like to make it absolutely clear from the outset, that while *RECIDIVIST ACTS* and *RESURRECTION* both dealt exhaustively with all things Oscar, *REVELATIONS* – although the first three and last chapters hone in on Oscar with the same precision focus – a few of the chapters are *not* all about Oscar. The merits of the case are carefully calibrated, especially in the first and last chapters, and plenty of *REVELATIONS* and stubborn mysterious emerge and persist (as the case may be) throughout those pages.

But the trial is also about to wrap up and so, having dedicated two full narratives to Oscar-Oscar-Oscar, I felt it time for this narrative to look beyond the Pretoria High Court. Let's look at society. Let's look at ourselves. Look at me, look at yourself. Let's not lose our sense of humor, but let's also get serious. Let's look at issues such as gun ownership, crime, collusion, objectification and what it means to live in South Africa. The reader may be interested in the slew of REVELATIONS that emerge in this area. I have to admit, some of the shockers I uncovered shook me to the core. Here's one.

Cape Town is the world's 20th most violent city.

The remaining top 19 are all South American cities.

Bet you didn't know that? I didn't either.

So I invite the reader to join me in stepping outside of the 'Strictly Come Oscar' narrative just long enough that we can gather a broad background, and then bring it back, and apply our insights – sometimes very global insights – to the finalising of this case. Please trust me. I promise you if you join me on the magic carpet of this narrative and you rub your eyes, and find yourself floating over Mesopotamia, there *is* a method to my madness. And I *will* bring you back to the case carrying treasures that are going to be necessary and useful.

Rub the magic lamp and the genie we've gone to fetch will float out. Ask the genie a question and what will we get? That's right: *REVELATIONS.*

Now, some of the first readers to complete this narrative have commented that the analysis I've done on crime actually supports Oscar's case. My response to that is that I don't have an agenda. I am not trying to make Oscar's case, or break it. I am simply shining a light, and using my curiosity, my education, Google and raw intellect to follow the rabbit holes, *wherever* they may lead.

As we go spelunking we may tunnel our way into the fabulous Maze of Collusion, an unseen network of subterranean corridors that convey the world's treasures and freights. We may fall into holes, and minefields, and raft the odd flood. Why does it have to be all about Oscar all the time? So yes, I have added social topics and commentary to the central chapters. Be patient, take a breath and push Oscar to one side for just a moment. Do that and we might just learn something! As pointed out previously, there are rhymes and reasons behind these writings – trust them!

Now, let's get through the acknowledgements and get this show on the road.

REVELATIONS is the fourth of five narratives on the Oscar Pistorius Murder Trial. It would not have been possible without the encouragement, support and commitment of several people. Megan Dale, Margaret Taylor, Vernon Baumann and Terry Wittwen – high fives for your reviews, suggestions, endorsements and general enthusiasm.

A special shout out goes to *Juror13* who has assisted me tirelessly from America, especially with the final (and arguably the toughest) research sections of this work.

I've made extensive reference here to Hagen Engler, Justin Divaris, Prof Tim Noakes and the efforts of numerous other writers, especially Ernest Becker. I hope I haven't quoted Becker too liberally.

There's a reason a narrative like this – *REVELATIONS* - needs to exist. A counterfeit narrative exists in the public domain. The only way to answer a counterfeit narrative *is* to counter it, which is what this narrative seeks to do. It must be emphasised at this point that very many media houses, editors and journalists were contacted with the information contained not only in REVELATIONS, but its precursors too. Most completely ignored the information presented here. A recent example is Rapport running a front page splash on Sunday 3 August, 2014, on Oscar's brother's 'serious car accident'. Is that how the media interrogates this trial? What's next? Uncle Arnold slipping on a banana peel? If I sound flippant, I'm not. I'm wondering if the media is flippant, and I'm wondering, just how flippant they can be? Or is the media flippant because they're simply serving the fickle tabloid tastes of the public?

Recently YOU/Huisgenoot turned down a story I offered them on motive in favour of discussing Oscar's feelings of worthlessness. The question is why? Why would media houses be interested in such soft, flimsy narratives? The answer may have something to do with:

a) A poorly informed, clumsily patched together media framework, beholden to money, beholden to a fickle readership most of all, beholden to the mere possibility of their cash cow undergoing RESURRECTION (in the legal sense, if no other)
b) A poorly informed media not fully aware of what reporting a case such as this involves, and thus easily cowed by threats, or implied, or imputed threats of litigation
c) A highly informed, highly strategic media machine, incentivised to drag a story out, for as long as possible, milking it for every possible cent.

REVELATIONS tackles this particular issue – the culpability and possible *collusion* of the media – in much finer detail.

Let's face it, consistent effort, leveraged by global media, has put Oscar's (I think) invalid narrative in place to begin with. What counterevidence is there to correct, and contradict, the extraordinary imbalances in these narratives? I will leave it to the *conscientious* reader – who also deserves special mention, and special acknowledgment – to evaluate whether *REVELATIONS* delivers on its promise.

*[**DISCLAIMER:** The entire contents of this narrative, though based in many instances on fact, and rooted in many instances in reality, are nevertheless speculations. Are they useful? Are they newsworthy? You be the judge.]*

Table of Contents

Explanations, Rationalisations and Acknowledgements 3
    14 Unanswered Questions 7
1. What exactly happened on 14 February 2013 at 286 Bushwillow Crescent, Silver Woods? 9
2. Is instant forgiveness justified? 12
3. Oscar's phone + Reeva's phone 15
4. Did Michelle Burger hear shouts of "help help help" after shots? 17
5. What was the 'shitty thing'? 18
6. Were there jeans on the lawn? 19
7. Is there a recording of Oscar's call to Netcare? If so, where is it, if not why not? 22
8. So what *is* his defence? 28
9. Is Oscar a unique athlete/an exceptional talent? 37
10. Did Reeva accept the invitation to go to Manchester, Brazil or Italy? 42
11. Was the media culpable? 53
12. Legacy Lifestyle…is it Objectification, and is Objectification evil? 72
13. Crime in SA – a credible threat? 83
14. Is Oscar guilty of premeditated Murder? 90
Sex Kitten? 104
Sex and Death 107
Love and Death 107
Glass Houses 118
Sultans of Spin 129
Crime in South Africa – up close and personal 156
Jail Time and Injustice 174
Author's Final Note: 192
The Method – and the Madness 194
Clinical Version of 'The Incident' 195
About the Author 235

14 Unanswered Questions

The ultimate aim of the (heroes') quest must be neither release nor ecstasy for oneself, but the wisdom and the power to serve others. – Joseph Campbell

Now we get to the heart of the trial. Evidence has been led. We have heard in detail the state's case, the defence's case, and how each in turn has cross-examined, tested and re-examined evidence, information and assumptions. At the end of all of that, we, society, must ask ourselves if that exhaustive analysis was sufficiently exhaustive. And we do that by checking the case against the unanswered questions that have arisen as a result.

Note: Liezl Thom, who calls herself *Journalist, Author, Presenter, Producer, Mother, Wife and Proud South African. Stubbornly Optimistic. Madly in Love with Life* has suggested a few questions of her own:

>*so many unanswered questions. why did the cops tell us there were text messages between her and Hougie but no evidence in court?*

>*why was no evidence lead wrt the bullet hole in his bedroom door? And*

>*why nothing said about the blood spatters above the bed?*

But I have not touched on any of these. I am not a private investigator, a cellphone wizard or a psychic. The point is there are many unanswered (and unanswerable) questions. I am going to focus only on those questions we at least have a hope of answering. And by answering them, perhaps we'll find ourselves on the path to *Revelations*.

Here are the 14 Unanswered Questions in bullet-point form:
1. **What exactly happened on 14 February 2013 at 286 Bushwillow Crescent, Silver Woods?**
2. **Is instant forgiveness justified?**
3. **Oscar's phone + Reeva's phone**
4. **Did Michelle Burger hear shouts of "help help help" <u>after</u> shots?**
5. **What was the 'shitty thing'?**
6. **Were there jeans on the lawn?**
7. **Is there a recording of Oscar's call to Netcare? If so, where is it, if not why not?**
8. **So what is his defence?**
9. **Is Oscar a unique athlete/an exceptional talent?**
10. **Was the media culpable? - Is there a <u>personal cost</u> to perpetuating a fake persona (to the media, to society, to the celebrities themselves, and to us as individuals)?**
11. **Did Reeva accept the invitation to go to Manchester, Brazil or Italy?**
12. **Legacy Lifestyle/Daytona Group/FHM/Nike/Oakley/tattoos …is it all Objectification, and is Objectification Evil?**

13. Crime in SA – a credible threat?
14. Is Oscar guilty of premeditated Murder?

The reader should use the questions provided in brief above and detailed below as a checklist to interrogate both the state's and defence's case. At the end of the day, the entire narrative of events – especially those on 13/14 February 2013 needs to be presented, evaluated, tested and finally – pronounced upon. First and foremost by Judge Masipa herself.

We, as South Africans, can be proud of Gerrie Nel, Barry Roux and Judge Masipa, in their professional and top notch introduction of the legal process to you and me, all of us ordinary South Africans.

Most reasonable South Africans will agree that both counsels and Masipa are not only well educated, intelligent and also eloquent practitioners of the law, but also great respecters of the law, how it functions and interestingly, how it can be manipulated.

Although they have all given a stellar reckoning of themselves, we, society, must hold ourselves to the same standards. The same excellence. We do that by paying attention, listening and learning. And as we follow this case we ought to apply high standards to this case, via *our own* deductive process. I invite the reader now to join me in doing exactly that. So let's jump right into the meat of it:

1. What exactly happened on 14 February 2013 at 286 Bushwillow Crescent, Silver Woods?

On 10 April, 2014, a day that happened to be a Thursday, Gerrie Nel, the state prosecutor in the Oscar Pistorius Murder Trial revealed the state's case for the first time. It was exactly 14 months to the day since Reeva's violent death in the early hours of Valentine's Day 2013.

Essentially, the state has only gone so far to state that Oscar Pistorius had argued with his girlfriend, Reeva Steenkamp, and that she "ran away screaming".

Just this, arguing on the one hand, and one of the two occupants of the house attempting 'flight' (or escape) suggests abuse and entrapment. Let's be clear on this. It suggests:

one person as perpetrator/attacker/abuser and

the other as victim/defender/abused.

We already know that in the *schema* of this story, Reeva was trapped. This was the reality, whatever one's version is after the event. We also know, within the same *schema* that ultimately, Reeva was the *true victim*. It may seem like overstating the obvious, but the simple result of this conflagration was that Reeva lost her life in a toilet. She was in a defensive posture when she was shot to death behind a closed door. This indicates that she anticipated what was about to happen to her just before it happened. Her 'petrified' screams reinforce this impression.

Reeva's last moments would have been unfiltered horror. Imagine a door bursting (exploding) with fragments of wood, bullets tearing through one's body and smashing into the confined space around you, fragments of wood and bullets and tiles penetrating one's flesh from all sides. And then another bullet (in a dark room) and another, and another. A total of three bullets caused massive attrition to the young model, yet Reeva did not die immediately. Reeva expired a short time later, due to catastrophic blood loss (ie 'she bled out' on the floor upstairs, not at the bottom of the stairs – the last chapter reveals how/why we know this).

Let's be very specific on this issue: to what extent was Reeva – in fact – *the true victim* of this incident? Irrespective of motive, or what really transpired, what we can immediately see is that sometime after 03:10 (but probably very close to 03:17) Reeva weathered three catastrophic bullets to her slim body.

Each bullet tore through her tissues with such destructiveness that each bullet individually was sufficient to mortally wound her. Each bullet had the potential to kill her through attendant blood loss.

The reader will reflect that the first bullet fired was on target, and shattered her right hip, making it impossible for her to stand. The second on target (but actually the third bullet of the four) ripped with such ferocity through her arm a doctor described it as 'equivalent to an instant amputation'.

Carice Viljoen, Johan Stander's daughter made special mention of this wound (effectively an amputated arm) that was 'bleeding so much', and it was her suggestion to stop the massive blood loss from it.

The third (but in fact the fourth, and final bullet fired) was the most devastating of all. For a third time Oscar's ammunition of choice, the tissue-shattering black talon casing, ripped through the top of Reeva's skull and exited through the other side of her head (at the back) below her ear. The path of this last bullet through Reeva's critical sentient tissues would have reduced the possibility for her resuscitation to virtually zero. It may have impaired her functions, but she may still have maintained very limited speech function in her final moments even *after* sustaining the path of this fourth bullet through her head.

Via City Press: http://www.citypress.co.za/news/gerrie-nel-youre-trying-mr-pistorius-working/

State prosecutor Gerrie Nel today confirmed he was building a case that Oscar Pistorius had had an argument with Reeva Steenkamp and that she then "ran away screaming".

This is the first time Nel has confirmed that the state believes Steenkamp and Pistorius had argued and that she then ran away from him in fear.

Within this question of what happened is another: did the argument flare up spontaneously at 3am or was it a long process of escalation? Why was Oscar on his stumps?
One cogent line of reasoning is that Oscar woke up (was in bed, legs off) and heard Reeva in the toilet. He then rushed to find out what she was doing, and she then locked the door. Well, we know Reeva had a late dinner, and from more than one ear witness, that the argument actually lasted a long time, and then escalated dramatically. One neighbour (Estelle van der Merwe) testified:

Via CNN's Emily Smith: *Nel asks if the voice that irritated her was a man or a woman. Van der Merwe says she heard a woman's voice.*

The Guardian's David Smith: *Van der Merwe nervous and sometimes struggling to speak.*

Via CNN's Emily Smith: *Van der Merwe takes a moment to collect herself. She says she heard people talking, then it stopped, then they talked again. It wasn't continuous talking. She says it sounded like two people who were involved in an argument but she couldn't hear the other person's voice.*

Via CNN's Emily Smith: *Nel: What happened to the voice you heard? Van der Merwe: After hearing the four sounds it was total silence.*

Via CNN's Emily Smith: *Shortly after the commotion she says she heard someone crying loudly.*

Let's summarise:
1. Long period of talking, arguing, very late at night/early hours of the morning.
2. The jarring of the woman's voice irritated her, she could not always hear the man's voice.
3. Four shots (exactly four), then silence.
4. Then a commotion (commotion may refer to attempts to break down door physically and with bat, ie banging and also Oscar shouting subsequently, but unclear.
5. After commotion someone (male or female)
6. crying loudly. Crying, not shouting or screaming.

This book, REVELATIONS, simply touches on this question – what really happened that night. The final chapter attempts to provide a full and final version to answer this question. The answer – it must be noted – needs to integrate all the (apparently) conflicting testimonies, times, noises and versions (including Oscar's) to be considered credible.

It is the author's position that the true 'revelation' of this book, is the description of the Incident itself in the final chapter. Arguably it may be the first and best exposition ever, better than any versions espoused thus far by the media, and better (in the sense of a complete, and finely-tuned narrative) than has been presented in court by *either* the prosecutor or the defence. Hubris? Time will tell!

2. Is instant forgiveness justified?

Curiously, at the time of writing [July 13, 2014 at exactly 6pm], two and a half weeks before the state's closing arguments would commence, Oscar broke his 5 month twitter silence. He tweeted three self-reinforcing (i.e. brand building) motifs. The first invoked religious themes:

pic.twitter.com/PHkiBF2KHn

the second was clipped from Viktor Frankl's memoirs of the Holocaust

pic.twitter.com/UFxSHfpavj

while the third invoked an appeal for societal solidarity:

pic.twitter.com/9e2fykp2E8

What Oscar conveyed to us essentially was:

*Psalm 34:18: The Lord is close to the **broken hearted**.*
*The **salvation** of man is **through love** and in love.*
***You have the ability** to make a difference in someone's life. Sometimes it's the simple things you say or do that can **make someone feel better** or **inspire** them*

So the message is very simple:

1. Oscar is sorry, and sad.
2. He deserves our love, this will be how we 'save' him (we must also bestow on *him* salvation/acceptance as part of our duty to humanity)
3. If we grant him a reprieve, in exchange he can and will resume his good work as someone who makes people feel better about themselves, ie acts as an inspiration.

In other words, the entire basis of this is emotional. We must feel sorry for Oscar, and this justifies our forgiving him. But there's a problem with his concept of salvation. It's not biblical; in fact a more astute version of how we attain 'salvation' (rescue from our troubles/sins) comes via Joseph Campbell:

It's only when a man tames his own demons that he becomes the king of himself if not of the world.

Has Oscar tamed his demons? Is he king of himself? Or does he simply wish to be reinstated as king of the world regardless?

Let's backup for a moment and look at where this 'religious fervour' comes from. It seems to be part and parcel of the philosophical fabric of the Pistorius Clan. Yes, it's real:

[Leonard] *Carr highlighted Pistorius' relationship with God as also noteworthy because of its apparent focus on "what God can do for him". Christianity is clearly a major priority of the Pistorius family, with the Twitter feeds of siblings Carl and Aimee prominently featuring Bible verses and expressions of religious fervour. Pistorius said on Monday that one of the things he liked about Steenkamp was that, as a strong Christian, Reeva "would pray for me every night" – though he did not mention whether this gesture was reciprocated on his part.* – Rebecca Davis, via http://www.dailymaverick.co.za/article/2014-04-10-analysis-will-the-real-oscar-pistorius-please-stand-up/#.U8LniRCSxOg

The question of forgiveness may seem an absurdly simple question with an absurdly obvious answer. Except neither is true. What we know is that Reeva's closest family (her father and mother, her cousin and uncle) basically extended instant clemency to Oscar, before they even knew the merits of the case. Why did they do so? Because of their own Christian convictions. This is of course wonderful news for Oscar. If Reeva's family can forgive him, why shouldn't we? After all, he's apologised. Surely that's enough?

Actually an apology for shooting someone to death is hardly enough. An apology, let's be absolutely clear, is not even an admission of wrong doing, and Oscar has been very careful to maintain that he did not intend to unlawfully kill. But then he contradicted himself, conceding he did have an intention to kill, and to do so unlawfully (we'll get to this more specifically later on.)

In RESURRECTION I mentioned, briefly, why forgiveness on the face of it, may seem morally good, but *ethically* indefensible. While one individual may feel a sense of beatific equanimity in extending clemency to a murderer (criminal/accused), and whilst this may help them sleep at night, this is not healthy for society. Why? Because in a society with a criminal element, failure to prosecute perpetuates recidivism.

Simply put: If a criminal commits an act, and you grant immediate clemency, what you do is excuse the act. Perhaps the intention is to behave within Christine doctrine, but let's face it, forgiveness of sin (especially murder) is God's business. The reason our societies have legal systems are to bring lawless (and mischievous) individuals and violators in line with the mores of society. In other words, it is good and right that those who break the law are punished. It is not good and right that we immediately and universally grant absolution to criminals (or accused persons) simply to assure our own 'rightness' with God. If one is going to bring Christianity into it (and this will be discussed in detail in due course), bear in mind:

The incident that riles Jesus Christ *the most* involves money changers. Merchants greedily going about their commerce, pursuing their *business* in the temple. Let's look at that for a second:

- Merchants
- Commerce
- Greed

Here's a picture:

http://en.wikipedia.org/wiki/Money_changers#mediaviewer/File:CastingoutMoneyChangers.jpg

Marcus Aurelius once said that *poverty is the mother of crime*. And 1Timothy 6:10: *For the love of money is a root of all kinds of evil. Some people, eager for money, have wandered from the faith and pierced themselves with many griefs.*

Is Oscar *eager* for money? Is he someone who deals with merchants, commerce, greed yet associates his life, and how he lives it, with the temple? Well, have a look at this infographic to appreciate the Pistorius' involvement in Empire building:

http://www.nickvanderleek.com/2014/07/the-pistorius-dynasty.html

Now, in the final chapter, dealing with the incident itself, the allegation will be made that the motive, the trigger behind the shooting, was to stop a phone call from taking place behind a closed (locked door). Say what? Yes, and the reason that phone call had to be prevented at absolutely all <u>costs</u> was the imputed terror of *lost income*, losing vast amounts of treasure, having a persona eclipsed by allegations of abuse, and thus *enormous revenues wiped out* in a heartbeat.

poverty is the mother of crime

Some people, eager for money, have wandered from the faith

love of money is a root of all kinds of evil

No compare these biblical tenets to Oscar's verse of choice:

The Lord is close to the broken hearted.

Well, it doesn't take a genius to see that broken-heartedness evokes a sympathy card, the 'ag shame' response, but what's left *unvoiced* is why Oscar is broken hearted? It's important to give a voice to it, so let's do it. Oscar is broken hearted (we imagine) because:

- He has shot to death someone he loved and someone who, we are led to believe, *truly* loved him
- He regrets how his life has changed and is broken hearted because he wishes to continue inspiring people

Can I be absolutely <u>fucking</u> clear on this point: Killing someone and being sorry about it isn't going to cut it. Not even close. And those who fall over themselves to extend clemency ought to visit a morgue for a morning, and have a look at the reality of a dead body, one that has bled to death. They should stand over the corpse and then make their generous proclamations of compassion.

3. Oscar's phone + Reeva's phone

Why was Oscar's phone not seized at the scene?

Why was Oscar's phone not seized for two weeks after the incident?

What was the final cellular activity on Reeva's phone?

Why did Oscar pick up her phone after dragging her body out the toilet?

What were Reeva's final whatsapp messages?

What happened to the allegations that Oscar was surfing porn?

> There was great excitement among journalists in the gallery on the arrival of police data analyst, Colonel Mike Sales, one of three policemen who flew to the United States earlier this year to meet with Apple to gain access to information on Pistorius's iPhone.
>
> Sales downloaded data from two iPads found in Pistorius's house, including web history and bookmarks.
>
> The iPad 3 he analysed only included browser history for the day of February 13 2013 up to 9pm. Records displayed showed several searches relating to cars and the last two items were a Google search for "free mobile porn" and a site called "youjizz."
>
> http://www.timeslive.co.za/local/2014/03/19/the-oscar-pistorius-murder-trial-day-13

Well, I can provide two answers to those questions, the first courtesy of *Juror13* and the second courtesy of Barry Bateman:

1. **20:04:17 – Reeva's last GPRS activity – 41,029 seconds (over 11 hours) – tower closest to Oscar's. This application remained opened throughout the incident and in to the next day. No details of what this application was, or its contents, were openly discussed in court. The Judge however does have access to this information.**

We also know via Cecil Myers (father of Reeva's best friend Gina Myers) that both father and daughter received an SMS from Reeva sometime between 22:00 and 22:30. The above factoid from *Juror13* doesn't necessarily include or exclude the SMS as part of the above GPRS activity. In order to address this question I have invited several experts in this area to comment, including Aki Anastasiou, however they did not wish to do so.

2. @barrybateman Barry Did #OscarPistorius slip up by saying,'wanted to know why Reeva was calling the Police'?
   (17.02) https://www.youtube.com/watch?v=l_hle5shsDY

   If you listen closely, Nel wants to know why Oscar was screaming, and in reply, Oscar's exact words are:

"I wanted to ask why...if she's phoning the police."

Because wasn't that what she was threatening to do?

4. Did Michelle Burger hear shouts of "help help help" after shots?

Dr. Johan Stipp and Oscar himself both testified to Oscar's shouting 'Help Help Help' after four shots were fired. Burger, when quizzed, explained these shouts as 'a mockery'. However she did not specifically state, as far as this writer has been able to ascertain, that the male voice shouted 'help help help' after the four gunshots.

This may not seem important, however it is of crucial import when piecing together the Incident itself, as it probably happened.

It should be noted though, that even without Burger's confirmation, both the state and the defence agree (via Stipp and Oscar) that the calls for help by Oscar occurred after the four shots were fired. This is another critical admission by Oscar. Why? All will be revealed in the final chapter, which explores the incident in detail.

5. What was the 'shitty thing'?

"To live fully is to live with an awareness of the rumble of terror that underlies everything." — Ernest Becker

In RESURRECTION it's established that whatsapp messages on 13th February suddenly change tone.

Reeva sends the following message on Wednesday: *"It's difficult to try and console you, it's a shitty thing and you're a nice guy..."*

What was the 'shitty thing'? Was it that Reeva wouldn't be involved in his career (as per instructions from Capacity Relations)? Was it that she would not be going with him to Brazil or Manchester, and so the 'shitty thing' was that he'd be travelling alone, for months. Is this why he needed 'consoling?'

6. Were there jeans on the lawn?

There's been speculation on some forums about a second pair of jeans lying outside (below the toilet window) on the lawn. Is it true? If so, did any other witnesses see it?

> http://forums.digitalspy.co.uk/showthread.php?t=1954969&page=179

Author's Note: *Juror13,* based in the USA, does a fine analysis of the trial (and incidentally, other high profile court cases) on her blog:

www.juror13lw.wordpress.com

> There is one thing I want to dig at, with *Juror13*'s assistance, above all:
>
>> is there definite information about the jeans on the lawn? Is it just hearsay? Or is it a matter of record/fact?

This is *Juror13*'s response, verbatim:

> *The jeans on the ground outside are not hearsay. When the official police photographer, Van Staden, was on the stand, these photographs were entered in to evidence. I have attached them for you to see however the quality is not great. I think I have better ones at home.*
>
> *In the first photo, you can see the toilet room window up above (the smaller window) and a dog standing below on the ground. The blue jeans are just behind the dog, to give you a point of reference. The second photograph is a close up of the jeans.*

So now we see it's <u>not</u> a case of jeans on the <u>lawn</u> but jeans outside, lying on the <u>paving</u> beside the lawn, directly below the toilet window.

Van Staden was not questioned by Nel about these jeans, nor was Oscar.

Great – more unanswered questions! Why not?

> [The images of the jeans] *were simply submitted as evidence along with the other crime scene photos for the Judge to view. Who knows if Nel will bring them up in closing, but since he didn't question anybody about them, I think he would have to tread lightly on any assertions he tries to make. (I think).*

Is he saving this for his closing arguments? Can he? I guess we'll have to wait and see. *Juror13* speculates:

> *My only guess as to why Nel didn't ask anybody is because the State has no clue why they are there, and <u>you always open up a can of worms when you ask questions that you don't know the answer to!</u> Maybe he felt it was better left untouched.*

They are clearly women's jeans. Therefore, they are either Reeva's jeans or another woman's jeans. That brings up several different questions:

1. *Were they thrown out of the window or were they left on the ground from outside?*
2. *Who put them/threw them there?*
3. *Were they actually left somewhere else outside and the dog dragged them to that point?*
4. *Do they belong to another woman? If they do and Reeva found them, did she throw them out in the midst of an argument about Oscar possibly cheating?*

We know that Mrs. van der Mewre heard arguing (a loud woman's voice) from 1:56am to 3am, off and on. Her house is situated in front of Oscar's, across the street and to the left (from an aerial perspective). On my blog, I have included maps/photos of where each individual ear witness was located in relation to Oscar's house.

*To me, Mrs. van der Mewre being the only one that heard the fighting, means that Oscar and Reeva were likely fighting in one of the rooms in the **front** of the house - the kitchen and the foyer are in the front. Reeva having food in her stomach suggests her/them being downstairs sometime very late in the evening/early morning. OR... maybe they were outside. Do those jeans support them being outside at some point during the incident? It's just a thought.*

If one considers how neatly packed Reeva's bag was, and that she was wearing Oscar's shorts (wasn't she?) it's possible that she tried to leave but was prevented in some way. Remember, her car was parked outside on the driveway. Did Oscar prevent her from changing into her other pair of jeans? Did *Oscar* throw the lighter pair of jeans out of the window? But we also know some of Reeva's toiletries were found in the bathroom. Oscar may have taken these out of her bag and placed them there, or Reeva may have wanted to leave and been prepared to leave them there. Either way, the jeans, the busted silver panel in the bathroom, the shot into the locked bedroom door, the front door unlocked, the blood spatter on the bedroom wall, the bathroom window open, the many ear witness accounts of shouting, screaming, crying, talking and arguing and the cricket bat marks on the toilet door all seem to sketch a portrait of a protracted domestic dispute. In sum, yes, Reeva probably wanted to leave and Oscar – for whatever reason – felt he could not let her go.

We also know that Mrs. Stipp testified that the screams that occurred a little later after 3am, right before the gunshots, <u>sounded like they were getting closer</u>[my emphasis]. *She even wondered if somebody was coming down the street. Based on all of the ear witnesses' testimony, there was clearly <u>movement</u>* [my emphasis] *during this fight/incident. Reeva and Oscar were not in one place the whole time. I feel very certain of that. That is why it's such an oddity to me that Oscar "apparently" was on his stumps during the shooting. If they had been awake and fighting, and moving around, I think it's so unlikely that he would be on stumps. I've often wondered if he had his legs on, but was kneeling during the shooting to give that lower trajectory. But that is not the State's position.*
Below is a link to the part where Van Staden shows the pics of OP's back yard that were entered in to evidence. Start the video at 18:00.

<u>https://www.youtube.com/watch?v=ovA-k3pO3Dk</u>

One other side note (unrelated to the jeans) about the <u>ladders</u> [my emphasis] that were found outside. Van Rensburg, the first officer/leader of the police who arrived on the scene, testified that when he walked out on to the bedroom balcony, he could see the ladders down below. In the third pic that I attached, the ladders seen on the ground appear to be close to the bathroom windows. There has been some confusion about this online as far as were the ladders under the bedroom window or under the bathroom window. The answer is actually neither.

The bathroom windows are to the right of the ladders and OP's bedroom balcony is to the left around the corner of the wall. If you walk out on to OP's bedroom balcony and go all the way to the left, you can see around the corner of the wall to that back yard area where the ladders are just below. That's how I believe Van Rensburg saw the ladders. Just figured I'd mention it in case it comes up in your research.

And in the fourth pic that I attached, the window that is circled in red, depicts the window that had a hole in the glass. This is the window on the ground floor, directly above the ladders. That hole had been there for some time. OP did not bother to get it fixed (further illustrating his <u>lack of concern</u>[my emphasis] for security). On the stand, he testified that he had bought the glass to repair it and was just waiting on his handy man to do the work. If an intruder had really been in the back yard, he would have just punched out the rest of that glass and hopped in that window. That would have been a piece of cake, especially with the ladders to stand on right there.

It's an interesting conversation that people have about the feasibility of OP really being that scared of a possible intruder. From everything I have read, it certainly seems like violent break-ins are an unfortunate part of culture in SA and I'm sure many people have had that fear at night. But the part that people miss is the rest of the story. They seem to stop there... he hears a noise at night, it's dark, he thinks it's an intruder, he acts. Yep, he's innocent. Ugh. But the story is FAR from that simple. Many of his supporters are completely ignoring the evidence of the case - the most damning being the ear witnesses and the ballistics evidence... and OP's own testimony!

7. Is there a recording of Oscar's call to Netcare? If so, where is it, if not why not?

[Disclaimer: In terms of written work, I am more an analyst and a compiler of data, rather than an investigator. In other words, I gather information and analyse it and then synthesise it and crystallise it into a – hopefully – cogent narrative. Investigative reporting is far more fact based, and hard news based. As such, the reader must bear in mind – especially in this section – that the information provided here is not 'investigative reporting' but a far more casual and often hypothetical synthesis of information.]

This information is copied and pasted directly from Netcare 911's own website [16 July 2014]:

Netcare 911 24 Hr Emergency Operations Centre

Netcare 911 leads the way in technology development with regards to emergency call taking and dispatching emergency resources in South Africa. Operating from Midrand, Johannesburg, the Netcare 911 24 hour Emergency Operations Centre has 100 seats and acts as the central liaison point for the management of all emergency situations.

One of the largest and most advanced Emergency Contact Centres in the southern hemisphere, this ?nerve? centre [note to the reader: these '?' were not inserted by the author] *utilizes the skills of trained Emergency Call Agents and Resource Coordinators to manage any pre-hospital emergency and Inter-Facility transfers.*

Registered Nurses, Paramedics and Medical Officers further enhance our service offering by using international triage (prioritizing) systems and custom-built South African systems to assess non life-threatening and inter-facility calls.

*Satellite tracking of all Emergency Vehicles in the fleet is integrated into mapping systems and a custom built Integrated Call Taking (ICT) and Integrated Dispatch System (IDS), which ensures the closest and **most appropriate response to every emergency call received*** [emphasis mine]. *Computer Telephony Integration further enhances the service offering to Netcare 911 clients by enabling demographic and contact information to be on hand in the event of an emergency call received from a **client pre-loaded on our database***. [emphasis mine].

As Africa?s [note to the reader: this '?' was not inserted by the author] *leading EMS provider, the investment in IT development and infrastructure, enables Netcare 911 to provide accurate measurement and reporting of actual response times to an emergency ?* [note to the reader: this '?' was not inserted by the author] *from the time a call is answered in the 24 Hour Emergency Operations Centre, to the time the appropriate resources arrive on scene.*

A custom-built Disaster Recovery Centre ensures business continuity and service delivery.

Digital voice recording of all telephone lines ensures an accurate audit of events [emphasis mine] *and allows for pro-active quality assurance and clinical governance.*

http://www.netcare911.co.za/live/content.php?Item_ID=4074

To attempt to answer this question - *Is there a recording of Oscar's call to Netcare?* - even more directly, at 12:06 and 12:09 on 16 July 2014, I made two calls from my personal cellphone to Netcare 911. The first call I made was to this number, appearing on Netcare's website:

Tel: 010 209 8009 (08:00-16:30)

The second to this number:

Netcare911 Head Office, Midrand

Telephone: +27 (0)10 209 8911

During the first call I briefly explained that I wanted to know if there was a voice recording of Oscar's Netcare 911 call (on 14 February 2013, at roughly 03:20)

The reader will recall:

At 03:19 he phoned Johan Stander to ask him for help as he was "struggling to pick her up".

He had already tried to phone for help on Steenkamp's phone in the toilet but did not know her password so had gone back to the room to fetch his own.

At 03:20 he called private ambulance service Netcare 911 and although he did not remember speaking to the operator, he remembered being told to take "Reeva to the hospital" and not wait.

He does not remember a call logged to security at 03:21. He ran downstairs to open the front door to let everyone in.

He went back up to the bathroom and picked Steenkamp up.

Here's the original report:
http://www.news24.com/SouthAfrica/Oscar_Pistorius/Oscar-tells-of-moments-after-shooting-arrest-20140409

Since there was no answer at Tel: 010 209 8009 (08:00-16:30) at 12:06 (midday in other words) I left a voicemail, including my number, who I am, why I am calling and a brief description. By 09:34 the following day (17 July), and the current time of writing, there was no call back to this inquiry.

I then called the second number, which is Netcare911's Head Office in Midrand, Johannesburg. The operator who took my call seemed just a run of the mill random operator. After hearing my request (simply to confirm that a recording of an emergency call existed) the call was transferred and dropped by itself (?) a few seconds later.

When I called back the same operator answered, I recognised her voice and asked to be transferred to a supervisor. I was placed on hold for about twenty seconds, and then the same operator came back on the line and said:

"They're not going to be able to help you with any details regarding Oscar Pistorius…"

An assumption must be made then, that a recording does in fact exist (or did exist). The reason these recordings are crucial is explained and dealt with in detail in the 911 Call Analysis I did for *RECIDIVIST ACTS*. These recordings are critical because they convey a real-time soundtrack of time-stamped audio, besides the 'realism' conveyed by the message itself. Vital to these messages are things that can't be faked (or accurately reproduced after the fact). Such as tone of voice. Urgency. And then what words are used in the actual call. And here Oscar's testimony is that the operator told him he should not wait for assistance, or attend to Reeva on the scene but:

"Take Reeva to the hospital"

In the *schema* of Oscar's own version, it doesn't take a trained paramedic to appreciate that if a genuine attempt was to be made to save Reeva Steenkamp's life, the first priority ought to have been to stem the massive blood loss she was suffering. A layman knows that anyone bleeding to that extent *should not be moved.*

The second priority is to treat the victim in situ, ie stem the bloodloss, and treat for shock and stabilise the victim.

It should be stressed here that if the intention – and motive – was to make sure Reeva did not live, did not in fact survive, would not be able to give any 'version' or 'testimony' then moving her first out of the toilet, and carrying her downstairs, and placing fingers in her mouth (in Oscar's own version she was still breathing shortly after sustaining the three bullet wounds) would make more sense. It should also be stressed that it was Oscar who insisted to the Stander's and to Stipp that Reeva be taken to hospital, and both Stander and Stipp (and Clarice Viljoen, Stipp's daughter) differed in what they saw as the best practical way to treat the injured Reeva Steenkamp (who was still alive at this point).

In fact Clarice Viljoen, as has been mentioned in some detail in *RECIDIVIST ACTS*, asked Oscar to fetch something to tie Reeva's arm "so it wouldn't bleed so much." It's unclear at this point who did fetch something to stem the blood loss, but what we do know is Oscar maintained a very careful vigilance over Reeva's dying body.

In the case of Stander and Stipp, recall Oscar's own testimony, insisting that Reeva be rushed to the hospital. Both Stander and his daughter wanted Oscar (wearing his prosthesis) to put Reeva down, and try to treat her on the scene first. Stipp later established, upon his arrival, that an ambulance had not yet been called. Once it was called Stander emphasised that the ambulance was on its way.

Recall that in the end Reeva – by his own version, and as per witnesses present – Reeva literally died in Oscar's arms. From his own version, at one stage (at the toilet) she wasn't breathing, but then she apparently started breathing again (at some unknown point) prompting Oscar to take her downstairs and get her to a hospital as soon as possible. She had to have been breathing otherwise why did Oscar have his fingers in her mouth (ostensibly to keep her airway open).

Now let's examine this part of his testimony and see if you notice something missing from his testimony:

http://ewn.co.za/2014/04/09/Oscar-Pistorius-trial-Reeva-died-while-I-was-holding-her

"I checked whether she was breathing. She wasn't. I picked her up and felt her blood run down my back."

He said he could see her arm was broken as he was pulling her out the bathroom.

"I pulled her out of the bathroom. I saw her phone in the toilet, and tried to call for help but didn't have the passcode."

Pistorius spoke slowly today in a soft voice and regularly paused as he kept his composure.

"I went back to my room, grabbed both my phones and ran back to Reeva. I called Johan Stander, a resident of the estate whom I'd become friends with, I called him to help me."

He said he couldn't pick Steenkamp up as he was scared he would hurt her more so he called Stander to help him.

"I called an ambulance service. I can't remember talking to them, but they told me not to wait for them. After speaking to the ambulance service, I ran downstairs to open the front door."

The athlete, who was sobbing and trying to hold his composure, said he ran back up to his bathroom, and picked Steenkamp up.

"I don't recall carrying her, but down the stairs the Standers arrived. I was shouting and screaming for them to help me get Reeva to the hospital. Stander told me to put Reeva down."

Pistorius said Stander had insisted they should get her to a hospital.

"I felt helpless waiting. I had my hand in her mouth to help her breathe and my hand on her hip to stop the bleeding."

Do you see it?

Have a quick squiz at his bail affidavit (16.16 and 16.17) and see if you notice something missing.

http://www.citypress.co.za/multimedia/full-document-oscar-pistorius-affidavit/

In his bail affidavit he refers to Netcare. Not once in his testimony in chief does he do the same. Not a single mention of Netcare, simply 'the ambulance' and 'the paramedics'. Who did arrive at the end of the day? Was it Netcare911? That also needs to be established for certain. What we know though is although Oscar claimed to have called them at 03:20, from his own version we also know that Stander and Stipp also both tried to call the ambulance. Here's the EWN report again:

Johan's daughter <u>Ms Stander</u> had then asked Pistorius for tape or rope so she could tie Steenkamp's arm. The Paralympian said Ms Stander told him Dr Stipp was coming to the scene.

Pistorius said he pleaded with <u>Stipp to help Reeva</u>. "It didn't seem like he knew what he was doing. He was overwhelmed."
He said Stipp had checked Reeva and left the house.

"She had already died while I was holding her, before the ambulance arrived."

In his testimony, he said he had stood back when the ambulance arrived. "The lady paramedic came to me, informed me that Reeva had passed."
<u>*The paramedic had asked for ID*</u> *and he had fetched it from Reeva's handbag in the bedroom which he claims he didn't go through.*

Interestingly from the report below (from TimesLive) we understand:

1. Oscar is asked (he has to be asked) by Paramedics to move away from Reeva's body

2. He keeps insisting to Carice Viljoen (incorrectly reported as 'Clarice' and Ms Stander at various times in the media) to take Reeva to hospital*

3. Viljoen tells him he should rather wait for paramedics to arrive.

Pistorius also called Netcare 911 and, when Stander and his daughter arrived, he shouted for them to help him get Steenkamp to a hospital but they told him to wait as an ambulance was on its way.

Pistorius testified that he had his one hand in Steenkamp's mouth to try and help her breathe and the other hand on her hip to try stem the bleeding, when a man, later identified to him as Silver Woods Estate resident Dr Johan Stipp, arrived but was unable to help him.

Paramedics then arrived and Pistorius was asked to move away from Steenkamp's body so they could work on her.

Pistorius said he screamed for Ms Stander to get Steenkamp to hospital, but she said to wait for the paramedics to arrive. He said he kept on insisting Ms Stander take Steenkamp to the hospital.

http://www.timeslive.co.za/local/2014/04/09/nel-set-to-crucify-pistorius-in-cross-examination

So simply around the question of "is there a Netcare911 voice recording" we have to also ponder:

1. Did Oscar call Netcare911 to begin with?
2. Did Oscar call ambulance services at all, to begin with?
3. Who did? Was it Stander, or Stipp? Stipp thus far, as state's witness, and a witness who tried to assist Reeva, appears to be the one who called the ambulance.
4. Why has this recording been glossed over by both the state and the defence (thus far)?
5. What is the significance of black bags under Reeva's body?
6. Stander said Oscar looked 'relieved' when he saw him. How does he know? Was it in his facial expression? Did he specifically cry, "I am so relieved to see you." I wonder if relief is appropriate when someone is bleeding to death and still dying?
7. The front door was open…why? Oscar says to let Stander in, but presumably with someone dying in your house, you open the door when you get to it. This polite and helpful opening of the door is a critical waste of time while Reeva is bleeding to death and apparently still breathing.
8. Oscar's car running?

In terms of the question 8, which I won't go into any detail here, what we see are allegations that Oscar wished to load Reeva's body in his brand new BMW (to…take her to hospital). One imagines (if you follow the debate at the link below) the black plastic bags, incredibly, were to make sure her bloodied body did not dirty the seats of his brand new car…

https://www.facebook.com/Justice4ReevaSteenkamp/posts/602248579853715

8. So what *is* his defence?

The best way to answer this, of course, is to ask Oscar. Which is what Barry Roux does. But listen to how Oscar doesn't really answer the question:

> http://nicolasvdl.podomatic.com/entry/2014-04-15T14_24_29-07_00
> My personal opinion of Oscar's defence is that it's simply "I made a mistake."

> http://www.iol.co.za/dailynews/news/you-made-a-mistake-1.1673364#.U8hnSxCSxOg

And Oscar's psychology is such that "a mistake" (even when one is dealing with the loss of a human life) is sufficient explanation. Furthermore, it would appear his Uncle Arnold and his entire family seem to support the idea that if you kill someone "by mistake" that's an acceptable excuse.

Actually, it isn't. Before we go into this question in finer detail, and before we really start to wade through all the Legalese, let's look at how Gerrie Nel interrogates Oscar on this idea of "a mistake' as a *sufficient reason* for shooting someone to death (through a door, using four bullets to execute that 'mistake'). First, let's remind ourselves what the word mistake means:

- Slip-up
- Error
- Gaffe
- Blunder
- Fault
- Inaccuracy

Do any of those words begin to describe *any version* of firing four bullets through a closed door with the presumption that a person is standing on the other side of the door?

If the reader feels this 'narrow' version – in writing – is skewing Oscar's narrative unfairly, let's examine how Oscar deals with the question when it is specifically (and repeatedly) put to him. Gerrie Nel does just this in the opening seconds of his cross-examination.

> https://www.youtube.com/watch?v=jvXf-N13xV4

The reader ought to heed Oscar's responses specifically between 0:30 and 0:50. Over the course of twenty seconds, half of which is Gerrie Nel speaking, Oscar repeats four times that he killed Reeva by mistake. That's an 'I made a mistake' *every 5 seconds*.

When Nel asks him to explain what he means by 'mistake', Oscar sums up his position by saying, in a soft, gentle tone:

> At 0:48: *"My mistake is that I took Reeva's life, My Lady."*

It almost sounds like he's admitting he took the judges pen when she wasn't paying attention.

"My mistake is that I took your pen, My Lady."

Oscar's *insistence* here is that 'taking someone's life' 'by mistake' is perfectly reasonable. Well, is it?

Nel emphasises the obvious, but it's a point worth stressing isn't it, given the absurdity of these answers.

> 1) Taking someone's life (ie killing someone) is *never* reasonable. One may act reasonably, but the actual *setup* that results in the death (especially when it happens through extreme violence, and due to lethal hollow point ammunition) of an innocent human being (whether in war, within rampant crime, or domestic violence) is *never* acceptable.
>
> 2) Killing someone (or as Oscar's puts it, 'I took Reeva's life') is not an ordinary, acceptable error. There may be extraordinary circumstances, but to kill someone, purposefully or accidentally, is – in either case – a very great tragedy. And in this case, clearly a travesty.

With my limited legal background Oscar's defence seems to be:

> 1. *'I thought someone was coming out to attack me.'* This is the so-called 'Swart Gevaar' defence - ie putative self defence against an imagined intruder. This is where one reasonably but unlawfully kills someone (by reasonably mistaking someone for an intruder)
>   http://constitutionallyspeaking.co.za/oscar-pistorius-criminal-law-101/
>
>   http://www.dailymaverick.co.za/article/2014-03-03-heart-of-oscars-defence-imagined-threat-of-a-black-stranger/#.U8ZfpxCSxOg
>
> 2. *'It was an accident'* – ie automatism. He didn't have to time to think, or think what he was doing. He didn't consciously pull the trigger four times. He was not aiming at someone.

"I did not intend to kill Reeva, my lady, or anybody else."

If he didn't intentionally shoot Reeva, or anyone else for that matter, then what did he intend? Nothing, he didn't intend anything. He simply–

Discharged his weapon four times because he was nervous?

Fired blindly at a soft muffled noise.

Screamed at the people, or persons, or intruder, or burglar, or attacker to get the fuck of his house, and then…fire four warning shots?

Let's make a pertinent note that in his first statements Oscar described his shooting 'style' or pattern as a 'double-tap'. Nevermind the pattern and trajectory and the ear witness testimony all contradict this, but if Oscar had fired *unintentionally,* a double tap is *less* likely. Why? Because a double-tap requires skill, concentration and a two-handed grip (to accommodate the recoil).

View this clip if you'd like to be absolutely certain you're following:

https://www.youtube.com/watch?v=Wbg2s2bfjhw

Another reason the double tap is important is, we need to know whether Reeva possibibly, or probably, screamed after the first shot. In other words, if there was the slightest pause after the first shot, the probability is that Reeva did scream.

The one M&G article interrogates this aspect quite well:

As the trial proceeds, it appears pivotal to the State's case to prove that Steenkamp had time to scream as Pistorius fired shots into the locked toilet cubicle. Nel has been leading detailed evidence suggesting that it is conceivable that he heard his girlfriend cry out but continued to shoot.
Last week the State called a ballistics expert who said tests showed that the first bullet hit Steenkamp in her hip, and the second missed.

[Author's note: The inference here is even if the interval was relatively short, although Michelle Burger suggests otherwise, but even if it was a short interval between shots, given that the second bullet missed, the period between the first shot and the fourth ought to have given Reeva time to scream. Even the first and third shots would not have been sufficient to prevent her from screaming, as both were some distance not only from vital organs, but from the chest, head and vocalising apparatus.]

Two further shots [three and four] *found her slumped in a defensive position, and struck her in the arm and head.*

[Author's note: the mere mention of 'defensive' ought to alert the astute observer that Reeva not only anticipated what was about to take place – by screaming – but having already sustained a wound, had both the prescience and a final precious moment to try to defend her mortal form from further, imminent desecration.]

In earlier testimony, the pathologist who performed the post mortem on Steenkamp told the court that it would have been "unnatural" for her not to scream after a bullet shattered her hip.

http://mg.co.za/article/2014-03-24-reeva-found-oscar-often-bad-tempered

The *last* bullet through the top of her skull, it is true, *would* have (and I believe, *did*) render/ed her virtually inert. But according to Burger's testimony there were:

1. "blood-curdling screams" which
2. reached "a climax"
3. followed by four shots
4. and the last 'petrified scream' ended shortly after the last shot
5. Burger also confirmed that she heard screaming during the firing of the four shots]
6. Johnson (Burger's husband) indicated he had been surprised when he heard Oscar's version. Why? Because <u>Oscar's version excluded a woman's direct participation</u> in the terror/argument/attack that he perceived.

Johnson testified that he had heard the woman's screams <u>intensify and that he then heard shots, with the last screams fading away after the shots</u>.

Although Burger had been adamant that it was <u>four shots</u>, Johnson said he recalled a "few shots" and <u>later told people it was five or six</u>.

[In the epilogue of this narrative I will explain why both apparently contradicting versions, why these apparent 'consistencies' actually both make absolute sense].

Johnson also confirmed that he had the impression that <u>somebody was being "attacked in their house"</u> and <u>he was later surprised to learn</u> that Pistorius had said that he'd shot his girlfriend by <u>accident</u>.

"It was difficult for me to believe ... unless it was a house break-in, because <u>I heard both a woman and a man screaming</u>".

http://www.citypress.co.za/news/tough-day-ahead-michelle-burgers-husband-oscar-pistorius-trial/

After all this we have to return to the original question: did Reeva scream at any time before, during or after the four bullets were fired?

If she did, we may have reason to suspect not only intention, but premeditation. Any pause therefore, in the firing of those four bullets could not only show intent, but a tactical approach based on expert weapons training. In others words, if one is trying to hit a target, and modifying one's stance and aim, and on his stumps Oscar may well have needed to do both, we can certainly not rule out an intentional act. Let's be clear:

The *RESURRECTION* narrative deals with a possible motive. *REVELATIONS* will ultimately deal with method.

It is interesting that although this subsection of Unanswered Question is titled 'what is Oscar's defence' when you Google 'Oscar Pistorius double tap' (and a 'double tap' is simply one method, one technique for discharging a firearm) the one thing common to most, if not all the media stories (see three links below) that come up under this search criteria is 'questions, contradictions and inconsistencies' in Oscar's version.

http://www.huffingtonpost.com/2014/04/15/oscar-pistorius-trial_n_5151111.html

http://abcnews.go.com/blogs/headlines/2014/04/oscar-pistorius-faces-contradictions-and-challenges-to-his-testimony/

http://www.bbc.com/news/27070096

The double-tap is not part of Oscar's defence, however at one point it *was*. Why? So Oscar could plausibly deny Reeva a chance to cry out. But the catch to that version is firing in a double-tap requires skill and conscious execution. *Conscious execution* implicitly contradicts this idea of the shooting being either involuntarily, or accidental. So the double-tap is not a non sequitur. It was simply a snare that the defence caught themselves in.

Now, in terms of that third link (from the BBC) the reader will note, Andrew Harding very helpfully provides his own list of niggling questions (within the 'accidental context'. Briefly, these are:

- Oscar Pistorius testified that - seconds before killing Reeva Steenkamp - he did not fire a warning shot into the corner shower in his bathroom because he was concerned about a "ricochet". Does that show **sufficient presence of mind** [bold emphasis by the author]*to raise questions about his "unthinking", "panicking" and "instinctive" shots at the toilet door immediately afterwards?*

- *Four shots... I am told the prosecution finds* **the number of bullets fired suspicious**[emphasis mine] - *that someone reacting in* **pure panic** *would normally shoot many more, and with much* **less directional control**. *Does the number, and direction, of shots imply a certain degree of deliberation?*

- *Has the prosecution produced any solid evidence to support its claim that* **Mr Pistorius intended to kill Ms Steenkamp**[emphasis mine], *or, as I am inclined to think from some background conversations in the courthouse, are they relatively indifferent about whom the athlete believed he was shooting at, and are primarily interested in* **proving he shot deliberately and with intent to kill**[emphasis mine]*?*

Mr Harding, I'm glad you've asked these questions. Intent will be answered (as far as one possibly can using a hypothesis) in the final chapter. As mentioned earlier, if *RESURRECTION* was primarily focused on *context* and *motive*, then *Revelations* is all about targeting *intent* and *method*. At this point it is too early to expand on either of these, further than making broad assessments. But by the time we find ourselves in the territory of the epilogue of this narrative, Revelations, we ought to be ready with a concise hypothesis.

For now though, the casual observer must be reminded that Oscar is not a lay marksman. His family own hunting farms, his family own arsenals of weapons, and Oscar, besides being a licensed owner, and besides regularly firing his weapons as hobby (and even at night, when he has insomnia), we're aware of video footage of him *actually performing advanced weapons training.*

More than this we have video footage showing Oscar's expert marksmanship with the same weapon he used to shoot Reeva Steenkamp to death.

Sky News [showed] footage of Pistorius firing a shotgun and using a pistol to shoot a watermelon, which [burst] on impact. Delighted screams and laughter from unidentified people are heard in the background.

Sky News reported the silver 9mm gun seen in the video is the same gun that was used in the death of model Reeva Steenkamp.

http://nypost.com/2014/02/28/oscar-pistorius-seen-shooting-in-gun-range-video/

We've seen him firing. We know he does so regularly, and thus knows exactly how to handle his firearm. He has also bragged on twitter about his accuracy.

In court, the prosecutor provided the license exam data which shows Oscar clearly understands the regulations around gun ownership.

http://www.theguardian.com/world/2014/mar/17/oscar-pistorius-tried-buy-seven-guns-trial

http://espn.go.com/olympics/trackandfield/story/_/id/8991348/oscar-pistorius-violated-basic-firearms-rules-experts-say

And from an excellent article by enca.com we get:

Nel then went through a number of questions Pistorius had answered during his assessment tests.

> 1. **You are alone at home** *far from police and security services. You happen to look out of the window and* **see two men jumping over your wall** *and making their way to your house. You are not expecting a visit because it is very late at night. Have they committed an offence that requires the use of lethal force? "The accused answered 'no'," Rens said.*

> 2. **The men break in through the burglar bars** *and remove your extremely expensive hi-fi equipment.* **Can you use lethal force then?**' *Rens stated that Pistorius had again answered 'No'.*

> 3. *If the same men became aware of* **his presence behind a security gate several metres away and instruct him to leave or they will kill him**, *issuing a definite verbal threat, Pistorius had again answered that* <u>he could not use lethal force</u>.

> 4. *Another question gave a similar scenario but this time with no security gate and the two men – one armed with a knife and the other with a gun –* **approaching him**

in a threatening manner. Pistorius had responded that he could legally discharge his firearm [if or] *because he believed his life to be in danger.*

5. To answer the question 'When can you use lethal force', Pistorius had written 'The attack must be against you and it must be unlawful. It must be against a person'.

6. Asked to explain target identification, Pistorius had answered: "Know your target and what lies beyond".

Questioned about the scenario in which two men had jumped his wall [or climbed through a bathroom window] *in the night and approached his house, Pistorius said the men had committed a minor property offence and the use of lethal force was not justified.*

When asked about the men being in his house [or in his bathroom, or toilet], *removing his equipment, Pistorius said lethal force could not be used because no life was in danger.*

In response to the question 'What does it mean to be muzzle conscious?' Pistorius had answered: "To know where the firearm is pointed".
http://www.enca.com/south-africa/oscar-trial-gun-love-and-recklessness-under-spotlight

For now, we will go no further than that on this very specific line of questioning.

The following mere *supposition* will have to suffice for the time being:

Would Oscar like us to believe he retrieved his firearm, approached a closed (in fact closed and locked door) and fired *accidentally?* Given the *contextual* evidence, does he realise the *absurdity* of what he's asking?

http://www.news24.com/SouthAfrica/Oscar_Pistorius/It-was-an-accident-Oscar-20140409

3. *'I was terrified'* – diminished responsibility due to anxiety/mental illness/GAD.
http://www.enca.com/south-africa/oscar-trial-state-calls-mental-observation-based-defence-case

Strictly speaking, these are Oscar's defences in terms of what he did on 14 February 2013. He may use two additional lines of defence, which may not have much of a bearing on the verdict, or even (possible) sentencing, but these would be applicable grounds for appeal. These are:

4. *'Abuse of privileged information.'* Unfortunately for the defence, the leaked video of Oscar on his stumps (broadcast by Australia television on Sunday the 6th of July, ironically the same day this writer gave an interview on national radio) was not even mentioned in court. If it had been, the defence, who had perhaps made and manoeuvred the video for exactly this purpose, could have claimed prejudice to their client's rights to 'private and confidential information' and the 'unfettered' administration of justice.

http://www.timeslive.co.za/thetimes/2014/07/09/oscar-keeps-all-options-open

5. *'Witnesses too afraid to testify'* – the argument that the trial is unfair due to 'trial by media'.

http://abcnews.go.com/International/oscar-pistorius-lawyer-complains-witnesses-testify/story?id=24463120

One does not need a legal expert to examine these so-called 'defences' (and implicit inconsistencies and contradictions) in order to feel they beggar belief. What is interesting is the symbolic import of Oscar's answer when Nel specifically asks him:

What was your intention? What did you want to achieve? [1:16:57]
https://www.youtube.com/watch?v=QxZYtDsMhIE

Oscar [1:17:02]: *I wanted to chase the people out of my house, my Lady*

When Nel asks 'why' he'd want to chase people out of his home Oscar switches tenses, and flips to a hypothetical:

"Yes, my hal[garbled]…if somebody's in your house, in the middle of the night I'm sure anyone would want to chase them out."

Except that's not what's happening here. This isn't about *chasing*, surely? Is it? Who in their right minds, especially a disabled person, with limited mobility, would be contemplating *chasing* (possibly armed, highly mobile, and probably not one but two) intruders?

Shooting, yes. Chasing? Improbable. And in the schema Oscar does zero chasing. He fires four shots through a closed (locked) door, effectively not only trapping the unarmed 'intruder', but – and this is critical – *preventing* their escape.

Is *chasing* a credible word then, even in this version?

Also worth noting is during this exhaustive cross-examination, in almost *every answer* Oscar gives, he says the words 'my Lady'.

A recent newspaper headline in the Citizen on 16/07/2014 (on the heels of a bar room brawl in Sandton, Johannesburg) provides some irony to Oscar's overall situation. The headline reads:

His own worst enemy

That headline should probably have been in all caps. Even in his own version, the enemy Oscar pursued (or didn't) purposefully pursue did not exist. A possible alternative version is actually not as far removed from Oscar's version as one might imagine. Why? In the schema of Reeva screaming behind a closed door, wanting to leave, traumatised, why not simply let her go?

Get the fuck out of my house!

These were the exact words Oscar used on the intruder.

The intruder was Reeva.

Thus in the reality of the situation? Get the fuck out of my house! Were the exact words used on Reeva. Anger. Betrayal. But why is she too afraid to leave? Why is she hiding in a toilet if Oscar, possibly, wants her out of his house. Why wouldn't she leave? Because of this:

"I'm scared of you sometimes and how you snap at me and how you react to me."

"You have picked on me excessively."

Are you not coming with me to Brazil? Or Manchester? Or Italy?

Get the fuck out of my house!

His own worst enemy

In the *schema* of the courtroom, Oscar even tells us *his exact words* --

[1:24] https://www.youtube.com/watch?v=fMsUK8mhGFw

--during the incident. Before the end of his murder trial, Oscar will almost certainly rue the day he did not follow OJ Simpson's courtroom strategy, courtesy of Roger Shapiro.

https://www.youtube.com/watch?v=e1DfpuTHGYg

Presenter[0:30]: If you were defence attorney for Oscar Pistorius, what would you tell Oscar to do?

Shapiro: Oscar, keep your mouth shut. Don't make any statements whatsoever. If you talk, I walk.

His own worst enemy

In *RECIDIVIST ACTS* I discuss how mountains of extraneous information is usually a key indicator of culpability. Giving too much information, or 'protesting to much', is highlighted in the adjoining *911 Call Analysis* as not merely *a* key symptom of guilt, but more often *the* key.

Note: The reader will be reassured that I have attempted (via The Oscar Trial Channel producers, and Linkedin) to make direct contact with Shapiro. I have been assured (by a contact at Carte Blanche) that my request for comment was passed on to Shapiro's PA. At this time no response has been forthcoming, however I anticipate this may change in due course.

9. Is Oscar a unique athlete/an exceptional talent?
The privilege of a lifetime is being who you are – Joseph Campbell

Is Oscar unique? Is he an exceptional talent? Here's a teaser? Is Michael Johnson unique? Is Lance Armstrong unique? Tyler Hamilton? Daryl Impey? Those are all good athletes, all unique in their own ways, all heroic in some ways and not so heroic in others. Is Oscar somehow different, somehow better than these names? Should we mention another world champion, the fastest man on two legs, Usain Bolt as a better approximation of Oscar's legend, and his legacy? Is that fair? I submit that it isn't.

Much of Oscar's *mythos* (and indeed his *schema*, during the course of this trial) is based on *who* Oscar is. Well, that's not quite right, is it? It's based on who he says he is, who we think he is, and as a result of this trade (what he says, what we think) there's another Oscar who thinks he is the product of our validation, of the endorsements, the money etc. Who Oscar is, then, is to a large degree who he thinks he is. And here's a hint at where that inner dialogue is heading right now:

> http://thejuice.co.za/top-stories/exclusive-oscars-club-night-turns-into-nasty-brawl-we-speak-to-oscars-team-and-the-person-involved-in-the-argument/

> Note:
> - the date of the story, 14July 2014 and
> - the timing of tweets 6:26 PM - 13 Jul 2014 6:34 PM - 13 Jul 2014

Oscar is still defending his brand! The original bible quote (since removed), around a theme of heartbrokenness was made at exactly 6pm.

Is Oscar unique? That was the original question. Let's start by examining a simple question. Who does *he* think he is? On Oscar's twitter profile (which as we've seen, suddenly blipped back to life on 13 July, the day before allegations of a bar brawl with a race car driver at the Viper Room) – he defines himself as:

South African Track Athlete. 400m Specialist. Personal Best of 45.07sec.

Nothing about Paralympiam. Or disabled athlete.

Perhaps that's not odd, considering Arnu Fourie's Oscar's not always healthy one-time roommate, whose identity – according to twitter – is:

> | *Professional athlete* | - *A gold medal is a wonderful thing. But if you're not enough without it, you'll never be enough with it* -

Is there a crypic message in there somewhere? If so, it is too cryptic for this writer to understand, and I'm pretty good at cryptic messages. If you doubt that, let's take one last look, this time at Alan Fonteles Oliveira. Who does *he* say he is on twitter:

http://www.nickvanderleek.com/2014/08/oliveira-real-hero.html

First of all I must admit right off the bat that this guy was very difficult to find. There are a bunch of Alan Oliveira's in the world, and I'm sure a whole bunch of Brazilian Oliveira's. There's even a pretty famous Brazilian footballer on twitter, that's an Oliveira – Diego. Guess how I eventually Googled this kid? By finding his full name on Wikipedia and then googling his full name + twitter. Alan, if you're listening, you need to sort out your searchability. Maybe call yourself @BrazilBladeKid or @BrazilRocketboy

Isn't it shocking that this kid (early twenties, a world record holder) has only 135 twitter followers. Well, he's only sent 6 tweets. Although he is Ossur's new #1 guy (Ossur is the manufacturer of those carbon fibre blades, based in Iceland) Oliveira doesn't seem too fussed about brand, and persona and self promotion. Even that Facebook link doesn't go anywhere. Which makes me wonder, having scoured the net for his account (something I'm not bad at), is this account, the closest one I could find, his actual account? Well, with no evidence to the country (yet, I'll update this if any emerges), let's assume this is legit. And get to the point. How does he – Alan Oliveira – describe himself:

Página não-oficial do atleta paralimpico Alan Fonteles Cardoso Oliveira, nascido em Marabá, medalhista de ouro nas Olimpiadas de Londres 2012 nos 200m T44.

I can't speka da Espana, but what I get from the above:
- Paralimpico
- Medalhista
- Olimpiades
- London
- T4

I like this guy. An honest hero! He says he's a medal winner at the Paralympics in the T4 discipline. Count me in as your 135th follower Alan!

Now, let's get back to Oscar. The reader must accept my apology at this point. As I am a flawed writer (in fact my LinkedIn shows a maximum of only 25 endorsements – for blogging, no less – as at 16 July 2014, and just 3 for writing, no jokes). This is evidence that I, like Thor, still have *much to learn* in this business, and especially need to remember, in terms of this narrative *it's all about Oscar.*

So, what do we already have? Oscar makes specific reference to his PB on twitter. It's not bad. That's an Olympic A qualifying standard.

And that's still his PB today. 45.07 – set on July 7, 2011 in Livigno, Italy. *RESURRECTION* describes the background to that time and place in great detail. But you can watch that race here, at the link provided:

https://www.youtube.com/watch?v=vGTyk7SFZsk
Note the number of views…13 000?

That's a *current* Paralympic world record, so why not say it? Why not say Paralympic world champion? Or 400m World champion? What we intuit from his profile is once again the perpetuation of a persona. What persona? The able-bodied persona. Even if we see Oscar compete as the superhero (the blade runner) when he is off the track he wants to be seen as able-bodied (not the short guy on stumps). Not the guy who runs events known as T4 or whatever the case may be.

He's a track athlete. And a specialist. He's hardcore.

But if that's specific, let's get specific in response:

- **Is Oscar unique and exceptional?** Yes, as a disabled runner, he is a world champion. His time is also fairly close to Michael Johnson's world record for the 400m. Watch it here.
https://www.youtube.com/watch?v=vVL7QLHn5y4&feature=kp
- How many views? 1.323 million. Johnson's record is almost 15 years old. Oscar's is going on 3 years old, and there are abundant signs that Brazil's double amputee sensation, Oliveira will eclipse this mark very soon (Oliveira already holds Paralympic world records over 100m and 200m). That's not all, due to advances in these prosthetic blades, and in the overall technology, Dr Ross Tucker believes the 400m world record, and certainly the Olympic podium, may soon belong to disabled athletes (plural). Does that mean Oscar is unique and exceptional?
- Does Oscar think he is unique and exceptional? Have a look at this link on Larry King Now. Pay special attention to the line of questioning (and good on Larry, a little gentle interrogation) from 09:42. Let the youtube clip run until 11:44 to get the full context.

https://www.youtube.com/watch?v=e3nuFArz0Rk

09:42 Larry asks Oscar if his prosthesis convey [gasp] any kind of advantage?

10:32 Larry: If there was an advantage, you'd win right?

Here it is at 10:41>>>"Well if there's an advantage, you know they've made over 30 000 pairs of prosthetics and there'd be a lot of other athletes running similar times. And yet there's no other athlete running remotely close to the times that I'm running."

10:43 Larry: You were defeated, as I understand it, in the 200 metres sprint, by Alan Oliveira, right?

Oscar [smiling sheepishly]: Yeah.

I'm afraid Larry has caught Oscar out twice on national (international) TV. Firstly, Oscar admits there are only 1500 athletes competing in the Paralympic Games. Yes, 1500, not 15000. He later suggests that out of 30 000 pairs of prosthetics (who knows where he's come up with that number) he's special because not a single athlete has come remotely close to his times. Both the numbers he is giving and the claim, are bogus. Oliveira, as we know, is not only close but beating Oscar's best times over the shorter distances. The only disclaimer open to Oscar is that Oliveira has not yet eclipsed his claim to fame – that 45.07 which still floats so prominently on his twitter page. But it seems not a little mischievous to make the broad (and let's face it, grandiose) claim that *not a single athlete has come remotely close to his times.*

Why does it matter? And does it matter *how* he occupies the headspace in our minds of the titular champion? Unparalleled, unchallenged? It matters a great deal! Because beyond making a good story, you can't very well have two or three disabled athletes running able-bodied races. That dilutes the hero-as-brand – that's not good for anyone. And who would want to share either the attention (as in media attention, and fan focus) or the treasure (as in corporate megabucks, sponsorships) if any other disabled kids wanted to sign up at the neighboring starting blocks? There are very high stakes and thus a tremendous amount riding on maintaining this bogus narrative. I have already weighed into it further here than is appropriate. RESURRECTION goes very deep into this subject matter, and also examines Caster Semenja as a secondary subject to test these interrogations on.

Before we abandon this section entirely, note this admission:

13:46 I never saw myself as having a disability

My classmates…said…this isn't something we're used to, this kid doesn't think he's any different [to able-bodied people]…if you don't let it control your life physically it shouldn't be anything to…to…to worry about."

Larry: You don't look at other people with legs and wish you could be like them?

Oscar: No, not at all, I'm pretty okay with my situation.

15:03 Did your dad get to see you compete.

Oscar's enmity with his father Henke is well documented. His response to his question (a dodge) shows how skilfully Oscar moves the narrative to where he wants it.

16:40 – 17:07 Oscar talks about a bible scripture on his back and summarises the message as 'don't preach a tale and not live it out yourself…'

17:08 Larry: Do you want to have a family?

Oscar [shakes his head with emotion]: Aah…I think that's one of the greatest things in the world. Yeah.

17:19 Larry: Does she have any difficulty with it [your disability/prosthesis]?

Oscar: No…no…I mean…I think that's really been um…you know in the past, with any girlfriend I've had, I think very quickly they've seen I don't have much of an issue with it [my disability/prosthesis] and at least to my knowledge [smiles] they haven't had any either.

There's a slight wiggle in Oscar's beatific smile at the end of this frankly less than credible statement.

Finally, notice how exceedingly *softly* and *quickly* Oscar says the word 'it' at 17:31.

Kelly Slater is possibly one of the greatest living athletes of our time. His heroism, though, is understated. A multiple world champion, how does Slater describe himself on twitter:

Welcome to my page where I make fun of things, point out absurdities and tackle serious subjects like the cutback

True champions don't talk about their singular excellence. True champions have an identity buried in the basements of humility, a humility borne out of exceedingly hard work. Which is why there is a suggestion, at least to this writer, that Oscar's achievements seem to have been achieved cheaply, and artificially, and thus (if this is true) his defence of these should (would) come across, at times, as artificial, and not always with the sort of candidness one might expect.

10. Did Reeva accept the invitation to go to Manchester, Brazil or Italy?

Follow your bliss and the universe will open doors where there were only walls. – Joseph Campbell

To answer this question directly I have emailed Gina Myers (Reeva's best friend) and also tweeted her sister Kim (the same Kim who asked asked, "How do you sleep at night?") for more information. Since I have to date [17 July 2014] not received any response, one has to make assumptions and use one's intuition in order to interrogate this question.

For the lazy reader, or – let me put it more politely – the reader who may feel in need of *an alternate form* of stimulation, and perhaps also those readers suffering from eye-strain, follow this link --

https://soundcloud.com/nick-van-der-leek/ofm-radio-interview-with-nick-van-der-leek-podcast

--to an audio stream of an interview I did with OFM radio's Johrne Van Huyssteen (recorded on, July 6, 2014, a particularly icy Sunday evening).

Listen to the whole thing, if you wish, but pertinent to interrogating this section, and this question [*#10 Did Reeva accept the invitation to go to Manchester, Brazil or Italy?*] the reader ought to focus on 6 minutes and 20 seconds within the segment: **46:17- 52:37** of the applicable track.

To summarise, Peet van Zyl appears to mask Reeva's response in a lot of obfuscation. By using the word 'excited' and by couching Reeva's response in very vague terms, Van Zyl doesn't commit to any specific facts. So Reeva may have been excited, or emotional, but did she actually consent, confirm or give her permission to being part of this trip (and thus, Oscar's career?) Well one person who ought to have known about Reeva's imminent jetsetting would have been very closest friend (and confidant) Gina Myers. While Gina Myers (thus far) has not pertinently answered the question/s I've posed to her directly (via email and twitter) I'm not sure if she needs to. She has already answered it, in her own words, here. When one is doing this sort of research and analysis, Google is a pretty good assistant:

Via **marieclairvoyant.com** [underlined emphasis by the author]:

Every time I travel now, I feel a hole in my heart. <u>It was our thing. To let each other know when we were leaving to catch a flight and when we had landed.</u> I travel for make-up jobs and <u>you travelled for your modelling career.</u> I know you won't get that message now, but I still check for that second tick [on whatsapp].

We met about six years ago when you were presenting for FTV Sandton. I had done the make-up for a fashion show and you interviewed me about the inspiration for the looks that evening. About a year later when we were both booked on a two-day photography shoot, we bonded. That was the first time I did your make-up. We understood each other. We developed an unconditional love for each other. And we laughed. A lot. It was very hard to not get along with you. You and your ridiculous sense of humour.

You were the kind of person who would drop anything to be there for a friend. Selfless and strong-willed. It was a given; that you'd persevere until you got something. I remember the time I called you when I landed in Jo'burg after a trip to Cape Town. You told me that we'd make a plan to meet for coffee the next day. When I walked out of the terminal, you were waiting for me. 'Surprise, my Gi!' you said. And then we both cried as if I had been away for weeks. It had only been three days. After returning from another trip for my first Elizabeth Arden meeting, I found you waiting at my house to surprise me yet again. I could never seem to return those surprises even though I tried a couple of times. When I tried to sneak up on you by arriving with a friend at the airport and hiding in the back seat, you got into the front, turned around and said, 'Hi Gi.' I know there won't be another surprise for me and yet I still hope.

The day you left for the reality-TV competition series, Tropika Island of Treasure, we both knew we wouldn't be able to see or speak to each other for about two weeks. The thought was agonizing. We lay on your bed watching Lana Del Rey's 'Ride' (silly idea in hindsight, as it's such an emotional song to begin with) and cried. We used to watch many YouTube videos together (you loved hip-hop and rocked high-tops, you were so gangster) and there are particular ones that will always bring back the best memories, but there was just something different that day; saying goodbye to you as we cried our eyes out.

I've tried to listen to it many times since but the words 'Don't leave me now, don't say goodbye' mean something very different now. Every night when we drank tea, you, Kimmy and I would dream up imaginary lands – places like Little Fillian where unicorns existed and feathers were floating everywhere. A place where we were protected and loved. You were our second sister, Alfi. You only moved in with my family and me last year September but you had always felt like family.

Do you remember when I got my biggest contract? Or the smaller jobs? You were the first person I would call. You were there for so many milestones in my life and career. You'd scream every time and I could hear you jumping up and down for me. We would feel extremely lucky if we got booked on the same job, and once the two of us, giddy little girls, worked together in a heavenly place called Indigo Bay in Mozambique.

Read the full letter here: http://www.marieclairvoyant.com/entertainment-news/celebrity/reevas-best-friend-gina-myers-writes-her-a-final-email

Given what we know (compiled and collected in the first three narratives of this series) Myers provides staggering insights not only into Reeva's mindset and philosophy, but also some critical factual data too. Before we get to that, let's pull that quote we started this section off with, from Campbell, back into this context. Remember it? *Follow your bliss and the universe will open doors where there were only walls.* Let's be absolutely clear. Reeva and Gina were following their bliss. And their bliss was the glamour, the fun, the adventure and the work involved in pursuing their respective passions. Which overlapped. For Reeva it was modelling, or Gina it was doing make-up for models.

Now: *Did Reeva accept the invitation to go to Manchester, Brazil or Italy?*

Well the implications of that 'acceptance', flying with Oscar to his various meets, being away from South Africa, her work and Gina, for days, weeks, possibly months at a time. It would mean postponing (at least) or giving up (at most) her own modelling career. If Reeva was following her bliss, why on Earth would she give that up at the drop of a hat? Well, if she'd elected to replace that bliss, something she had worked on for several years, with Oscar.

Let's be frank. Love makes fools of us all. Was it *possible* that Reeva may have traded in her dreams, her most cherished desires and friendships, for a rollicking adventure with one of the world's most famous men? Yes, it was possible. Was it probable? It may seem as though we can't answer that, how could we possibly intuit Reeva's own intentions (towards her own life, and how to live it, and her philosophy towards life) on 14 February 2014? Well *of course* we couldn't answer it if we didn't *try*. But when one applies a little effort, and a little digging, the answer is closer (and. more articulate) than one might imagine.

This was perhaps not written *on* the 14 February 2013 (perhaps it was), but it certainly was written *for* the 14 of February 2013. What is it? It's a statement of intent. It's a statement of purpose. It is who I am. And who I will be. It's Reeva's own mission statement. What's more, it isn't a willy nilly private mission statement, it's a public *raison d'tre*:

8. *Being loved by others, although an amazing feeling to have the appreciation of others, does not define your place in the world*.[Inserted by the author: In other words, do not seek validation for yourself from others, or through external means].

9. *Accept who you are. Acknowledge your absolute "CAN DOS" in life and work on your "MAYBES" so that you can be a better person for the ultimate upliftment of those around you.*

10. *No matter how many people say that they "love" you, if you do not love your person then you will never step outside of the physical you. The physical you can only do so much if your mental you is lost inside of all the confusion.* .[Inserted by the author: Reeva is not lost, she's enlightened in her own life, and circumstances].

11. *Be brave. Always see the positive. Make your voice heard. Your physical seen. And the presence of your mental you felt. Its that culmination of your person that will leave a legacy and uplift.* .[Inserted by the author: Does this sound like a person ready to give up their career to be someone elses media sidekick, to be an 'also-run', a 'runner-up', in branding terms, a 'handbag' to Oscar's Superbrand?].

12. *I hope that you have the most amazing Valentines Day and that you are spoilt with love and roses and chocolates. Go home and tell your parents, siblings, neighbours that they are appreciated.*

You will go to bed with a happy heart and open mind for the future. .[Inserted by the author: Reeva was happy and fulfilled and secure in her life, and open-minded about the future. As Gina Myers says *Selfless and strong-willed,* but not so selfless to give herself up, and not so strong-willed not to care about the consequences of defining her purpose, her career, to Oscar, as she probably did to Oscar on 13/13 February 2013].

Did Reeva accept the invitation to go to Manchester, Brazil or Italy?

Cecil Myers: "Reeva told me he pushed her a bit into a corner; she felt caged in."

Reeva's cousin Kim Martin met up with the couple in Cape Town shortly after Christmas 2012: "We spent about two hours together. I thought he was a nice guy, but when Oscar walked away from the table, I asked Reeva, 'Are you happy?' She smiled and said hesitantly, 'Yes.' But I could see something in her response. And she said, 'We will have a chat.' I felt there were things that they had to deal with. They looked good together – happy together – but there was something that she could not talk to me about at the table. She said, 'We will talk about it another time.' But we never did."

Remember, the Tasha's incident happened shortly after this, in January. The upshot of this was that Reeva, now part of Oscar's inner circle, was asked to keep one of his secrets. The implication would not have been lost on her. Oscar's secrets were worth millions (to Oscar). And so, if at that stage Reeva had any revelations she'd intended to share with her cousin, she may have second-guessed them on the grounds of:

    a) Maintaining the trust and confidence of her very influential friend
    b) Want to maintain a powerful relationship, perhaps also a loving one, and one that might in time mean something, or otherwise prove valuable to her (personally and/or professionally.

In *Reeva in her own Words* we see a Reeva demonstrably good at maintaining discipline in social media, something measured, and restrained, rather than a blabbermouth. If we look at Reeva's circumstances we see persistent financial difficulties with her parents. Even her closest friends say she never spoke about this, not because they were not urgent, but probably the opposite. Exactly those difficulties were on her mind on 13th February when she called June Steenkamp to arrange payment of her DSTV, so that her mother would see her daughter on television.

On the night she died, when she was on her way to Oscar's house, we talked about her sending us money to pay our cable television bill.

http://www.mirror.co.uk/news/world-news/oscar-pistorius-trial-reeva-steenkamps-3434188

https://www.youtube.com/watch?v=-MedbKo8mgs

Karyn Maughan, presenter [@ 4:09]: Throughout her childhood and adolescence [and adulthood] Reeva's parents struggled to make a living in Port Elizabeth's horseracing world. But s*he gave little away about these difficulties*

Janet Badenhorst, family friend [@ 4:21]: She just took it in her stride…that's how she was…*she didn't outwardly show that there were problems.*

Did Oscar ask Reeva to keep his secrets? Well, he asks *a lot* of people. And not only to keep secrets, but take the fall on his behalf.

Murder accused Paralympian Oscar Pistorius sent a message to his girlfriend, Reeva Steenkamp, asking her "not to say a thing" about the gun incident at Tashas, the high court in Pretoria has heard.

11 January 2013, Oscar via WhatsApp: *"Angel, please don't say a thing to anyone. Darren [Fresco] told everyone it was his fault. <u>The guys promised they wouldn't say anything</u>,"* Captain Francois Moller read from a WhatsApp message Pistorius sent to Steenkamp on January 11 2013 at 3.03pm.

RS: *I have no idea what you're talking about:) But thank you for telling me, I appreciate it.*

http://www.citypress.co.za/news/oscars-whatsapp-message-reeva-angel-please-dont-say-anything/

19 January 2013, RS: …just appreciate that I'm not a liar

27 January 2013, RS:…We are living a double-standard relationship, where you get mad about how I deal with stuff, when you are very quick to act cold and off-ish, when you aren't happy…**I do everything to** make you happy and to **not say anything to rock the boat** with you.

Barry Roux made the assertion that by far the majority of the messages were loving. Perhaps a more accurate assertion would have been by far the majority of the *remaining* messages were loving.

Police cellphone analyst Captain Francois Moller began testifying on Monday afternoon, the 24th March 2014 in Oscar Pistorius's murder trial in the High Court in Pretoria.

https://www.youtube.com/watch?v=T2UovSRmpDI

@ [1:35] Moller quote Reeva's 27 January Whatsapp message: "…and I'm sorry if you think that little of me."

SABC Presenter Chriselda Lewis: When details of the text messages were being read out in court, Oscar Pistorius turned red in the face, and looked down. Reeva's mother June Steenkamp, kept leaning forward, looking in his direction, but the athlete, never looked up.

So what we see is Reeva, the rags to riches girl, trying to make it big, trying to emerge but also trying to not 'rock the boat' of the star who was 'besotted with her', and yes, she was naturally good at keeping secrets. Her secrets. His secrets. Good at keeping secrets, but also principled, conscientious and strong-willed. Good at keeping secrets, but also self-possessed. Good at keeping secrets, but also someone who had experienced abuse before. Good at keeping secrets but also someone who later that day would speak out against abuse.

Who was Reeva? By her own account:

5. *I was in an abusive relationship at the same time (his mother used to abuse him) and all together these factors encouraged my move to Jozi.*
[...]

7. I lost a lot of self worth during my last year in PE before I moved to Jozi and it took some serious soul searching to remind myself of my value in this world

*11. Be brave. Always see the positive. Make your **voice heard**. Your **physical seen**. And the **presence** of your mental you **felt**...*[Emphasis mine]

Who was Reeva? Someone very good at keeping secrets but also clear on *what* secrets should *not* be kept. Let's take a long, thorough look at who she was, and how she saw herself on 14 February 2014:

Who received flowers/chocolates/cards/messages/tweets/etc today (February 14) for valentines day.

Tell them what I received, [what did she receive?] make a small joke about this. And then tell them that receiving those things is very special <u>but not receiving anything doesn't define you as a person or make you less valued!!!</u>

1. I was raised on a small farm just outside of Cape Town. In a way I was blessed and privileged to be away from the pressures of city life and <u>I grew up to appreciate the simpler things above the superficial.</u> [Had Reeva finally seen through Oscar's world, seen that it was little more than superficial persona?]

2. I will chat about life on the farm, <u>having no money</u> but being blessed with amazing parents who never allowed me to be aware of my circumstances. Some "looking back now" points somewhere after this would fit in.

3. After moving to PE and deciding <u>to study Law despite our financial situation, I worked hard to be acknowledged</u> as one of the top 15% academics at university so that my studies could be 80% covered by bursaries and <u>I worked to pay off the rest</u>.

4. I broke my back towards the end of varsity. Learnt <u>mobility</u> [Reeva had also experienced 'lack of mobility' firsthand] *again and made a <u>massive life decision</u> with regards to my <u>career</u>. I will elaborate on this part of my journey.*

5. <u>I was in an abusive relationship</u> at the same time (his mother used to abuse him) and all together <u>these factors encouraged my move</u> to Jozi.

6. Despite my height disadvantage and the difficulty in general of breaking into the modeling industry, I put my head down and <u>worked hard towards my dream</u>.

7. I lost a lot of self worth during my last year in PE before I moved to Jozi and it took some <u>serious soul searching to remind myself of my value in this world</u>.

8. <u>Being loved</u> by others, although an amazing feeling to have the appreciation of others, <u>does not define your place in the world</u>.[but being loved by others did define Oscar in a very personal way; his fanbase meant he was accepted as 'able-bodied' despite 'it' [his invisible disability. The love of others had come to define him personally, and he'd realised a woman could play an important role in his career, to define the next chapter, an add another dimension to his exploding brand]

9. Accept who you are. Acknowledge your absolute "CAN DOS" in life and work on your "MAYBES" so that you can be a better person for the ultimate upliftment of those around you.

10. No matter how many people say that they "love" you, *if you do not love your person*[does Oscar ultimately, and honestly, love or accept who he is?] *then you will never step outside of the physical you.* The physical you can only do so much if your mental you is *lost inside of all the confusion.*[Is that what happened on February 14, 2013? Oscar got lost in his own persona, lost and confused by his own, self-made, contrived *mythos*?]

11. *Be brave. Always see the positive. Make your voice heard.* Your physical seen. And the presence of your mental you felt. Its that culmination of your person that will leave a legacy and uplift.[Was this the terror Oscar felt. That whatever was agreed, bargained, guaranteed through the toilet door, Reeva would (and ultimately *could*) make her voice heard…An unconscionable risk?]

Did Reeva accept the invitation to go to Manchester, Brazil or Italy?

16:25 https://www.youtube.com/watch?v=-MedbKo8mgs

Was it in the realm of possibility to give up her life, and join Oscar? Play the supporting role in his career? It's not only my analysis, and Reeva's own account that answers this seemingly subtle question with absolute clarity. Karyn Maughan uncovered the selfsame narrative when she did her research. The answer is almost self-evident:

Reeva was someone *focused on her career*

But she loved Oscar, didn't she? Wouldn't this have subsumed her career focus?

Actually, if Reeva was focused on her career, she was, although interested in romance, far more circumspect about love and relationships than many would like to acknowledge.

17:59 https://www.youtube.com/watch?v=-MedbKo8mgs

She was unsure; she was uncertain whether she should pursue the relationship

In December Oscar phoned from Cape Town and said to Reeva (who was in JHB) over Christmas and New Year 2012: "I need you to be with me. Will you come down…?"

She told me, she sat down with this message and thought, "should I, shouldn't?" she was torn (toying?) between the two. And in the end she said, "Stuff it, I'm going…"

What does this show? Reeva's resistance and hesitation contrasting with Oscar's pleading with and pestering her. And the stakes of his 'pestering' only went higher and higher after that – moving in, travelling together, being part of his career. On Valentine's Day it all came to a head. Or more specifically, a halt. Reeva told him, no, I can't be part of your adventure, certainly not to the extent *you* want.

Now, let's ask the question again: *Did Reeva accept the invitation to go to Manchester, Brazil or Italy?*

What if she didn't? What if Reeva didn't accept *any* of these invitations? What if Oscar saw this non-acceptance as *rejection*? What if that rejection awoke in him a deep pain, and deeply buried resentments against the strictures of able-bodied society. And beautiful women, Oscar had found, never stuck around very long. *The Mirror* provides a useful summary of Oscar's own comments to the media on his romantic life and experiences with the opposite sex:

In his last interview [published in Sarie magazine, February 2013 issue http://mediaslutza.com/2013/01/25/sarie-february-2013/]

before gunning down Reeva Steenkamp, Oscar Pistorius told how he had yet to find the right girl – despite dating the stunning model <u>at the time</u>.

His bail hearing in Pretoria has been repeatedly told how much in love the couple were, with claims she was "unlike any girl he had ever met".

But in the interview published just weeks before tragedy struck, he told how <u>he found it hard to trust</u> after his previous relationship with student Samantha Taylor <u>ended sourly</u> – allegedly <u>with him threatening</u> to break a man's legs.

By the time he sat down to answer questions, Pistorius and Reeva were already <u>dating but</u> the pair had <u>yet to go public</u>.

[**Author's note**: why had they not gone public after 3-4 months? And why, ultimately would you not? I am currently starting on a new project, and have been asked to not go public about it. When I asked 'why not', I was told, 'Because it would be uncomfortable for both of us if ultimately, nothing came of it…']

He told February's edition of Afrikaan[s] women's mag[azine] Sarie: "It's difficult to find the <u>right person</u>, one who is <u>reliable</u> and <u>will keep your private things private</u>.

"It takes a very special person to be in a relationship with a sportsman. It's not an easy life.

"<u>You need someone who</u> either <u>can travel</u> with you or is <u>super-accommodating</u>.

"It is a challenge, yes. <u>I have not yet found the right person, but that's OK</u>."

http://www.mirror.co.uk/news/world-news/last-oscar-pistorius-interview-before-1723955#ixzz37vStO5Bb

Is Oscar stretching the truth here? If he says it's 'OK' that he hadn't found the right person, well, personally, I find that a little doubtful. Let's assume this line of reasoning is possible and reasonably possible (for the moment). If it is, we may assume even further that when confronted by a real resistance to his plans, he became angry, possibly, and snapped at Reeva. She wanted to leave, then his anger, his sense of betrayal only escalated. You're dumping me! On Valentine's Day! Get the fuck out of my house.

Let's face it, the couple had had their problems, and although somewhere in the centre they had something good going, along the edges, the fringes, things weren't hunky dory. Recall June Steenkamp's ominous commentary:

"She said, they were fighting a lot. And this was a very new relationship. Very early to be fighting a lot. She didn't elaborate on what they were fighting about. But she said, 'We, we are fighting a lot'. That's what she said. Which is unusual for Reeva. There were no fights with (ex-boyfriend) Warren ever. Or anybody else. Or, or, even... personal fights maybe with friends and things, she didn't... wasn't one for fighting. But she said, they were fighting a lot."

She didn't elaborate on what they were fighting about...

Except what we know, from Reeva's own words:

You fucked up a special day for me ... [Selfishness]

I just want to love and be loved. Maybe we can't do that for each other. [It's all about Oscar, Reeva's feelings, hopes, career is inconsequential]

Right now, I know you can't be happy and I'm certainly very unhappy and sad. [He's moody, needy, insecure and difficult to please].

You have picked on me excessively ... [He's critical]

I do everything to make you happy and you do everything to throw tantrums ... [She's considerate, he's conceited]

I'm the girl who fell in love with you ... but I'm also the girl who gets side-stepped when you are in a shit mood ...[She's trusted him, but feels betrayed and abused by his moodiness and disassociation]

I get snapped at... [He's insensitive to her feelings; his hopes, desires and feelings are at centre-stage]

And to Cecil Mysers:

She felt caged in *by his attentions...*

Trapped...

Pressured...

"She told me he pushed her...into a corner."

Now let's listen to Oscar...

https://www.youtube.com/watch?v=fMsUK8mhGFw

[52:30] Nel to Oscar after court adjournement due to Oscar becoming 'emotional': "That's why you cried [because] you don't understand the implications."

Next, we'll examine this link...

https://www.youtube.com/watch?v=fMsUK8mhGFw

[16:40] Oscar: "I heard the door slam whilst I was shouting and screaming..."
[23:52] Oscar: "I was thinking of all the possibilities. The worst things that could have possibly happened."

Oscar's own version gives us: a door that slammed. Was it an intruder than slammed the door? No, in the true schema of the evening, Reeva slammed the door.

According to The Telegraph:

By January, [Oscar] said, the relationship became more serious. "We started really seeing a future together," he said. "We discussed me moving to Johannesburg. I was besotted." [That may be true, they discussed a future together. Big plans. Travelling together internationally, living together, making a life together. But then, on February 13, the future Oscar had pinned his hopes on, the future he had been pestering her about, always calling her...fell apart. The 'shitty thing' was the realisation that *none* of it was going to work. Not some of it, none of it.]

On the night she died, Steenkamp shelved plans for a trip to the cinema with a girlfriend and offered to cook him supper. [She also cancelled an engagement with Nimue. A trip to the cinema on February 13 seems like a clear statement of 'I'm not really that interested in you romantically. Given that she spent the night at his house on 12 February, and that on February 13th Reeva recommended he spend the night with his family, there's clear intention from Reeva – that she wanted him to back off, at the very least, slow down.]

They both had a "taxing day" so, after chatting and checking over a modelling contract, they went to bed.

[Oscar admits they were discussing a modelling contract that night. It may not have been a contract about modelling, but they were almost certainly discussing contracts, and obligations – if any – towards one another in a work sense. Reeva would have told him Capacity Relations did not wish to involve Oscar in her brand, an admission that would have disgusted and nauseated him.]

http://www.telegraph.co.uk/news/worldnews/oscar-pistorius/10751743/Oscar-Pistorius-trial-athlete-was-besotted-with-Reeva.html

Roux: Would you say there was a point where it became more serious, in the relationship, and if so, when was that?

Oscar: Um...I think we both had um...we both had things that kept us back. [Such as our brands respective brands?] In our relationship. In getting to know each other. Um...we both came out of difficult relationships before. [0:35 Kim Martin, with a doubtful, almost cynical expression, glances at Gina Myers]. I think if anything, I was more into her than she was, at times, with me. [0:46 Kim Martin, a severe look on her face, appears to mutter, "Well, no wonder."]

Did Reeva want to go to Brazil, Manchester and Italy? It's unlikely. Telling Oscar this was likely what fuelled the argument that lasted through the night. When it escalated to the point that Reeva wanted to leave, the dynamics shifted. Oscar became abusive, and Reeva suddenly held extraordinary power. Suddenly she was the able-bodied person goddess, towering over him, stronger than him as a person, and a woman, and evidently (despite her 'nothing brand, a brand that was nothing without his') he still wasn't good enough for her. And now that he had shown his true colors, she held that whole career, that whole persona in her slim fist.

Had he known Reeva better he would have realised he could – indeed – have trusted her with his secret. Except, Reeva was less coy about abuse. And unfortunately, this secret (and Oscar's knowledge of her class, her discretion, but also her principles and strong will) would cost her her life. If her brand was worth nothing, and his was worth millions, hers was expandable.

It was her strong-will that Oscar feared, if he allowed her to live, would ultimately destroy him. Ironically, despite extinguishing her life (and extinguishing her in his own version), Reeva has persisted.

She has emerged through her whatsapp messages, she has emerged through her own stubborn refusal to die (even after sustaining three bullets, she has emerged through her powerful presence even beyond the grave).

If there has been any real *RESURRECTION* here, it has been hers, not his. The phoenix in this story is Reeva, not Oscar. The reality of Oscar is not a superman, but a legless man. Not a hero but a dwarf-like apparition no one recognises. If Oscar's desperation to be accepted as an able-bodied celebrity was powerful, Reeva's dream burnt far brighter, because her flame was borne from authentic fire.

While, beauty, popularity and external validation mattered, she was wise enough to know – wiser than Oscar, certainly – that one's own esteem for oneself was a far greater treasure to protect. In this department, Reeva was exceedingly rich, and Oscar spiritually bankrupt (despite the oft quoted bible verses to the contrary).

If Reeva seems to have demonstrated an eerie prescience in her art, in these last words, she demonstrates it again:

Go home [but she didn't] *and tell your... neighbours* [Burger, Stipp] *that they are appreciated...You will go to bed* [but not Reeva] *with a happy heart and open mind....*

> http://www.standard.co.uk/news/crime/the-valentines-day-speech-pistorius-girlfriend-reeva-steenkamp-never-got-the-chance-to-make-8496896.html

11. Was the media culpable? - Is there a personal cost to perpetuating a fake persona (to the media, to society, to the celebrities themselves, and to us as individuals?

Myths are public dreams, dreams are private myths – Joseph Campbell

In many ways the media is like racing cars. You have different engines plying their trade on the same track, some engines are undoubtedly better than others, some drivers have talent, others simply know the rudiments of driving. Some racing teams are out there to win, others are simply out there to make a living. Some want to change the world, some simply see racing (or rat-race reporting) as a means to an end.

In 2014 the media is in dire straits. From top to bottom, the turmoil is there. And underlying this sea-change in the media industry is the encroachment of digital flatteners, those democratic forces (social media, the internet wanting to be free, Google search, digital techs ability to be shared and copied at no expense) which effectively overrun the print medias guardians and gatekeepers at every turn.

What is being guarded? Treasure. Profits. Print media was, once upon a time, one of the great moneyspinning industries. Think of Fleet Street. And Clark Kent and Lois Lane at the Daily Planet. Peter Parker at the Daily Bugle. And Batman's girlfriend Vicky Vale at the Gothan Gazette. Why would entire comic franchises place the alter egos of their super saviours (or their girlfriends) at newspapers? Because they were sexy once. They were where it was all happening.

There is still money to be made in the media of course, but it's more diffuse in the 21st century, and it's no longer concentrated in print. Content, though, will always be king, whether in print, digital, audio, or audiovisual form. The industry though, in its entirety is contracting in terms of profitability, as the extent of content (and especially free content, and free conversation – which is arguably the most compelling content/communication of all) expands.

Twitter's impact on the media landscape is not small or incidental. In fact, it could be argued that a single twitterfeed from the inside of a courtroom (someone like Barry Batemen) is sufficient. Why does one need a dozen journalists repeating the same dry facts from the horses mouth? Well, we do need more than Barry Batemen, so that we can interrogate the news, and get a better picture. Which is why some journalists, such as CNN's Robyn Curnow are more focused on insights, and observation – than facts necessarily. Even so, with a small battalion of local and international press attending trial, all tweeting (for free, presumably, and t's certainly free to the public) there are going to be winners, and losers. And the challenge is to monetise this, when budgets are shrinking.

Thought leader and social media expert Sarah Britten said recently, words to the effect that Oscar's brand is still worth a lot of treasure. And that Oscar still sells a lot of newspapers. Britten chuckled at the end of this, saying, "unfortunately, this time the money's just not for Oscar."

That's not necessarily true. The leaked video of Oscar on his stumps we know was purpose-made and sold, possibly for a million dollar paycheque. A book or movie deal could be bought or sold by Oscar, at any time for tens of millions. An exclusive scoop for a single story could be auctioned to the highest bidder.

This craven idea of the media, and its opportunists, spinning cash out of murder (alleged?) is not new. Aileen Wurnos, the 'Monster' portrayed by our own Oscar-winning (okay, bad pun) Charlize Theron, is a case in point. It does happen that murderers and the media join hands to become a hot new circus act. Of course, these dalliances usually end in tears.

> Via Wikipedia:
>
> Wuornos said to Broomfield in the interview, "You sabotaged my ass! Society, and the cops, and the system! A raped woman got executed, and was used for books and movies and shit!" Her final words in the on-camera interview were "Thanks a lot, society, for railroading my ass."
>
> Broomfield later met Dawn Botkins, a childhood friend of Wuornos', who told him, "She's sorry, Nick. She didn't give you the finger. She gave the media the finger, and then the attorneys the finger. And she knew if she said much more, it could make a difference on her execution tomorrow, so she just decided not to."
>
> Wuornos was brought into the death chamber on October 9, 2002. For Aileen Wuornos' last meal, she requested a "single cup of black coffee," not KFC as was once reported. Her last words before the execution were, "Yes, I would just like to say I'm sailing with the rock, and I'll be back, like Independence Day with Jesus. June 6, like the movie. Big mother ship and all, I'll be back, I'll be back." At 9:47 a.m. EDT, Aileen Wuornos died.
>
> Suffice it to say, Wuornos did not return 12 years ago or since, via mother ship or any other means.
>
> *More here:* http://en.wikipedia.org/wiki/Aileen_Wuornos

But Wuornos was not the first to shoot the fast-acting steroid cocktail that is true crime content into a flagging industry. When Jack the Ripper terrorised London in 1888, the 'Ripper' wrote letters to newspaper editors, the first case to create "a worldwide media frenzy" as Wikipedia describes it.

> More here: http://en.wikipedia.org/wiki/Jack_the_Ripper#Media

The 'Ripper' was never caught, and once theory is that he was not an individual but an amalgam of several killers. His persona may even have been concocted by the media to begin with. If the *theory* of concocting a persona was gaining traction in 1888, we, the unsuspecting public must assume a full skillset in crafting narratives over 125 years later.

Remember, the media not only report news, but they must anticipate it. And thus like formula one, or stock car racing, media houses and journalists have to have a plan, have to pace their race, have to spar with competitors, pre-empt them or, if they are at the front, possibly collude to retain their dominance. Collusion implies co-operation. Everybody wins (well, amongst the frontrunners), and a treasure is shared equitably.

Recall that major media houses in South Africa were ready to sell Nelson Mandela's death narrative while he was still alive. Each time he went to hospital, journalists gathered like vultures around the hospital. Some readers may recall a hovering camera fitted copter swooping pterodactyl like around Madiba's hospital window. At the first word of his passing, they could send word to their editors to greenlight torrents of pre-recorded (pre-assembled) coverage. It was all about been first.

And when he did pass, all preparations were in place, and all day radio and TV stations played their pre-recorded interviews. And reaped the benefit of their investment.

> **Disclaimer:** The most honest way I know to interrogate this question of 'culpability' and 'integrity' in the media, and by the media, is to offer my own, firsthand experience in terms of the media. Obviously I am biased towards my own interests and own efforts, and the reader should bear this in mind from the outset.
> But the reader should also bear in mind why this writer is a true freelancer. Why? In order not to have to be beholden to the strictures of this industry, or the narrow-mindedness and singularity of the editor-as-boss-and-final-word scenario, which I experienced at one time when I worked in a newsroom (and was authorised to produce no more than two articles in two years).
> As a writer, and analytical person the reader should also be made aware that while I a writer, am a curious person, I draw the line at covering funerals, and weddings. Hence I took absolutely no interest in reporting Mandela's poor health or funeral. Call me cynical, but the milestones of death and marriage seem to me the most farcical of all in our society, when they really ought to be the opposite.

Right, so now we get to it. Having danced around the topic across a few pages, it's time to get specific, and more personal than I am completely comfortable with, on this question:

> *Was the media culpable?*
> *Is there a personal cost to perpetuating a fake persona*
> *Is there a personal cost to the media,*
> *Is there a personal cost to society,*
> *Is there a personal cost to the celebrities themselves,*
> *and is there a personal cost to the media to us as individuals?*

When we ask, was the media culpable, the full import of the question needs to be spelled out. What we are doing is questioning the honesty and integrity of the media (within a contracting period of the industry's history) in reporting the Oscar Pistorius case.

RESURRECTION demonstrates a media complicit in perpetuating and leveraging a false narrative (that Oscar's competing against able-bodied athletes is 'fair' and beyond circumspection).

I provided Mike Finch (editor of Runner's World) as a go-to example of a fawning editor who took the news of Oscar's bloody recidivism on February 14, 2013, without flinching.

If one considers the other two bodies of my work on this case, the *entirety* of both narratives – *Reeva in her own Words* and *RECIDIVIST ACTS* – both were published on this platform, ie Kindle (non-print, it should be pointed out) because none of it made the cut with print editors.

[**Note:** Aspasia Karras, a one-time colleague and currently the striking brunette editor of Marie Claire magazine was the singular exception. Karras did publish a précis version of *Reeva in her own Words* in their May 2014 issue, and also punted the Reeva story on their cover. Karras also appeared on Carte Blanche's Oscar Trial Channel to discuss this article specifically.]

The author of these works – *Reeva in her own Words* and *RECIDIVIST ACTS* – may be (and should be) biased, which means the reader ought to draw his/her own conclusions on the merit this content could have/would have/should have held within the realms of print media. That's newspapers. And magazines.

The reality is the author submitted these materials across the media spectrum and although there were a few voices of excitement and acceptance, ultimately the bottom-line message was: "We will not be publishing your story."

The reasons could be fivefold:

1. *Content is substandard* (which would be a perfectly reasonable response for not using it)
2. Content is of an acceptable standard but may be *legally problematic* (see earlier comments in this section on the sub-judice rule)
3. *The local and international media suffer from acute ADD (Attention Deficit Disorder) fail to see the bigger picture and are otherwise unaware, and/or ignorant* of what is best practise when reporting on the law, legally and/or ethically, specifically in South Africa. But the media aren't alone in this.

For the sake of clarity ADD is defined (by Wikipedia) as:

'Predominant Inattentiveness' characterized primarily by inattentive concentration or a deficit of sustained attention, such as procrastination, hesitation, and forgetfulness.

More specifically, ADD behaviours are:

Procrastination; *delaying or avoiding starting projects that require vigilant mental effort* (such as reading an eBook like this in its entirety)
Difficulty sustaining concentration *on conversations or briefly losing attention on someone speaking*
Hesitation to sustain concentration *in planning and organizing for the completion of tasks*
Hesitative responses, doubt, and delayed execution *due to inattention remembering information*
Difficulty finishing projects *or completing assignments because many tasks simultaneously on the go*

Forgetting to complete tasks *and details after temporary switches to more stimulating tasks*
Difficulty finding misplaced tools after task switching due to bypassing adequate memory storage
Sustained information processing is slower than others causing information gaps that inhibit execution
Problems remembering emails, appointments, obligations*, or instructions*
Difficulty learning new projects when concentration deficits cause desire to multitask or daydream
Distracted from persevering *during work; difficulty holding onto a job for a significant amount of time*
*Change plans to the inconvenience of others due to forgetting or **not fully aware of the bigger scenario***
Difficulty transitioning to new task *or activity due to obsessive behaviour*

Author's note: My unscientific opinion is that due to the enormous varieties and quantities of media, and the dearth of platforms broadcasting these barrages of info-noise at us, we become sitting ducks. The problem is the lack of filters and systems for organising the deluge of media. Because these filters aren't in place the average suburban user by definition suffers various levels of mild and extreme ADD at different times.

Put simply, *any person with a smartphone* seems incapable of remaining focused on the here and now even for a modest length of time, and is virtually incapable of focused attention or concentration for greater lengths of time (an hour or more) because the phone's notifications tend to be the absolute first priority for most users (even if the notification causing the distraction turns out to be a belated smiley faced sent via whatsapp.)

In other words, ADD is part and parcel of a growing societal malaise.

Bertus Preller, a divorce lawyer, and a friend, has highlighted *social media* propensity as the main culprit driving loving partners to distraction. It is – GASP – a *major* modern cause of divorce in contemporary families; you have been warned!

    4.   *The media have colluded/are colluding* in order to draw out this narrative, to its very last drop of blood, to maximise the potential treasure trove of the story (ie greed is the overriding objective)

    5.   *The media are playing it as smart as they possibly can* (their behaviour is thus impersonal but 'strategic' in the business sense).

If it is #4, then:

    1. The media are pretending not to know, and not to have insights into this case, in order to profit from this (in other words, their deception enriches them, at our expense, and the media purposefully has attempted to turn journalism in 'soap opera'; which is short episodes that slowly move the narrative forward, in order to perpetuate the longevity of the narrative, but not the narrative itself.

The reader should familiarise him or herself with the 'storytelling' nature of soap opera narratives here:

    http://en.wikipedia.org/wiki/Soap_opera#Story_and_episode_structure

And:

http://en.wikipedia.org/wiki/Soap_opera#Plots_and_storylines

2. To perpetuate soap opera, the media must avoid both factual reporting, and insightful analysis. An open-mindeness for drama and above news analysis means the narrative is perpetuated, because it remains open-ended. The Oscar Trial Channel has been very straightforward in limiting discussions about motive, and innocent/guilt. While on thje face of this these may seem couched in legal incentives (some of which are valid) it is also clearly in the media's interest to leave these discussions until the absolute last moment (ie after sentencing).

If this seems like an assumption, here is an editor of one of South Africa's largest selling weekend newspapers revealing his position on this issue:

I have not read Nick's e-book, although he has offered articles it to us for publication. Interrogation of Oscar's motive ought to happen in court; there is no evidence before us or the judge at this stage to suggest there was a particular reason Oscar may have wanted to rid the world of Reeva. But of course we remain open to any leads or evidence that may reach us.

At this stage we will not take up your offer to publish your piece, but please do not hesitate to approach me again.

And a UK journalist:

No. I think he's an idiot [Nick vd Leek].The reason the SA media will not publicise his book has nothing to do with Brand Pistorius and everything to do with the sub judice rule. Your mate is very likely to find himself in contempt of court at the very least. At worst he may have handed Pistorius his Get Out of Jail Card. If Oscar is convicted his lawyers can now seek a mistrial on the grounds that your mate has prejudiced the outcome. If that fails they can seek an appeal on the same grounds.

When I approached the Editor in Chief of Guardian Newspapers, and author, Alan Rusbridger, pitching the idea of a 'plausible motive', Rusbridger referred me to the Guardian's Africa correspondent, David Smith. This was a setback, because I thought it was odd that Smith followed me to send me to send a Direct Message on twitter (July 7), and then immediately unfollowed me. It's suspicious because why, if you are following 22 000 people on twitter, why would you particularly care to unfollow a random 22 001 tweeter?

But since Rusbridger, in London, had alerted his man in Johannesburg, to my pitch Smith then made contact via email on July 13th:

Thanks. I'd be interested to hear your theory about the motive. Jealousy leading to an argument?

I made a little dig at Smith at this point, reminding him that despite his interest, I had (or thought I had) emailed him on an earlier occasion, but that email was never acknowledged.

[It now appears no email was sent, despite Smith direct messaging his email address.]

I don't remember receiving an email from you previously and, when I do a search in my inbox, I can't find anything from you. Perhaps it went to the spam folder. Anyway, I can't quite tell from your email or attachments what the proposed story actually is.

When the pitch was explained, I appended these two words to the end of it:

make sense?

Smith: *Yes it does, thanks, but it's not something I would write about in a news report. I hope the eBook continues to do well.*

Why not? Not newsy?

Smith: *No, more comment/opinion.*

Of course, the entire eBook series is just that, isn't it? Opinion. And the media are more interested in facts. Right? Criminals and serial killers have always sold newspapers. Because facts sell, not fear. Newsy insights are what matter, not outrage. It's information that counts, not emotion. Right?

Well, the Guardian does seem to be a newspaper that's more interested in news than emotions, analysis, comment or opinion.

On July 16th, the Guardian published this [commentary about 'Brand Pistorius']
http://www.theguardian.com/commentisfree/2014/jul/16/brand-pistorius-tweeting-brands-pr

In April, the Guardian published this commentary about 'being hooked':
http://www.theguardian.com/commentisfree/2014/apr/15/watching-oscar-pistorious-trial-reeva-steenkamp

Is this news?

In *RESURRECTION* I have quoted liberally from the excellent investigative reporting of two journalists.

Sokolove and McEvoy are arguably the only two journalists that have had the courage and insight to reveal the 'real Oscar'. Can their insights, analysis and firsthand experience be called 'news' or 'comment'? And if it is comment, does that mean it has no merit, or no meaning? Or is comment all about the credibility (or the accord the media give to the credibility) of a particular author?

If the reader has not studied *RESURRECTION*, the particular articles that interrogate (that is challenge, examine, test and investigate) the authenticity of Oscar's narrative (and the media's narrative of Oscar, by extension) are noteworthy:

1. I'm done talking about my legs – Oscar by Jonathan McEvoy, Daily Mail, August 2011 [prior to London Olympics]
http://www.iol.co.za/sport/athletics/i-m-done-talking-about-my-legs-oscar-1.1121468#.U8tuhRCSxOg

Updated 14 February 2013:
http://www.dailymail.co.uk/sport/olympics/article-2027614/London-Olympics-2012-Oscar-Pistorius-I-wouldnt-want-run-I-cheating-I-believe-purity-sport.html

2. The Fast Life of Oscar Pistorius, by Michael Sokolove, New York Times, January 2012 [prior to London Olympics]
http://www.nytimes.com/2012/01/22/magazine/oscar-pistorius.html?pagewanted=all&_r=0

3. Oscar Pistorius and the Olympics: The Controversy Continues, by South Africa's Sport Scientist, Dr Ross Tucker, Runner's World, 18 Julky 2012 [during the London Olympics]
http://www.runnersworld.co.za/columns/ask-the-experts/oscar-pistorius-olympics/

In terms of interrogating the validity of Oscar's narrative (exhaustively covered in *RESURRECTION*) it's hard to choose which of these three is the best. Is it news? David Smith would likely say 'No'. Were there many articles questioning Oscar's competing in the able-bodied Olympics? If they were, the tone was broadly supportive. After all, the point is that by selling Oscar, you also sell newspapers. By selling Oscar, you also sell the Olympics. In other words, there is an incentive to sell, an incentive to monetise, and this exposes the media's fatal flaw. This is the media's bias – and underlying motive – it's real *raison d'tre* made manifest.

But the above links are all pre February 14, 2013. Has the media really interrogated *itself*, or taken any trouble to interrogate the Oscar case, since February 14, 2013? There's not much evidence that it has. One symptom of this is the ongoing 'all about Oscar' saga. It's all about Oscar, with one exception: as long as there's no real attempt at probing particular lines of questioning (such as along the lines of culpability, motive, or even method).

Part and parcel of the media's culpability then is their failure to pay any meaningful attention to the real victim. This can partly be explained, no doubt, by the reluctance, resistance and reticence by Reeva's closest family and friends to share their firsthand insights in her life. Perhaps it is distasteful. Perhaps it is not moral or ethical. Perhaps these disclosures are contractual and thus can only be revealed to select (paying) customers in the media. And let's face it, book deals are going down in a big way. Seven books, is it, are being written?

[**UPDATE 14 November 2014**: Including *Reeva: A Mother's Story*, by June Steenkamp, published on November 6, 2014…

http://www.amazon.com/Reeva-Mothers-Story-June-Steenkamp-ebook/dp/B00NNR0X3G/ref=pd_sim_kstore_3?ie=UTF8&refRID=1JCXT3STFXGDJNCRP97G

….Update Ends]

More on that in a moment.

[**UPDATE 14 November 2014**: The reticence – both in court and in terms of the media – by the Steenkamps turned out to be a 'sort've contract' with Oscar after all. In exchange for

R6000 per month from Oscar, the Steenkamps were expected to not testify in court in aggravation of sentence. And also not to disclose these payments. Thus, during sentencing, Oscar's defence could claim – in mitigation – the victim's family were 'secretly' receiving payments, and so they did.

As a result of the agreement, neither of Reeva's parents testified in aggravation, but after it was revealed they were receiving money from Oscar, the Steenkamps declared they would be paying every cent of the 'blood money' back. At this point it's uncertain if this has occurred or not.

http://www.theguardian.com/world/2014/oct/14/reeva-steenkamp-parents-payments-oscar-pistorius

http://www.dailymail.co.uk/news/article-2831193/Reeva-Steenkamp-s-mother-reveals-torturous-decision-accept-6-000-blood-money-payments-Oscar-Pistorius.html

....**Update Ends**].

The question remains, in the mainstream media, why is there still so much mystery (and anonymity) surrounding Reeva? Who was Reeva? Where is *her* voice? With so much information in the public domain, why haven't we heard it? Why has no one really vouched for Reeva since Cecil Myers did?

Meanwhile Oscar's validators are coming out of the woodwork. Arnold, Azzie, Arnu, Derman, Leo and not least of all, the media itself. On Twitter, when his profile tweets to life, his adoring fans are back, begging him to follow them. Gushing in their support. Bible verses make news headlines. And a brawl, complete with (another) press statement from his family, and from his PR spokesmen, Michelle Burgess.

Why does Reeva in her own Words evidently, not matter?

One article that stands out from the clamour to participate in this persona is The Telegraph's *Oscar Pistorius: from 2012 stardom to murder trial* by Paul Hayward.

11:49PM GMT 14 Feb 2013
Oscar Pistorius is the Blade Runner who united disabled and able-bodied sport. He bestrode the Olympic and Paralympic Games of London 2012 like an advert for the human spirit.

But his cartoon hero status will be inadmissible when he appears in court in Pretoria on Friday charged with murdering his 30-year-old girlfriend.

The death of Reeva Steenkamp from gunshot wounds at Pistorius's home in a gated community in South Africa was a tragedy with only one true victim: the law graduate, entrepreneur, television presenter and model who died at the hands of perhaps the most famous runner after Usain Bolt, whether accidentally or by design.

Either way, one of the most romantic sporting tales of modern times has been engulfed by darkness. Pistorius was emblematic of London 2012. He was an inspiration who had defeated

those who tried to stop him running on the main Olympic stage. He was the man who bounced across the gap between the two London carnivals.

Now, the world convulses in shock and Pistorius enters the dock as South Africa's justice system pieces together the grim events of Wednesday night and Thursday morning: Valentine's morning.

Memories of Pistorius in London remain vivid. Few nights went by in the media zones of the Olympic Stadium without his excited chatter moving along the line of cameras and voice recorders. Often he would tell his uplifting tale for an hour before finally padding away on his carbon fibre blades. We stage-door-johnnies would marvel at his appetite for publicity, his willingness to answer the same question endless times. Some nights he would give 20 interviews. Whole races would go by and Pistorius would still be talking. The tone was always the same: buoyant, affable, proud.

Pistorius was his own PR department for the amazing story of how he broke down the barriers of Olympic sport. "I'm not disabled, I just don't have legs," he liked to say. This was a personal movie about one man's refusal to be held back by a physical calamity. But it was also **a broadcast to the world** [emphasis mine]: to amputees and people with other debilitating conditions. He was throwing open the doors of sport to all.

He was a symbol[emphasis mine], a moment in history, **a one-man parade of the human will** [emphasis mine]. He reached the semi-finals of the Olympic 400m before moving on to win silver in the T44 200m, gold in the 4x100 relay and gold in the T44 400m at the Paralympics, where he was a combination of poster boy and elder statesman.

His voice box was always working, his smile never extinguished, except for the day he stirred up controversy by accusing fellow Paralympian runners of adjusting the length of their blades to gain an edge. Even then he managed to present himself as the guardian of the sport, a fierce advocate of fair play....With the filmic grandeur of his story came a celebrity profile, not only in South Africa but across the world. A large PR industry grew up around him and he became a billboard regular. Advertisers loved him because **he conveyed a message deeper than money** [emphasis mine] or medals. Here was an athlete on the cutting edge of science, propelled not only by technology but his own courage. London 2012 was his chance to join Bolt and co in the worldwide consciousness and he expended every ounce of spare effort to make his story heard.

With all this swirling in our heads, the news that Pistorius had been charged with the murder of Miss Steenkamp at his home in the Silverlakes complex in the Boschkop area of Pretoria arrived as two possibilities: accident or crime.

Either way it has wiped out the sporting narrative [emphasis mine].

To leap from recollections of Pistorius sharing the London stage with Usain Bolt, Mo Farah and Jessica Ennis to an image of fatal gunshot wounds was indeed a shock. Whatever the truth, this is one more good reason to stop thinking the lives of top sportsmen and women are somehow superhuman and blessed.

The jolts keep coming. In the last few days alone we have heard allegations of **industrial-scale match-fixing in football** [emphasis mine] *and a "widespread" performance-enhancing drug problem in Australia. In Madrid, a major doping trial is sucking in sports beyond cycling, itself reeling from the* **Lance Armstrong scandal** [emphasis mine]. *Paul Gascoigne, one of the most talented English footballers since 1966, has put his life at risk through drink.*

Strictly, there is no connection between these events and the terrible news about Reeva Steenkamp. But they tell us not to think the gods of the sporting world lead better or simpler lives...Pistorius was the one the whole world knew. But he will no longer be known as the Blade Runner: the man who led disabled sport into the bright lights. His global renown will be much darker now. He will always be the man on "cheetah blades" who picked up a gun and, whether by accident or deliberately, dispatched a woman to oblivion.

In that sense his part in London 2012 already reads less like a triumph over adversity than a cautionary tale.

http://www.telegraph.co.uk/news/worldnews/africaandindianocean/southafrica/9871914/Oscar-Pistorius-from-2012-stardom-to-murder-trial.html

What's interesting is this comes from the British media, and behind a paywall. In South Africa, publications such as South Africa's largest magazine (Huisgenoot/You) would rather sympathise with Oscar's feelings of 'worthlessness' and his 'suicidal' feelings.

[**Update November 2014**: *A recent article in Huisgenoot/You examines how Oscar may begin again ,find love again, and rebuild his life. It also bemoans the difficulty Oscar will have trying to train 'optimally' whilst in jail...*]

In fact, if the reader feels there is any uncertainty about the media, and South Africa's media in particular in their sticking to the 'it's all about Oscar' tune, have a look at virtually every article on Huisgenoot's website:

http://huisgenoot.com/kategorie/nuus/oscar-pistorius/

But there's a difference between media strategy (ie doing good media business, point #5 above, which Huisgenoot may be guilty of) and ignorance, which this writer places in the realms of poor (substandard) reporting.

Is London's The Telegraph an example of a 'good' publication, and Huisgenoot, an instance of a 'bad' publication? Things are never that cut and dried. Just like car racing, a race car is only as good as its driver, and the driver, is to some extent only as good as the crew supporting the driver behind the scenes.

No matter how good a job the race car crew does, or the capabilities of the engine, or the quality of the tyre, a bad driver can wreck all of it.

In my opinion (and that's all it is) on the 4th of March, The Telegraph's Aislinn Laing makes a subtle but critical error in her article: *Oscar Pistorius murder trial: Witness heard argument before shots*

> Laing writes: *Miss Burger told a packed Pretoria's high court on Monday that she heard a woman screaming and shouting for help, then a man shouting for help, then the woman screaming again before shots were fired.*
>
> http://www.telegraph.co.uk/news/worldnews/oscar-pistorius/10675289/Oscar-Pistorius-murder-trial-Witness-heard-argument-before-shots.html

Also listen to the audio clip at the above link to follow Laing's 'reasoned' reporting on this particular issue.

It may be a difference of opinion, but it may also come down to a difference of fact (and thus poor reporting, and poor following of the court proceedings, despite being present in court at the time). I must apologise for bringing myself into this, but I must also emphasise at the same time that the reasoning here, though intuitive, is necessarily subjective. In other words, Laing, at the end of the day, could have reported accurately, and I could be wrong.

But I don't believe that. Part of the problem here is Burger's obtuse testimony, and Nel's failure to verify elements of it (unless it was a strategy to obscure this point until he revealed the strength of his hand during closing arguments). This is an interesting question which will likely be answered sooner, rather than later.

The point is, although Burger (who is a doctor, and arguably the best, the most credible and most accurate of all the state's witnesses) mentions a woman and man shouting for help, my impression is that in her explanation, muddled sometimes by the interpreter, she simply means to make the point that:

1. A woman shouted for help.
2. A man shouted for help.

But the way Laing 'frames' it, suggests that Oscar and Reeva both shouted for help, and then shots were fired. Even within the schema of Oscar's version, this doesn't sound right (because Oscar said Reeva never once cried out, let alone shouted audible words for help).

It must be emphasised that the reader follow the more than slightly subtle line of reasoning here. The portent of this seemingly inconsequential piece of evidence is critical to the final chapter, where the incident, it's psychology and methodology, itself will be revealed (as a hypothesis).

While Laing can be forgiven for repeating Burger's admittedly unclear testimony, she appears to have missed its strategic value. Barry Roux, however, did not.

http://www.nickvanderleek.com/2014/07/reeva-couldnt-possibly-have-screamed.html

Previously, I have highlighted his strident response to Burger, where Roux took pains to extricate out of the state's witness the incongruity of a scenario where not only a woman shouted for help, but also a man. How could she explain it, he asked? Burger finally addressed his question by reluctantly answering, that she did not know, could not speak for

Oscar, but suggested it might be "a mockery". To reference this, see audio clip at the above link, @ **0:49**.

This response animated Roux perhaps to the greatest extent we've seen during the entire trial. It even prompted Nel to jump up and protect his witness from further 'badgering'.

Here's additional reportage on the same point. Note the sequence is slightly, subtly different here compared to Laing's version of events as revealed to the court:

"She screamed terribly and she yelled for help.

"Then I also heard a man screaming for help. Three times he yelled for help."

Thinking it was a violent break-in, Ms Burger said her husband called the private security firm guarding their upmarket housing estate in Pretoria's eastern suburbs, before the pair heard more shouts.

"I heard the screams again. It was worse. It was more intense," Ms Burger told the court, her voice cracking with emotion.

"She was very scared.

"Just after her screams, I heard four shots. Four gunshots. Bang ... bang, bang, bang."

Note: Despite the inference one might make here, Burger does not specifically say a woman's screams, then a man's screams, *then shots*. She first establishes that she heard a woman and a man, referring to the entirety of the night. In RESURRECTION I clarified that both Oscar and Stipp clearly state that the man's three screams for help occurred after the gunshots. If anyone ought to know, it is Oscar. This evidence, the timing of the man's screams *after the shots*, let me reiterate, is absolutely crucial in our attempt at piecing together motive, intention and the method behind the madness of that took place early on Valentine's morning in 2013.

Burger: *"It was very traumatic for me. You could hear that it was bloodcurdling screams."*

Pistorius lawyer Barry Roux repeatedly and pointedly challenged Ms Burger, picking at potential inconsistencies in her account.

http://www.abc.net.au/news/2014-03-03/oscar-pistorius-pleads-not-guilty-to-murdering-girlfriend/5296068

Now, let's go to the reporting by elements of the South African media on that day, 14 February 2013.

I recommend the reader follows this link to get the gist of my argument:

http://www.nickvanderleek.com/2014/07/reeva-steenkamp-was-my-homegirl-but-not.html

In summary, Hagen Engler, the former editor of FHM wasted little time (possibly no time at all) in getting his 'in' with the media, that he was the go-to-guy for content on his 'homegirl' Reeva. Why his timing is interesting, is we know Beeld broke the story (officially) on twitter at 08:03 and Radio 702's Aki Anastasiou 5 minutes later (08:08).

http://grubstreet.co.za/2014/07/08/stuff-sans-the-eye-candy-talks-to-shifting-publishing-trends/

If the *Daily Maverick's* clock is wrong, and it may not have been, then this story ought to be a scandal. And it would scandalise not only Engler, but all and sundry at the *Daily Maverick*.

Although I did email the editor *of Daily Maverick* on July 12 2014 (see below link) to verify whether the time the article was posted *was* in fact 07:28 AM on14 February 2013, and I also emailed Engler to verify the same, neither have responded to date (20 July 2014). ADD?

To be honest, I find it unlikely. No, not ADD, that's actually very likely. No, the likelihood that the article was posted in the evening does bear out in the actual *schema* of the day. Why? Firstly, I have discussed this with at least one other freelancer, and it seems more likely that the error is – after all – simply in the juxtaposing of AM rather than PM. This makes sense when one looks at the time the article was tweeted for the first time (early evening) and I have contacted (over twitter) some of the first responders to these tweets, and thus far all were unanimous that their responses were in the evening, rather than the morning.

So we see, if one is serious about 'interrogating a narrative' one has to apply the same open-minded reasoning to one's *own* narratives too.

http://www.nickvanderleek.com/2014/07/first-tweet.html

Note the times and dates of the tweets in response to Engler's story at the above link. And, for interest sake, note the date of an email sent to the editor of the *Daily Maverick* (which has to date not been acknowledged).

If we're asking whether the *Daily Maverick*, a particular publication (and it's really no more than just a particular *online* platform) if they are 'culpable' of anything, the answer appears to be, 'not really'.

Does that mean they should be left off the hook? The answer is probably the same, 'not really'. Here's why:

In my attempts to investigate the correct time this article was posted, I not only contacted the *Daily Maverick* editor, and Engler, but also one of its reporters, Rebecca Davis. I did get a response out of, but not the sort of response I'd expected. Personally, until this interaction, I held Davies in high regard for her insightful articles and analysis, especially this one:

http://www.dailymaverick.co.za/article/2014-03-03-heart-of-oscars-defence-imagined-threat-of-a-black-stranger/

I have highlighted that article on more than one occasion in this series, and, ironically, am about to do so for the last time in question 13 (not the next, but the penultimate question).

Suffice it to say, the following interaction on twitter with Davis and Brodie did not leave me with a particularly flattering impression of either ladies, and the reader will notice took me the low road, and didn't mince words with them either:

Rebecca Davis @becsplanb 14 Feb 2013 "Though [Reeva's] personality sparkled like the night sky, she was carrying a bit of extra weight." - Necessary??
http://www.dailymaverick.co.za/opinionista/2013-02-14-the-reeva-i-knew/...

Nechama Brodie @brodiegal 14 Feb 2013 @becsplanb in context, yes. should we pretend such things don't matter?

Rebecca Davis @becsplanb 14 Feb 2013 @brodiegal It just seems so ICKY in an obituary!

Nick van der Leek @HiRezLife 13h @becsplanb @brodiegal got to say Brodie in this context you absolutely lack common sense.

@HiRezLife why are you going through & commenting on 17-month-old tweets???! @becsplanb

Nick van der Leek @HiRezLife 5h @brodiegal @becsplanb Because I'm doing research. And frankly, you're a woman right, you should be ashamed.

Nechama Brodie @brodiegal 4h @HiRezLife you're asking dozens of twitter users what time they RT'd @HagenEngler's piece for the DM last year! it's freaky @becsplanb 5:01 AM - 13 Jul 2014 ·

Nick van der Leek @HiRezLife 4h @brodiegal @HagenEngler @becsplanb actually what's more freaky is the time of the actual article you're defending. 07:28am.

Nick van der Leek @HiRezLife 4h @brodiegal @HagenEngler @becsplanb but please, keep defending yourself.

@becsplanb 2h @HiRezLife Please stop bombarding me with these messages. I have absolutely no idea what you are on about!

One would think that a cursory glance at a tweet might answer the question (I have absolutely no idea what you are on about!) but Davis apparently elects not to do this, either because the line of questioning is:

1. *substandard* (which would be a perfectly reasonable response for not responding)
2. standard is acceptable but may be *legally problematic*
3. *acute ADD, unawareness or ignorance*
4. *media collusion*
5. *The media are playing it as smart as they possibly can*

I will leave it to the reader to decide which is the most likely in this case.

Before I wrap up this section, and there are really volumes and volumes of data that are applicable, let's highlight a few stories that we know, in retrospect, were flawed, dead ends or otherwise defective. Off the top my head:

1. *Pistorius 'DID beat model girlfriend with a cricket bat' before he shot her, police tell horrified family - and relatives have seen her extensive head injuries*
   Key quote:

Olympic sprinter Oscar Pistorius crushed his girlfriend's skull with a cricket bat before shooting her dead, police have told her family.
Details of the post-mortem examination of South African model Reeva Steenkamp were withheld from last week's bail application hearing.

But grieving relatives who saw her body before Tuesday's cremation in Port Elizabeth described horrific injuries from the cricket bat, and entry wounds from 9mm bullets fired by Pistorius.

They were also briefed about the model's death by police and lawyers from the state prosecutor's office.

http://www.dailymail.co.uk/news/article-2283507/Oscar-Pistorius-DID-beat-model-girlfriend-Reeva-Steenkamp-cricket-bat-shot-her.html#ixzz380UgCaCr

2. *Oscar Pistorius murder charge: 'steroids found at athlete's home'* [by Aislin Laing]
   Key quotes:

Police asked for blood taken from Mr Pistorius to be tested for steroids, **City Press** *claimed, in anticipation that his defence team might claim he acted in "roid rage" – an aggressive condition associated with taking large doses of performance-enhancing drugs. A source told* **The Sun**: *"Steroid drugs were found at Pistorius's home together with evidence of heavy drinking. That's why police have specifically ordered that he be tested for steroids."*

The case has provoked an intense bout of soul-searching in South Africa about the high violent crime rates that lead many people to keep guns at their homes.

http://www.telegraph.co.uk/news/worldnews/africaandindianocean/southafrica/9877016/Oscar-Pistorius-murder-charge-steroids-found-at-athletes-home.html

3. *Hougaard: Oscar has nothing to do with me.*
   Key quote:

It was reported this week that Steenkamp and Oscar Pistorius started dating just three days after her split from the Blue Bulls scrum half.
It is also believed that Hougaard contacted the blonde model soon before Pistorius shot and killed her in the early hours of February 14.
"It has nothing to do with me," Hougaard told City Press at the launch party of the Daytona Group's KwaZulu-Natal branch. Daytona is the official agent of Aston Martin, Rolls Royce and McLaren in Africa.
Hougaard and Pistorius move in the same social circles, and both met Steenkamp through Daytona's chief executive, Justin Divaris.
Divaris' girlfriend, Samantha Greyvenstein, knew Steenkamp through modelling – and Divaris was one of the first people Pistorius called after shooting her.
At the Daytona launch party on Thursday evening, hostesses draped in black kept champagne glasses brimming. Among the cars showcased was a Rolls Royce Ghost with a price tag of R5 million.
Speaking to City Press, Hougaard was happy to elaborate on his love of cars.
"I'm mad about cars. From a young age, it's always been a passion of mine," he said.
He looked dapper in dark jeans, a black shirt and gel-slicked hair. He said he enjoyed attending Daytona functions for business opportunities and to meet new people.
Divaris said the Umhlanga branch had made four sales in its first three weeks of operation – two Aston Martins and two McLarens. He refused to comment on Pistorius, though, merely saying: "He is my friend, that's all I can say".

Far away from such glamour, the athlete's legal team and brother, Carl, had coffee and toast with anchovette at Caught Coffee at the Pretoria Magistrates Court on Tuesday.

Pistorius' 10-minute appearance sparked a media storm, with journalists from around the globe piling into the court to chronicle him staring ahead detachedly. His trial was postponed to August 19.

The owner of Caught Coffee, Hannetjie van Rensburg, said the case had greatly inflated the shop's turnover. "It's the biggest media circus I've seen in seven years of being here. With the Nair hearings, profits doubled."

http://www.citypress.co.za/news/hougaard-oscar-has-nothing-to-do-with-me/

So...

Was the media culpable?

Yes, in both the pre-killing narrative, and after the incident, the media seem to be colluding to the same agenda. Draw the story out as far as possible. This may not be in the public interest, but in the media's interest, as a business resolution.

Is there a personal cost to perpetuating a fake persona?

It could even be argued that Reeva was a victim of her 'model' persona. Is there a personal cost? Think of Michael Jackon, Tiger Woods, Lance Armstrong, Princess Diana. The media and a celebrity persona are like a strange lopsided dance between Batman and the Joker. It's not necessarily conscious or consciously co-operative, but there is no doubt the one enables the other. And the costs are huge.

Is there a personal cost to the media?

If the media is more beholden to money than to the public interest, then that personal cost is higher than we can afford. The media act as barometers of the public conscience, or should. Money clouds these perceptions, reflections and conceptions.

Is there a personal cost to society?

The Penguin in *Batman Returns*, 1992: *You gotta admit I played this stinkin' city like a harp from hell.*

Is there a cost to maintaining a soap opera? Is there a cost to maintaining an artificial narrative way beyond it's sell-by-date? Arguably, the cost in wearing through our attention spans with junk information, or non-news as news, is the highest cost of all.

Is there a personal cost to the celebrities themselves?

Yes, there are costs, some of which they pay with their lives, but there are also benefits, endowments which can run into millions and multi-millions of dollars. So if there is a cost, it appears most media players carry them in order to enjoy the benefits. What is most deleterious about this behaviour is that because we treat these celebrities as models, because we aspire to be like them, we also impute into our own lives this 'truth' (which is actually a lie) that money is more important than authentic living. Or put differently, living a lie, and an unhappy lie, is worth it, and a small price to pay towards the only real reward, which is 'material' happiness.

And is there a personal cost to us as individuals?

This is a question only the individual can answer.

But this link:

http://www.couriermail.com.au/sport/commonwealth-games/no-love-for-volatile-oscar-pistorius-from-exsouth-african-teammates-at-commonwealth-games/story-fnntmmqu-1226995243624?nk=a53ee31299c64538c6f27629820ddc5e\

shows that even athletes and officials close to Oscar, who admit to being aggrieved by him (Fourie being one) are nevertheless too cowed by impressions of moneyed power, moneyed media and moneyed celebrity, lest they find themselves isolated and victimised.

"We all knew he had a different side to him but it was rarely placed on public view. He played the media beautifully while he was running.

Though Fourie later denied the claim, many believe it was true. There were other reports that during Pistorius' days on tour other runners did not want to room with him and that he sent vile text messages to male and female journalists.

Many South African journalists refused to criticise him during his athletics career for fear of being seen a cynic trying to tear down a national hero.

"When he admitted to a 'fight or flight' instinct where sudden loud noises such as a car backfiring freaked him out I wondered how did he cope with the starter's gun when he ran?" the official said.

"If he was so scared of loud noises how did he ever get out of the blocks after the bang? I'm serious. The question should have been asked."

Whose fault is it when one man behaves unacceptably, yet even his detractors do and say nothing? There is an adage that goes: *evil flourishes when good men do* (or say) *nothing*.

In this sense, the media, the public and even Oscar's detractors are co-conspirators. Why? Because silence is consent. It's tacit support.

Is there any cost *greater* than investing large fractions of one's time, energy, attention, hopes and often one's treasure, in something (or someone) that is a fraud? Imagine the crisis when your partner turns out to have deceived you about their sexual orientation, or religion, or any other fundamental truths. When the identity of a person or the authenticity of a narrative that is important to us turns out to be counterfeit, it calls into question our own identities, and our ability to question, and discern what is true about ourselves and the world, and what is not. Is there a personal cost? Of course there is. Anchored reference points begin to float and our definitions, our values (for and of *ourselves*) are set adrift. This can be an alarming process, but if we have the strength, the resolve and the integrity to interrogate these mutable reference points in ourselves, it becomes a vital journey filled with revelation and enlightenment. Yes, we might even learn from our mistakes, if we pay attention to them. And when that happens, there's transformation. Or in a word: *Resitutio*.

12. Legacy Lifestyle/Daytona Group/FHM/Nike/Oakley/tattoos ...is it Objectification, and is Objectification evil?

Your life is the fruit of your own doing. You have no one to blame but yourself. – Joseph Campbell

For this section, it isn't necessary to spell out all the details here. This has been inferred in the section above, especially immediately above. Lance Armstrong is a good example of a man who got carried away (and arguably *with*) his own narrative. But controlling a narrative is not the same as an authentic narrative.

Although this is a subject worthy of further research and investigation [hint to Barry Bateman, Karyn Maughan, Debora Patta] due to the secrecy of Francois Hougaard, and the media's silence on this issue, I will do no more than make a cursory observation.

Firstly, whilst it's been made abundantly clear that Reeva Steenkamp was managed by Capacity Relationships, what has been left out – a gaping hole in fact – of her story, is that Reeva herself represented the cause of *Legacy Lifestyle*. Francois Hougaard also belonged to this stable (although appears to no longer), and Reeva had recently attached her brand to it in the weeks and months leading up to her death.

Visit the *Legacy Lifestyle* website here:

http://www.legacylifestyle.co.za/

WELCOME TO LEGACY LIFESTYLE...
THE REWARDS YOU'VE EARNED WILL PAY FOR THE LIFESTYLE YOU DESERVE
Legacy Lifestyle is about big money, luxury brands, and broad ambassadorial duties. It is Reeva's connection to *Legacy Lifestyle* that actually defines her 'emergence' as a real player, in South Africa's elite inner celebrity circle. This is also the reason behind her wanting a new definition for herself. Instead of the FHM bikini model label (something she had aspired towards for at least three years), once she achieved this label she wanted to be seen as a 'classic model' instead. This is also what *Legacy Lifestyle* wanted. Would Reeva, as a brand ambassador for *Legacy Lifestyle* be able to endorse a particulasr brand of luxury watches, or a particular airline, or brand of hotel, or line of apparel etc as Oscar's girlfriend?

If Oscar, sponsored by Nike, flew with British Airways to Manchester, and Reeva sat beside him, and she was contractually obligated to play ambassador to Oscar's brands (in return for airfare, accommodation etc), how could she also endorse her *Legacy Lifestyle* brands, such as Cross Trainer and South African Airways?

See the conflict?

http://www.legacylifestyle.co.za/partners.cfm

Now, look at the personalities on their current list. Do they strike you as celebrities, individuals in their own right, or the partners of celebrities? See the problem?

http://www.legacylifestyle.co.za//personalities.cfm

Objectification

- *to treat as an object or cause to have objective reality*
- *to give expression to (as **an abstract notion**, feeling, **or ideal**) in **a form that can be experienced by others*** <it is the essence of the fairy tale to *objectify* differing facets of the child's emotional experience — John Updike

From **The Urban Dictionary**:

A hair colour sometimes associated with unintelligence when in fact intelligence is not affected noticeably by hair colour.

Example: She's blonde...who cares?

From Wikipedia: In social philosophy, objectification means treating a person as a thing, without regard to their **dignity**.

[Author's note]: As a photographer (of people, places and things) I can write with some authority, and firsthand experience on this broad idea of *objectification*.

In my opening salva, let's be clear: a photographer very broadly must try to capture the object his lens is pointing to *in the best light*. In other words, you're trying to show your object in the best way you possibly can, yes, and a good photographer can cheat a little, and pretend something is bigger, brighter, rounder, (insert-your-pleasure here)-er than it actually is.

Is is actually mesmerising how talented young women often are at traversing a range of narratives, a visual spectrum ranging from innocent schoolgirl to Cosmo covergirl (early thirties). Is is impressive, and not a little scary. The merest movement of a shoulder strap can transform a silly little girl into a seductive, self possessed temptress.

It is also the photographer's job – without crossing professional or personal boundaries of course – to show off the assets of his client to full effect. The model may sometimes ask if she is showing herself off to full effect, and the photographer may have to give pointers to help her do so. This applies to light in eyes, how the face/skin appears in the context and balance of the portrait, how the proportions and shadows match up etc. A good photographer knows how to emphasise all of it, the features, the background, the colours, the clothing, and perhaps spice it up with something that catches (or at least attracts) the viewe.

Laymen and members of the public would be amused to hear how family members, boyfriends, onlookers will often shout impatiently from the sidelines (at model and photographer) to get on with it, 'show your body', '*gooi* the moves', "give some attitude' to get the required sexualised effect. Sometimes some of the whitest skin emerges reluctantly into the sunshine. On one occasion, when I was shooting a calendar, and the theme was explicitly 'sexy girls with cute animals' one young cheerleader arrived with her mother, and simply wouldn't give me anything sexy. Obviously her mother was the deciding influence, and I certainly wasn't going to interfere with that. Curiously, another woman (another mother, and a mother of two boys) arrived with the animal that we'd be featuring in the shoot.

Recognising my debacle, the 'second' mother then stripped down the model, revealing her shoulders, and waist, and a sideview of her breasts. The model's mother did not seem to mind this (as long as it came from another woman), and of course, the shots taken of the cheerleader in this setup (they were the last photos of the day, and just a handful) made it into the calendar. No surprises there for me, but it's an interesting scenario, isn't it?

We may not be consciously aware of society's socially acceptable margins, but subconsciously we must be, and failure to adhere results in social poking, ridicule, insults and isolation (ie social punishment/death). Hence these should not be ignored, and should be antagonised with due care and consideration.

It's astonishing how passing traffic, and perfect strangers, and passer-by suddenly become part of a shoot, as though this weren't an invasion of privacy (which in any other scenario, it would be). Why? Because there is not a small sense, from the public, of being entitled to anything that is objectified. Let's face it, if objectification is the motive, the goal is a public audience.

It's true that in many instances a photographer imbued with a creative and artistic appreciation for things bright and beautiful seeks to edify above all. Yes, there is something sacred and precious in the splendid, those things that – at least for a moment in time – appear to repel life's endless rusts, attritions, and wrinkles.

But it's also true that when I photograph beautiful young women, one tries to address the conventional tenets of beauty. As such I find it easy to photograph women. Men are far trickier simply because a male-oriented society seems to care less about treating men as sexual objects, even if men tirelessly and gratuitously objectify specific portions of their own anatomy.

With women there is a faux subtlety, despite the grandeur (and recent more is more) of the ever-popular female bosom. If there is an area of the female anatomy that is objectified, surely the bosoms play a central role. Revealing the shapes, emphasising the cleavage – yes, that **intermammary cleft or the intermammary sulcus** – all these contrive to communicate not just attractiveness, and fertility, but availability. In other words, ease of use, ease of access, accessibility.

When a woman flaunts to a camera, is she flirting with the object, the man behind the object, someone specific in the audience? Is she truly objectifying herself, or does she mean to communicate a more subtle message (via an admittedly overt tone) namely: I am here. I am beautiful.

On one occasion I photographed the daughter of a pastor in a particularly cheeky and titillating fashion (legs open, church in the background) and when I asked the model what she thought of the message she was communicating she admitted:

- she was a virgin
- did not want to antagonise her father or the church
- did not want to advertise her availability (sexually or otherwise)
- but did want to show herself, generally, as an appealing – ie beautiful – young woman
- her intentions, broadly were, she said, to find a 'trou man' (an eligible bachelor, not for dating, but for a good, honest to goodness marriage

In other words, woman may hijack society's own narrative to further their own agendas. Is misiniterpretation possible? It happens all the time.

Let's come back to the tactics a photographer and model employ to communicate their message effectively. As I've touched on earlier, the way breasts are shown or not shown is a key part of the symbolic contract – which the photographer and model collude in, to hook the viewer/publication/client/sponsor.

Sex sells, and believe it or not, sex can be commoditised. Ask J-Lo, Miley Cyrus, Madonna, Lady Gaga and each and every supermodel. A woman's cleavage, it should not be news to anyone (least of all women themselves) is a precious commodity. Heard the saying:

if you've got it, flaunt it!

http://www.thefrisky.com/photos/10-kinds-of-cleavage/cleavage-71510-m-jpg/

Society wants more, and FHM was all about flaunting sexy youing booty. But the reveal must be done with tact, timin, strategy and the right setting. It must be…tasteful. Why? Because this is a sensitive area and society is ~~neurotic~~ insecure especially in this area, so if you rock too many boats, elements in it waste little time in reactionary payback.

I have experienced this so often with shoots posted to facebook, I've long since found my own 'rule of thumb' which seems to keep ex-boyfriends, parents, jealous rivals and rival photographers envious but not angry on the one side, and interested parties, married stalkers and the anonymous social media mob (along with the client herself) thrilled on the other.

It's astonishing how something that's decided by a random tannie to be 'too sexy' can flare up into nuclear Armageddon on facebook. Astonishing, silly, but not unimportant, and also, important to acknowledge if you want to stay in this business.

Society punishes those who make forays for power (social power, which is attention) excessively. What's 'excessive'. Well it is one of those 'floating' concepts. It's like the definition of promiscuity.

What's the definition of prosmiscuity? Anyone who is having more sex than you are.

Amusing yes, but true, no?

Showing off one's assets (ie objectifying oneself) is also to some extent relative to the age, self-perceived desirability, relationship status, social standing (social power), perceived attractiveness and capability of the person (usually another woman) criticising the model.

We know in *Reeva in her own Words*, and via her Twitterstream, that Reeva was often maligned by other women. As a male photographer I find these vindictive responses oddly silly, because the maligner is clearly exposing themselves for jealousy, nastiness and also that they feel themselves 'outshone'. It seems clear to me, however other women seem to wish to impress not only other men, but also other women, and thus they try to reconcile (explain, validate themselves) even, and often especially to those who invalidate them. But there is an agenda at play. I won't endorse you, because if I do, I lose my sense of validation and my (perceived) spot on the pecking order. The pecking order is a valuable thing. It is society's agreed ranking of where you fit in, what echelon of the social order you belong to (desirable, delicious but ditzy, desperate or dead in the water). One's position is not necessarily a true reflection of oneself, but, let's face it, how one objectifies oneself, how effectively one does so, can certainly propel one either way along the sliding bar. Importantly, it is not so much men who decide where the women fit in, but the individual woman (how she sees herself) and her collaborators and detractors, as a whole. [*End of author's – photographical – note/s*]

So, let's not kid ourselves, objectification is not only real, but plays a valuable role in society. There is a clear contract between society and individuals in terms of give and take – society wants certain select individuals to 'pretend-make-themselves- available'and these individuals (actresses, actors, models) do so, often in exchange for treasure.

Let's face it, the ultimate form of objectification is pornography? Why does it have such a stigma? Why does porn have a stigma, but not glamour modelling? Because porn openly sells the mindless animal psychology.

A cursory glance at the "Adult Entertainment" section of any classified newspapers shows what clients demand from practitioners of the world's oldest profession:

- busty
- Boobs 36DD
- Hot sexy blue-eyed blonde
- Young sexy stunner
- classy

While most people enjoy their own 'animal instincts' from time to time in private, and may intuitively and intimately know and share the animalness about themselves and their lovers (in measured doses) public displays are considered vulgar and inappropriate, and not without good reason. Society considers obviously prostituting oneself not an acceptable average expression of our values or standards towards each other. And Reeva seemed to have similar reservations as we've already seen in exhaustive detail (see *Reeva in her own Words, RECIDIVIST ACTS* and *RESURRECTION*) The impression that the public/society portrays, that humans-as-sexual-animals is shameful, or an aberration, or a minority of cases may, interestingly, be a mass delusion, or a communal deception, as sexuality is by it's very nature both natural and anima-like (ie instinctual, more mind*less* than mind*ful*) . In other words, the animalised (rather than humanised) sexual impulse may well be the average for humans, and statistics showing a third of all internet traffic to porn sites appears to bear this out.

However, society wishes to legitimise itself (which is to say validate, formalise and authoritatively) and to do so it attempts to place itself in a position above such reproachful (yet natural) activity, which is probably a good thing. Why? Because private animal instincts are fine, private one on one sexual behaviour is fine, but public purpose, societal instincts, social drives need to be more altruistic, and as such have to be consented to, regulated, and refined into a form of social contract for more sophisticated group behaviour. If this sounds like Greek, here's the dumbed down version:

Should a son have sex with his attractive girlfriend in the lounge, in front of his father or mother? Why not? Because certain stimulating behaviours stimulate inappropriate responses, and society has learnt over time that certain members need to be protected – even – from themselves.

This, let's be fair, is for the good of both society and its members.

Otherwise, this could happen:

http://perezhilton.com/2013-06-25-adore-trailer-naomi-watts-robin-right-penn-sex-young-men#.U85LPBCSxOh

Having said that, society as a whole is inching closer towards what I call *Pornogrifisation*. The word appears not to exist, but it should. Pornogrifisation is the conscious or subconscious attempt to *pornify* society. The link above, has a decidedly porn theme, yet the actors, Robin Wright and Naomi Watts are by no means out of the mainstream. There are many many additional movies one could highlight that appear to reinforce this trend, but here's a shortlist:

- Vicky, Christina, Barcelona (and many more movies by Woody Allen)
- Rumor Has It
- Eyes Wide Shut
- Sex Lies and Videotape
- Basic Instinct
- Pretty Woman
- Lolita
- Natural Born Killers

What these films, some of them pretty watchable, basically do the opposite of *purify*. Pornogrifisation does many, if not all those things that are objectionable about objectification, but especially:

a) Making adultery or unfaithfulness into a taboo

b) Making incest or social taboos (underage sex, group homosexual sex, sex without precautions including sex without a condom) appear conventional

c) Tattoos and piercings are important ploys in objectifying the flesh (Oscar and Reeva participated in at least one of these).

d) Associating the half naked body with devices or accessories or items of clothing, even jewellery is another.

e) Dressing the body up in overly elaborate scenarios (role-plays) that are not necessarily realistic and are closer to porn standards and fantasy than to one's actual role/function in society.

f) Turning the body into a public sex object (ie not nessesarily appearing nude or semi nude in a context of running, or bikini modelling, but in a more generalised way)

g) Collaborating in public sole-playing (with sexual theme, and with a particular partner, to advance a particular – and usually sexy - scenario)

If the reader thinks objectification is wrong, or unnatural, please allow me to set the record straight. Even in nature, animals objectify themselves to make themselves appear better than their rivals to possible mates. This applies across the animal kingdom, from Impalas, to Baboons, to Peacocks. Lions do it. Even in the insect world strutting one's stuff is important (ask any male praying mantis). Why is it important? It's important to the survival of the species that the female chooses the best mate. One that will look after her and/or be abke to defend/provide for a possible brood. Weaver birds literally collect a harem based on how many effective nests they build, and necessarily, on how quickly they can do so. More than that, it comes down so very vivid song and wing shaking displays. So objectification, strutting, dancing, 'pulling moves' isn't nonsense.

Humankind, it may be humbling to remember, is still part of the animal kingdom. We must procreate like other animals, and we must also attract mates (to some extent, like other animals). Is there tension when one's supposed mate is attracted by a rival? Just Samantha Taylor.

"Hell hath no fury like a woman scorned."

Ironically Oscar Pistorius' Murder trial probably revolves around the fury of a *man*'s scorn. But the pertinent point here is simply that the scorn and derision woman direct at each other usually has little to do with *objectification per se*, and more to do with attempting to manipulate, manoeuvre and *control* new talents, new beauties, new threats, new pretenders (by older women, by those recently sidelined or passed over, by those once golden cheerleaders fast approaching their own meretricious obsolescence.) Joan Rivers is a case in point, and we'll get to her in a moment.

In human pair bonding, as Swartzenegger (playing an object himself) once called it, symbolism is also an important device that is 'suggestive' of intention, but not necessarily intention itself. Hence, while a reader might encounter a model half naked within the pages of a magazine, and whilst a model might smile seductively at a photographer (more specifically the camera lens), it may come as a surprise to both that in the real world, the models real affections are targeted and specific. The 'generalised' objectification is thus a pretense, and one society (the media, models, photographers and the consumers of these) perhaps fail to appreciate.

Do I still need to belabour the point? If a bra strap is lowered off a shoulder, openly or cautiously or teasingly, allowing more of an unknown woman's bounty to be seen, there is an imputed symbolism in this salacious revealing of what is generally held to be private. Is that symbolism true? Of course not. We are dealing with a model. A representation of reality. Is it reality? Is the model flirting, personally, directly with us (does she know our names, a numbers)? No.

So now that we are clear on objectification in the modelling/fashion/photographer sense, let's expand our viewfinder to look at it in a broader societal sense.

According to the philosopher Martha Nussbaum, a person is objectified if they are treated:

- **as a tool** for another's purposes (instrumentality);
- as if **lacking in** agency or **self-determination** (denial of autonomy, inertness)
- as if **owned by another** (ownership);
- as if **interchangeable or exchangeable** [see below];
- as if **permissible to damage or destroy** (violability);
- as if there is **no need for concern** for their feelings and experiences (denial of subjectivity).

Rae Langton adds three more features to Nussbaum's list:

- **reduction to body**: the treatment of a person as identified with their body, or body parts;
- **reduction to appearance: the [reduction] of a person primarily in terms of…how they appear to the senses**;
- **silencing: the treatment of a person as if they are silent**, lacking the capacity to speak.

[**Updated 22 July 2014:**] Obectification is commonly ascribed (by women) to men. However, it seems more politically correct and even acceptable for women to objectify one another, or rather, as form as in-group-out-group bonding, as in this case:

http://www.channel24.co.za/TV/News/Joan-Rivers-shocks-with-sickening-Reeva-Steenkamp-joke-on-Fashion-Police-TV-show-20140722

"The last time I saw a blonde with red streaks in her hair she was laying on Oscar Pistorius' bathroom floor," said Rivers

The objectionable term here is 'blonde'. In other words, an entire person, an entire life, reduced to *hair colour*. Of course it goes further than that. Associated with the *blonde* cliché is:

- stupidity (as in 'I was have a *blonde* moment' or 'a dumb blonde')
https://www.youtube.com/watch?v=JtkX3OyPF4Q
- sexiness
- glamour, the most glamorous partners are blonde (Rod Stewart, Tiger Woods, Seal, Sean Penn arguably subscribe to this archetype of attractiveness)
- many celebrities fully utilise this popular archetype to advance themselves, such as Dolly Parton (who is a brunette) and our own Patricia Lewis
http://www.ecr.co.za/post/patricia-lewis-hidden-secrets/

Reeva herself changed her hair colour in an effort to 'typify' or 'objectify' herself as a sort of bikini-girl sex goddess. On twitter Reeva describes herself as:

SA Model, Cover Girl, Tropika Island of Treasure Celeb Contestant, Law Graduate, Child of God.

It should also be pointed out that the term 'model' which is the same term used for people of a certain type, and automobiles (and ordinary product categories) actually means:

- replica
- mock-up
- copy
- reproduction
- mould
- form
- sculpt

The last word – 'sculpt' can also be used 'interchangeably with 'fashion'. As in to 'fashion' something out of nothing, to mould a person, or product…

In other words, it is unfair to attach this idea of objectification to Oscar, as though he were its sole purveyor. Objectification is part of the currency of a consumer society, and thus, our ordinary materialism (things being more important than beings).

If we do demonise Oscar for this, it is a sort of voyeuristic way of attending to those things that we demean, and that we demean, during the course of our lives in society (but are perhaps too invested to admit, even to ourselves). Oscar provides a convenient vehicle in this regard, as a sort of cautionary tale for society. More on this particular lining of interrogation in *Restitutio*. **[End of 22 July 2014 Update]**

Meanwhile, it is a curious thing, this idea of Oscar's *alleged* 'objectification' is the exact topic of a Sunday Times newspaper story today [the time of writing being 20 July 2014]. In fact the writer of the News24 article actually uses the words '<u>object</u> of his [Oscar's] attention' in the article:

Paralympian star Oscar Pistorius stunned guests at a private party shortly after the Valentine's Day shooting of his girlfriend when he openly hit on a Reeva Steenkamp lookalike. According to the Sunday Times, the object of his attention was Kesiah Frank who bears an uncanny resemblance to his slain girlfriend. Frank, a <u>blonde model</u>, was an <u>FHM cover girl</u> and also holds a <u>law degree</u>.

The newspaper reported that fellow partygoers said Pistorius was drunk after having knocked back a few drinks and shooters. He then <u>targeted Frank</u> and only gave up after all his advances were rejected.

http://www.news24.com/SouthAfrica/Oscar_Pistorius/Oscar-hit-on-Reeva-lookalike-weeks-after-shooting-20140720

And via the Sunday Times:

Johannesburg clinical psychologist Leonard Carr said the family should probably rather have characterised Pistorius's behaviour as "self-sabotaging".

"He shows a consistent lack of judgment and a lack of impulse control. What his behaviour shows is someone who does not have control and has a severe lack of judgment ... how he has been behaving shows there is something seriously wrong."

...His boasting about his family's influence in the South African military is another massive untruth. Company searches show the closest link his family have to the army is through a company belonging to his uncle, Theo Pistorius, who builds and supplies armoured cars.

N4 Trucks says on its website it "re-manufactures" armoured military vehicles that are mostly used for policing, guarding and peace-keeping efforts.

http://www.timeslive.co.za/local/2014/07/20/partying-oscar-hit-on-reeva-double-just-52-days-after-shooting-girlfriend

Now consider the reality of a lifestyle that supports objectification. We'll briefly revisit the link posted previously rounding off question 12:

"It has nothing to do with me," Hougaard told City Press at the launch party of the Daytona Group's KwaZulu-Natal branch. Daytona is the official agent of Aston Martin, Rolls Royce and McLaren in Africa.
Hougaard and Pistorius move in the same social circles, and both met Steenkamp through Daytona's chief executive, Justin Divaris.
Divaris' girlfriend, Samantha Greyvenstein, knew Steenkamp through modelling – and Divaris was one of the first people Pistorius called after shooting her.
At the Daytona launch party on Thursday evening, hostesses draped in black kept champagne glasses brimming. Among the cars showcased was a Rolls Royce Ghost with a price tag of R5 million.

http://www.citypress.co.za/news/hougaard-oscar-has-nothing-to-do-with-me/

Daytona Group describes its positioning as follows:

The luxury lifestyle concept stems from the idea that luxury living is not just about owning luxury items; it is a way of life. We have embraced this concept knowing that high-end clients consume exclusive brands from vastly different retail and service arenas, yet these brands often reflect similar needs, desires, buying patterns and personalities.

We have established a group of companies that provide the world's most sought-after brands and, in doing so, catered for the different needs of our valued clients.

http://www.daytonagroup.co.za/about.html?page=12

You caught that, right?

brands often reflect... desires...and personalities

In other words, you objectify a person, with a brand, and you brand a person, with an object. The reader should reflect that as is the case with most people, cars are very important in how we objectify ourselves, and also communicate our personality. This was highly evident in Oscar and Reeva.

The following text comes courtesy of 2Oceansvibe (ironically a site that pushes brands, lifestyles and its own objectifications…):

It has been reported that Oscar Pistorius, murder accused, bought himself a McLaren supercar as a Christmas gift to spoil himself for the" good year" he had during 2012. The supercar comes at the small fortune of R3,5 million. Pistorius told the Sunday Times:

*I drive a McLaren – **a gift I got for myself for this Christmas** [emphasis mine] and the next one.*

*But, in the affidavit presented before the court on 19 February 2013 Pistorius listed the value of his movable properties to be just over R475 000. These movable assets include household furniture and effects, cars and jewelry. Which would lead you to believe that he either forgot about that R3,5 million supercar he bought for Christmas, or he deliberately lied to the court and everyone else. Alternatively, the **McLaren could be a loaned or rented vehicle**[emphasis mine], in which case **Pistorius is only guilty of massively misrepresenting himself** [emphasis mine] to his fans and friends.*

Or, perhaps the vehicle is entirely owned by a financing institution, and is not property of Pistorius at all?

Justin Divaris is the CEO of the Daytona Group and fought back on twitter claiming that it could not have been a sponsored car and that Pistorius purchased it. He also happens to be a well-known friend of Pistorius, and even went as far as to provide the court with a positive character witness of Pistorius during his bail hearing.

@mandywiener False. Oscar wasn't sponsored by McLaren. He was purchasing a car like any other customer. McLaren do not sponsor cars.
— Justin Divaris (@daytonagroup) February 22, 2013

He was sponsored it*. Mclaren didnt want their name brought into the case. The deal was *that at the next Olympics he'd run on Mclaren blades. See the piece on the Tasha's shooting and how Divaris said "it will affect the Mclaren deal"*

Note: *10:45*:* http://www.99fm.com.na/live-updates-oscar-pistorius-back-in-court/

http://www.2oceansvibe.com/2013/02/25/the-question-of-the-supercar-was-pistorius-lying-to-his-fans-before-reevas-death/

Enough said.

13. Crime in SA – a credible threat?
Poverty is the mother of crime. – Marcus Aurelius

Despite being a topic of vital concern, to South Africans above all, this narrative will deal with the issue only briefly. Three areas will be highlighted:

1. **Swart Gevaar** – are white people ~~un~~justifiably scared about being murdered in their homes at night?
2. **SA Statistics on Intimate Femicide**
3. **On the Ground, at the Grassroots, in the Suburbs** – is crime in South Africa a factor in the life of the 'Reasonable Man'

Remember those partners in (journalistic) crime, Davis and Brodie? Well, Davis' key idea in her discussion re: the idea of a 'swart gevaar' is this:

So the trial will revolve around Pistorius' intention: essentially, the psychology of a man who claims to have been driven by fear to shoot before asking any questions. This claim inserts a third body into an all too familiar narrative of domestic violence. This imaginary body, of the paranoid imaginings of suburban South Africa, has lurked like a bogeyman at the periphery of this story for the past year. It is the threatening body, nameless and faceless, of an armed and dangerous black intruder.

It is this "third" body that will be the most important, even though, as everyone knew as soon as that now famous bathroom door was opened, it did not exist. That was Steenkamp dying there and she had made that fatal female error of being in the wrong place at the wrong time.

And yet it is this imagined intruder that will be central to Pistorius defence. It is this chimera that is going to be the focus of all the court's attention.

Say what?

this imagined intruder…will be central to Pistorius['s] *defence. It is this chimera that is going to be the focus of all the court's attention.*

I'm not 100% what the word 'chimera' means, but it is undoubtedly a fancy word. Of course, if anyone has been living (or perhaps) reporting in a sort've daydream, it's possibly Davis herself. First off, I don't recall any mention, anywhere, during 30+ days of evidence of a 'black' intruder. Oscar himself only mentions 'intruders, burglars, attackers, people, persons', nothing about race.

I've touched on this before, and the essence of it is, you can't make use of this 'chimera' if the judge is black. Davis seems to have forgotten to figure this in her reasoning. And for the same reason the Griekwastad defence turned into a limp biscuit. In an Apartheid era court, the charge of a 'farm attack' may have been accepted to less circumspection. But it's not the

Apartheid era, and in the boy's own version, there is curiously little or no suspicion even from him, not the tiniest bit of opportunism, to fingerpoint his own farmworkers.

In Oscar's version, there's also not even the merest suggestion that his own domestic workers may have been involved, or may at the very least have 'made noises' that terrified him in the dead of night. Not even mentioned. So what has been central to Pistorius' defence? What has been the focus of the courts attention? Well, not Davis' the 'swart gevaar'.

Not let's turn our attention so something Brodie wrote for the excellent website edited by well known investigator journalist Julian Rademeyer (who also edited the same article).

The question is, are South Africans ~~un~~justifiably afraid of crime. Which is it, are we justifiably or unjustifiably afraid of crime?

If Brodie is somewhat out of touch when it comes to speaking ill (or less than well) of the recently deceased, as she tweeted in Reeva's case, she's better at interrogating exaggerated crime statistics.

Writing for Africacheck.org Brodie calls into question South African musician Steve Hofmeyr's claim 9In June 2013) that the number of white South Africans killed by blacks would fill a soccer stadium. And further:

...that white Afrikaners are being killed "like flies" ... Is a white South African farmer being "slaughtered every five days?" Would the number of whites "killed in SA in black on white violence" fill one of the country's largest football stadiums?

These are some of the claims made recently by Steve Hofmeyr, one of South Africa's most popular, and controversial, Afrikaans singers and performers. In a post on his [blog](#) and [Facebook](#) page titled "My tribe is dying", Hofmeyr made several sweeping statements about South Africa's murder rate and the quality of life of white Afrikaans-speaking South Africans.

Within a day of it being posted, Hofmeyr's blog entry and a [pie chart](#) that he used to support some of his claims were "liked" by more than 2,000 Facebook users. A similar number also shared the post on their Facebook pages.

Hofmeyr, writes Brodie, *then went on to make the following statements on Twitter:*

- *"[Old](#) SA averaged 7039 murders/year from 1950. New SA averaged 24206 (SAP) or 47882 (Interpol). Sorry Columbia (sic). We still champs."*
- *"[When](#) SAP claimed 26000 murders in 96, Interpol counted 54000. A lot of bodies to lose in stats."*
- *"[There](#) is a discrepancy of 10 000 murders per year between government and MRC figures!"*

Several readers asked Africa Check to investigate the accuracy of Hofmeyr's various claims, among them that:

- *Whites are being murdered at a rate faster than any previous period in South Africa's history.*
- *A white farmer is murdered every five days.*
- *During apartheid, black-on-black violence was responsible for the majority of black homicides, with only a fractional percentage of black murders due to government forces.*
- *"Whites killed by blacks since apartheid 77.3%". This is unclear as Hofmeyr has not indicated what factor the percentage is of however Africa Check assumes Hofmeyr is stating 77.3% of all white homicides (since 1994) have been perpetrated by blacks.*
- *The number of whites killed by blacks in South Africa is equivalent to, or more than, the number of seats at Soccer City stadium, which has a maximum seating capacity of 94,736.*
- *There are significant discrepancies between murders reported by the South African Police Service and other agencies and that these discrepancies have been used to hide or obscure the "truth" about murder in South Africa.*

Let's skip ahead to Brodies' conclusions:

Hofmeyr's claims, she writes are "grossly incorrect".

Hofmeyr's claims ... grossly exaggerated the level of killings.

Well, I'm not sure if you can use the word "grossly exaggerated" (referring to domestic crime) in one sentence then hedge your comment in the next sentences stating *South Africa certainly has one of the highest crime rates in the world and one that is characterised by a particularly high rate of violent crime. This is not an area where degrees of comparison offer any form of comfort. South Africans are affected daily by crime.*

This makes me scratch my head. Hasn't Brodie's research been all about rubbishing the controversial Afrikaans singers claims? They're not incorrect or inaccurate, or out by a few percentiles, but "gross exaggerations". Gross exaggerations imply we are better off paying no heed. Really?

South Africa remains gripped by its fear of crime. In the 2012 Victims of Crime Survey, about 35% of households believed that crime had increased since the previous period.

Again, it's hard to get to the meat and potatoes of Brodie's point here.

If *about 35% of households* that's about a third *believed that crime had increased* I'm not sure if it matters what the minutiae of the crime stats actually reveal. It shows a society clearly terrorised by the criminal element. South Africans are often dismissive of the criminal element, that is until a foreigner visits our neighbourhoods and finds our pavements devoid of pedestrians, our parks vacant, and the perimeter walls of the average suburban home blocked by palisade walls. These 'fortress-like' fortifications are often reinforced with additional safeguards, including electrified perimeter fencing, alarm systems and controlled access communities. Any South African who thinks this suburban arrangement normal – warning to sensitive readers – is *fucking* retarded.

Any journalist who thinks by picking apart a few crime statistics they are *really* dealing with the societal paranoia that clouds our neighbourhoods should perhaps consider a career in social work, or as a prison guard. Barry Ronge, if I recall correctly, once said that 'paranoia' about crime in South Africa is entirely justified. As a survival instinct.

I will deal with this subject in further detail, and more personal detail, later in this narrative. But I hope at this point I have made clear that outrage against crime – of any sort – in this country is justified. Journalists who frolick so luxuriously with crime stats obviously have little appreciation or experience of crime firsthand. I wonder then, if they are qualified to write or speak to us in a representative manner?

I mean, is Hofmeyr out of line for lying or exaggerating, or is Hofmeyr (who is not a journalist, let's be fair) out of line for reporting worrisome crime rates in South Africa, and against whites specifically, as intolerably high? Which is it?

Brodie's facile counterargument reminds me of the counters alcoholics use. "Smoking is worse." Or the counter smokers use when the deleterious effects of their habits are highlighted: "Alcohol addiction is more dangerous than smoking."

What I find tedious with this disassociated style of arguing, is that in the interests of intellectual superiority, and dogmatism, there's no gracious and humanitarian acknowledgement of the common problem we're all facing. There's too much crime. Nd we're fearful in our homes. Is that too large a point to admit in public? Does have to be so permanently anal, that one must score points about accuracy – even on this topic? Sadly, it seems so.

Because Brodie finishes off with this flourish:

Public figures like Hofmeyr, who disseminate grossly misleading information about crime patterns, only serve to contribute to this underlying fear. In addition, such misinformation creates or entrenches existing racial divisions and perpetuates an unfounded fear and hatred of other races.

http://africacheck.org/reports/are-white-afrikaners-really-being-killed-like-flies/

Brodie suggests our *underlying fears* have no basis, and further, seems to be saying Hofmeyr is entrenching racial divisions. If that's true, then what about Davis?

Have these perceptions of a 'swart gevaar' been thumb sucked, do they have absolutely no bearing in reality? Brodie seems to think so.

But let's skip back to Davis:

*If the prosecution is unable to prove its case beyond reasonable doubt, the judge will have to **weigh up whether this fear of an imagined intruder is reasonable** [my emphasis] and therefore a mitigating factor.*

*The fact remains that this default to extreme and paranoid violence, **whatever its psychological origins, has been so dangerous for women and children for so long in this country**[my emphasis].*

Let's back up for a moment. Shrien Dewani. He hired black hitmen to take out his wife, Anni, during their honeymoon. There seems to be a very real plot here, by Dewani, to mischievously utilise the widespread (ie popular) notion that murder is so commonplace in South Africa, that when someone is killed, the actual mastermind plotting and pulling the strings (including the purse strings, and who may well *not* be black) has a real chance of getting away with murder. Why? Exactly because of this 'swart gevaar' stereotype.

Brodie seems to miss this entirely. Stereotypes, like clichés, are grounded in reality. They may not be perfectly true, but they are often basically, or broadly part of our reality.

Most reasonable South Africans, and even many unreasonable one's, ought to agree with that at least. Next point:

2. SA Statistics on Intimate Femicide

I won't go into detail here. The reader can familiarise his/herself with the data at this link:

http://www.dgmt-community.co.za/sites/dgmt/files/documents/everyeighthours.pdf

Key details from these statistics are summarised as follows:

   a) Definition: **Intimate femicide**: The killing of a female person by an intimate partner.
   b) Intimate partner violence in now the leading cause of death of women homicide victims
   c) South Africa's intimate femicide rate in 2009 was more than double the rate in the United
   d) Furthermore our intimate femicide rate is most likely an under-estimate
   e) findings show no evidence of the impact of interventions or national efforts to prevent gender-based violence.

Key takeout: The large and significant decrease in gun related homicides in 2009 compared to 1999 provides **very strong evidence of the impact of the gun control legislation** that has been implemented since 2000.

In this regard, and I am a huge proponent of stricter gun control, this article by Koketsi Moeti is too my mind far more useful to this debate:
http://www.thoughtleader.co.za/koketsomoeti/2014/06/12/pistorius-and-the-unfinished-gun-ownership-debate/

*According to Adele Kirsten, an independent small arms control analyst: "There is good evidence that **one of the most effective violence prevention interventions is to strengthen national gun laws**[my emphasis]. Since the introduction of SA's Firearms Control Act in 2000, there has been a 50% reduction in gun deaths, from 34 a day in 1994, to 18 a day in 2009. Evidence that South Africa's Firearms Control Act (2000) has saved thousands of lives has been presented. The research, which was published in the March 2014 edition of the reputable American Journal of Public Health, shows that more than 4 500 lives were saved from gun violence in five SA cities between 2001 and 2005."*

In a CNN interview she goes on to share how **there is overwhelming evidence globally that having a gun in the home increases the risk for injury and death through suicide, intimate partner violence and accidental death**[my emphasis], *noting that "in South Africa, there is relative certainty that a gun will be taken from its' owner in an armed robbery, feeding the illegal market".*

Based on research, Gun Free South Africa says that **in South Africa a civilian gun owner is up to four times as likely to have their gun stolen than to use it in self-defence**[my emphasis]. *This is affirmed by research undertaken between 2006 and 2009 by the Institute of Security Studies, which showed that "armed gangs often targeted homes where owners were believed to have guns in their possession, in order to steal them", putting more people at risk of becoming victims of gun violence.*

Next Point:

1. **3. On the Ground, at the Grassroots, in the Suburbs** is crime in South Africa a factor in the life of the 'Reasonable Man'

The answer is obvious isn't it? The answer is self-evident isn't? Which is why Brodie's claims that crime can be 'grossly exaggerated' is something worse than woeful.

A series of eBooks could be devoted to this subject alone (and probably should be), but I find the subject matter not only intimidating but grossly dispiriting. What is the prime reason well to do South Africans wish to not live in the country of their birth? What is a prime reason this writer would move overseas if the VISA requirements were less inaccessible? Crime.

To even suggest crime is not a big deal in South Africa is tantamount to social treason. It ought to have the same social stigma as Holocaust denial. But the spindoctors who came up with Proudly South African as a tourist trick, well, somehow, being proudly South African (whatever that means) evokes in the most misguided an additional sense of, is it, *patriotic protection* (?) of our scandalous crime statistics.

I am not sure if any South African can pore over these names and in the same breath, declare themselves proudly South African. To be proud one needs an unblemished record, surely, not one blemished in buckets and buckets of our countrymen's blood.

http://whisnews21.com/2013/02/01/70000-whites-murdered-in-south-africa-since-1994/

More info here:

http://www.statssa.gov.za/publications/P0341/P03412012.pdf

I have indicated previously that I will, later in this narrative, share my own firsthand experiences of crime. For now, have a look at this story. It was one of two stories making the front page of the local newspaper this week. Any guesses what the other story was about? Yes, crime.

A few days ago, (at the time of writing it is a Sunday), on Tuesday the 15th to be precise, my best friends – they have two young daughters – were victims of an armed robbery at their home in Houghton. It was also not the first time they found themselves face to face with intruders in the supposed 'safety' of their own home.

http://www.volksblad.com/nuus/2014-07-18-pj-wil-help-n-rooftog

14. Is Oscar guilty of premeditated Murder?
I think the person who takes a job in order to live - that is to say, for the money - has turned himself into a slave. – Joseph Campbell

It would be premeditated if (cumulatively):

>-there was an argument
> - there was screaming
> - there was a motive
> - there was an intention to kill
> - there was a trigger
> - the last two or more could have taken place over a period of seconds

(premeditation involves planning, and planning can be anywhere between moments and months to many years).

Some commentators have begun speculating that the state prosecutor will *not* attempt to prove premeditated murder. They, mistakenly in this writer's view, suspect that there is not enough evidence to support this view. Really?

The state prosecutor, in my view, has never deviated either from the idea of intent and/or motive. Why? Because the defence, in my view, simply has no case. It never had a case to begin with. A man shoots to death a woman behind a closed door, and fires four bullets. It is up to the defence to provide a version that is reasonable, justifiable and defensible (that is, lawful in some way) and thus also, reasonably possibly true. Have they done so?

Not even close, to my mind.

In fact, a far better defence strategy would have been to rely on police bungling, which was successfully argued in both the OJ Simpson and David Baine acquittals. The defence certainly had some *cause célèbre* here. But given the highly publicised nature of the case, the defence possibly felt themselves hopelessly outgunned by the state's slew of experts, including police experts, Captain Mangena being one of obvious stars of the trial.

Credit must also go to Nel for his astuteness in warding off this entire line of questioning, firstly by:
- Removing Hilton Botha from the roster of witnesses (and making his partication almost irrelevant)
- Having Oscar point out tampering
- Highlighting Oscar's 'tampering' with the scene at ever possibly turn (including the bed/duvet, the bathroom, the toilet, the door, his un-confiscated phone and last, but not least, Reeva's mutilated body (which he transported from the crime scene and kept a vigil over, he even had his fingers down her throat. Reeva remained in his custody until the last moment when Stipp and the paramedics arrived, to find she had just recently died).

But how can it be *premeditated*?

We will investigate this in-depth in the final chapter, which describes the incident, the motive and the method, but for now, we'll gloss over the basic merits of the case. At the end of it I will provide a very brief reason why it looks – quite obviously actually – like premeditated murder. So let's get to it.

On March 10, 2014, a week into the trial proper, CNN provided the following summary:

Three bangs. Four shots. Nine witnesses.

The Olympic and Paralympic track star killed his girlfriend in the early hours of Valentine's Day last year. He fired four bullets through the door of a toilet room she was in. Three hit her; the final one in the head, and she died.
The overarching question in the trial is why he did it. He says he thought she was a burglar and made a tragic mistake. Prosecutors say the couple argued and he shot her in anger.

http://www.cnn.com/2014/03/07/world/africa/pistorius-trial-week-one-wrap/

Hold on. What was that?

Prosecutors say the couple argued and he shot her in anger.

I'm not sure if that is what they're saying.

The couple argued? Yes, the prosecutors and witnesses do allege that.
Oscar was angry? Yes, if there was arguing it's likely Oscar was angry, Reeva may have been angry too, or they were both angry. And other emotions too – disappointed, fearful, unhappy, let down, betrayed etc. Anger was one emotion of that night, no doubt, but so was fear. It is my position that Reeva was terrified, but Oscar was terrified too.
And I will provide my own supposition as to why Oscar shot Reeva not out of anger, but out of fear.

Before we get there – to the fear – let's bury our minds and noses into the key contextual issues. To do that, head on over to this link:

https://www.youtube.com/watch?v=9FYJwto6cDI

This was 3rd March 2014, Day 1 of the trial. The link is useful for a number of reasons, not least of which:
- Oscar's plea explanation/s (ie his defence, his plea 'not guilty' etc) are laid out
- The admissions are presented (facts not in dispute by both counsels)
- State advocate Gerrie Nel opens up the state's case with arguably the best witness (of either counsel), Michelle Burger

At this link

http://www.channel4.com/news/pistorius-murder-trial-five-dramatic-moments-so-far

the reader can appreciate at the glance the media's (well, Channel4's) assessment of the case, but only as far as May 06, when Roger Dixon began his somewhat disastrous testimony. It's clear from this framework that the state has a lot more blue building blocks, certainly in the first half of the trial. We also know that the defence's case *after* Dixon stuttered in terms stumbling experts, and less than stellar witnesses – including neighbours – but appeared to get a shot in the arm when Specialist psychiatrist Professor Merryll Vorster took the stand. Could a Generalised Anxiety Disorder be enough to acquit Oscar? Could it be used to argue reduced capacity? Could it be used to argue in mitigation of a possible sentence?

Yes to all of the above, conditional on a consensus that Oscar did in fact have GAD, or some other pre-existing condition. Given that Oscar was competing at an Olympic level, and able to plead a very difficult scientific case before the International Court of Arbitration (as I argued here:

http://www.biznews.com/oscar-pistorius-trial/2014/05/oscar-pistorius-able-bodied-mentally-disabled-analysis-whether-fastest-man-legs-fit-appear-court/)

it doesn't really take an expert to make an assessment. Which is why Nel could be quite confident in referring Oscar for evaluation, thereby further embarrassing – is that too strong a word? – the defence strategy. In any event, Nel seems to have torn each defence to shreds, whether Oscar's or his expert's.

One of the more obvious tactics that backfired was, I think, Vorster's confident (and, at the time it seemed 'reasoned') claim of a pre-existing anxiety. Someone frightened by noises yet the same someone who bestrode Olympic stadiums and ran to glory and triumph but not before coming under the obeisance of the starter's gun.

So we saw the state called the defence's bluff, and sent Oscar for evaluation, and the results were that his state of mind at the time of the shooting were essentially 'normal'. Ie Oscar had an appreciation of right and wrong, knew the difference and would have (could have, or possibly should have) known the difference.

Interestingly, Meryll Vorster has come the closest – in my opinion – to revealing the true state of Oscar's mind on February 14, after 3am. Although she highlighted a Generalised Anxiety Disorder, incorrectly and irrelevant in the sense of it being 'generalised', Vorster comes perilously close to touching on the motive, as I think about it. Because anxiety did play a decisive factor. It did, but not for the reasons anyone has led us to believe thus far, and certainly not – I suspect – for the explicit reasons Oscar has given.

The question is what does the state believe, what does it know and what can it prove? It should be emphasised to the reader that belief is one thing, knowledge is another, but a court runs essentially on the currency on what can be proved, and reasonably proved at that. This is why experts will express their opinions, beliefs, knowledge on an issue and then more experts will be called to challenge these expert opinions, and then the judge must make a reasonable assessment from these arguments.

The astute reader, and certainly the reader who has gone through *RESURRECTION*, and *RECIDIVIST ACTS*, will know what I'm actually playing at here. What was going on in Oscar's mind on the night and morning of the shooting? In due course we'll examine that thoroughly, not only what was going on in his head, by the psychology of his bail affidavit, and what probably took place in real time (the incident itself), and why it happened.

We'll get to that, but I suspect the prosecutor will stick with the easier-to-prove version which is not necessarily accurate as to what happened exactly, but for the purposes of a courtroom, good enough. In other words, not absolutely true, but sufficiently true, or to use the parlance of the court 'reasonably possibly true'. Of course, in the final analysis it is up to the judge (and her two assessors) to decide whether in fact, it is.

But that's out of our hands, so let's get back to *our* narrative.

After Dixon, the remainder of Oscar's defence (the ballistic expert, the screaming defence via their audio expert, Oscar's agent etc) – none of it was particularly compelling, was it? In fact what the reader ought to reflect on is the PR quality of Oscar's defence. It starts with a tearful public apology to Reeva's family and friends (meanwhile one can't be sure if he apologises to Reeva herself) and ends with Oscar fingering Reeva's Valentine's Card to him (which, ironically, he did not even open that day, or night, or for several months). Of course, there were no similar exhibits (Valentine's cards, or gifts) from Oscar to Reeva.

It's also noteworthy that the defence went to great pains to show that Reeva loved him, and rather a lesser focus on whether Oscar truly loved Reeva. The implication here is that Reeva being Reeva, who *wouldn't* love her? And conversely, Oscar being Oscar, how easy would it be for any woman, able-bodied or not, model or teenager, not to be in a relationship with him necessarily, but how easy was it to *remain* in one with him for any length of time.

Oscar admits exactly this – the difficulty of being in a genuine relationship – in his interview with *Sarie* magazine and to Larry King on *Larry King Now*.

But we've already covered all that. The time is nigh to cut to the quick of it. So let's head on to this link:

https://www.youtube.com/watch?v=QxZYtDsMhIE

This is a critical section of testimony, all of which can be mined for chestnuts, oopsies and major inconsistencies which do not do Oscar (or his defence) any favours. State prosecutor Gerrie Nel can (and will) do a far better job mining these and compiling these than I can. What must be highlighted though is there is a world of difference between what is said in court, and what can be proved, and a good prosecutor (or defence for that matter) needs to remain objective to the provable facts if they want to secure a victory over the other.

Which facts are **not** in dispute?

At **25: 38** of the above Youtube link state prosecutor Gerrie Nel reads Exhibit A, the 'admissions' into the court record. These, briefly and roughly, are as follows:

- The deceased is Reeva Rebecca Steenkamp, aged 29 on the day of her death
- The day of her death was 14 February 2013
- Her death was as a result of multiple gunshot wounds sustained on the same day
- The location is described as 286 Bushwillow Street, Silver Woods Country Estate, Silver Lakes, Pretoria

- The gunshot wounds sustained by the deceased were inflicted by the accused
- The body of the deceased sustained no further injuries from the time of her death until the post mortem examination was conducted on her body
- On 14 February 2013 the accused was resident at 286 Bushwillow Street, Silver Woods Country Estate, Silver Lakes, in Pretoria
- On 15 February 2013 Dr Gert Saayman correctly recorded his autopsy findings…as Exhibit B, the post morten report
- The photo album…depicts images of the post mortem examination annexed as Exhibit C
- The accused formally applied for bail in the Pretoria Magistrates Court…and is a true reflection of the evidence led [Bail application marked Exhibit D]
- The accused was adequately represented throughout his bail application by advocate Roux SC and advocate Oldwage on the instruction of Ramsay Webber Attorneys
- All the accused's rights were explained to him (in terms of the Criminal Procedure Act)
- Photo album 1 [Exhibit E] are Warrant Officer van Staden's images, images 1- 171.
- The photos depict a scene that was contaminated and/or disturbed and/or tampered with
- Contamination will be dealt with in terms of Hilton Botha and other photographs where necessary
- The photographs are admitted, but not as a true reflection of an 'uncontaminated' scene
- The accused will specify instances of tampering
- Photo album 11 is marked as Exhibit F
- Images 915-951 were compiled by Warrant Officer Van Staden and depicts aerial photographs of the accused's residence
- It will be [alleged] that the various distances to the balcony will be contested by the accused
- Images 1131 – 1141 are further photos taken by WO Van Staden depicting scenes at Tasha's Restaurant, Melrose Arch [Exhibit G]
- Exhibit H – van Staden's images taken on the R25 highway in the Modderfontein area
- Exhibit J includes a copy of weather conditions for the night 14 February 2013 [due to a typing error there is no Exhibit I]
- No blunt force trauma [Exhibit J]
- Blood analysis of the accused's blood (no alcohol or other illegal substances) [Exhibit K]
- Urine analysis showed no positive result for anabolic steroids, stimulants or diuretics.) [Exhibit L]
- Count 3 (at Tasha's restaurant), admission: the shot went off whilst the firearm was in the possession of the accused
- Count 4, the accused was not in possession of a license for .38 calibre rounds of ammunition.
- Confirmation by Defence of 'Admissions' concluded at **35:52**.

In this case, even to the casual observer, the objective facts clearly favour the state in terms of what did objectively happen on 14 February 2013. Because we know
- There was a single victim, known to the accused
- The accused, the only occupant of his own residence
- Fired his own weapon

- Through a closed door
- Thereby killing the deceased (his girlfriend)
- Four bullets were fired
- The deceased sustained three severe wounds
- And died on the scene

Before we move on we should take note of Gerrie Nel's opening address at 36:15 (which he – I think – tried to avoid giving, and thus giving away too much of the state's case…). But since Masipa insisted, Nel put it on record that:

"My Lady and learned assessors, this matter deals with an incident that took place in the early hours of 14 February. The accused, state's version, shot and killed the deceased at 286 Bushwillow Street – as indicated. They were the only two people in the house, my Lady. There were no eye witnesses. The state's case is based on circumstantial evidence that [inaudible] includes:

- Evidence as to what the accused's neighbour's, as well as in the neighbouring estates, heard.
- We will lead ballistic and forensic evidence.
- We will also argue that there are certain inferences to be drawn from the scene.
- My lady, we argue that the accused's version during the bail application and today [plea bargain] cannot be reasonably possibly true.
- Should be rejected
- And as the only inference, from the circumstantial evidence, would be:
- That the accused shot the deceased with direct intent to kill her." [in the background, behind Nel, Oscar shifts uncomfortably on his seat]

At **37:48** Nel calls his first (and arguably) best witness, Michelle Burger. Note the extremely subdued tone of her voice, and the difficulty she has in trying to get her message across thanks to the oral fumblings of the less than over-qualified interpreter.

But Burger, a lecturer in construction economics (the words describing what she does already sound portentous) soon finds her voice.

At **43:00** Nel asks her to recall the incident that took place on 14 February 2013, after 3am. How does she remember it?

Burger **[43:58]** speaking in Afrikaans: "U edele, net na drie het ek wakker geword van 'n vrou se verskriklike gille."

The rough translation:

My Lady, just after three I woke up from (as a result of hearing) a women's terrible screams.

Author's note: I recall at this point, when the case was unfolding in real time, thinking that if Burger was a credible witness, and if her testimony was credible, and if *this aspect* (a woman's screams) was credible, and verifiable (and true), it was case over for Oscar. That's within 45 minutes of the commencement of his case. Why? How can one say that? Simply because in Oscar's version there is absolutely no concession or even a possibility that a woman screamed. Oscar's version is that it was him and only him who screamed, and that his screams sounded like a woman. In order words, if a woman *did* scream, by inference, Oscar seems to be lying, and by further inference, they *were* arguing, and by further inference, not only is his story about a burglar manufactured and untrue, something *else really happened that night that involved an argument*. In other words the subsequent (and intentional) shooting of the deceased to death (Reeva) can be predicated on a woman's terrified screams, and a domestic argument. In theory, we have all of this within 45 minutes. QED?

Let's leave Michelle Burger and jump across time from Monday March 3 (Day 1 of the Oscar Pistorius Murder Trial) to April 14 (Day 21). We're going to look at a specific point on Oscar's 6th consecutive day of cross-examination.

Here's the link: https://www.youtube.com/watch?v=QxZYtDsMhIE

Move the slider to this section:

1:14:00 – 1:15:20

For reference, just prior to this section in the audio, Oscar tells Roux that he 'doesn't know' why he didn't mention the window opening (a sliding sound) in his bail, but simply referred to it as a 'noise'. Nel is quite bemused here, accusing Oscar of tailoring his evidence, but more than that, of pretending not to follow his line of questioning because he is 'making inferences' in order to pre-empt the implications of his [Nel's] line of questioning.

Note at **1:14:05** Oscar says, "My Lady I don't know how a tailoring of evidence would make any difference if I heard a window sliding and [inaudible] and I heard a window sliding and hitting a frame. I don't understand how that changes anything."

What Oscar's actually asking here – just not in so many words – is this: "If I did tailor my testimony, so what? What's the sound of the window got to do with anything?"

Nel asks why was the window opening and slamming against the frame was not included in the plea explanation. Oscar says, sounding positively morose, "I *ff* [inaudible] I don't know, my Lady."

Nel responds saying, "You're the only person who can tell us, but you don't know."

Now we get to **1:14:43**

Nel [pinching his eyes shut, trying to concentrate]: "Now, that's the noise you heard whilst you were in the bedroom.
Oscar: "That's correct my Lady."
Nel: "That particular noise [the window] caused you to take immediate action.
Oscar: "That's incorrect my Lady."
Nel: "What caused you to take immediate action?"
Oscar: "As I said before, I stood there for a brief moment, and I froze [Judge Masipa's make another note] and I wasn't sure what to do. I didn't want to cross the passage immediately…because I wasn't sure if the people or persons were coming down the passage…and then I ran to get my firearm, my Lady."

Nel: "Okay." **1:15:19**

Nel in response to Oscar's correct, a little sarcastically it must be noted, tells Oscar that he stands corrected again, and jots down that 'you were frozen' and 'you waited' and 'then you ran'.

Recall which question we are interrogating right here, right now:

But how can it be <u>premeditated</u>?

Premeditated means:
- Planned
- Calculated
- Thought-out
- Intended
- Deliberate
- Conscious
- Studied

Now with that context in mind, look at these words:

- Took a moment
- I froze
- Wasn't sure what to do

In a word, what did he do after hearing the 'galvanising' sound? He *waited*.

This is the point Nel is trying to impress upon the court, and he succeeds.

At about **1:15:35** Oscar recounts collecting his firearm from *under* his bed, "I took the holster off, I turned my body back to the passage and as I started *walking* I told [he corrects himself] I said to Reeva to 'Get down.'"

Waited.
Walking.

- Planned
- Calculated
- Thought-out
- Intended
- Deliberate
- Conscious
- Studied

"Then I made my way *as quickly as I could* to where the wall enters the passage" [quickly to flee Reeva answering him from the bedroom perhaps?]

Waited.
Walking.
As quickly as I could...

If we discount for a moment what happened after that, does this sound like someone operating from a perspective of:

- Automatism?
- Anxiety?
- Anger?
- Fear?

Or self defence?

At this point, and given the context (which is Oscar's version, no more than that) there are no signs of automatism, or fear or anxiety sufficient to cause freeze, flight or even flight. I am no psychiatrist, but here is someone standing right beside his prosthetic legs when he decides to move away from them (his legs), and instead prioritises a sound as a threat, and instead of escaping, and protecting Reeva who is – though invisible – right beside him, decides to confront the threat whilst on his stumps.

Does he confront the threat in a panicked state? No. Is he crying and screaming? No. If anything he is shouting for the police, but it's fairly measured shouting, and not more than two instances essentially of 'call the police' and 'get the fuck out of my house'.

Has he confronted sounds before in his home in a strategic, tactical manner, yes, he's told us as much on twitter on November 27, 2012 [since deleted].

http://www.washingtonpost.com/news/morning-mix/wp/2014/03/17/oscar-pistorius-once-went-into-full-combat-recon-mode-to-fight-perceived-intruder/

So why should this night be any different? After all, he's armed, and in his own home. Self defence, ironically, is what Oscar is getting at, and in my assessment, yes, that was what motivated him in the objective events of the day (*self defence against Reeva*, or what she was about to do), as it turned out. We'll get to that.

Before we move on to the next link, the reader that is particularly susceptible to OCD should have a look at **1:17:45**.

OCD definition [via Wikipedia]:

<u>Obsessive Compulsive Disorder</u> - **anxiety disorder** *characterized by* **intrusive thoughts** *that produce uneasiness, apprehension, fear or worry (obsessions), repetitive behaviors aimed at reducing the associated anxiety (compulsions), or a combination of such obsessions and* **compulsions***.*
Symptoms of the disorder include excessive washing or cleaning, repeated checking, extreme **hoarding***, preoccupation with* **sexual***, violent or religious thoughts,* <u>**relationship-related obsessions**</u>*, aversion to particular numbers and nervous* **rituals** *such as opening and closing a door a certain number of times before entering or leaving a room.*
These symptoms can be **alienating** *and time-consuming, and often cause severe emotional and financial distress.*

*The acts of those who have OCD may appear **paranoid** and potentially **psychotic**. However, OCD sufferers generally recognize their obsessions and compulsions as irrational and may become further distressed by this realization.*

Oscar sounds like he wants to burst out crying, because Nel is poking hole after hole in his version. What the OCD reader might want to look at is Oscar insisting on how he is holding his firearm. Why? Simply because it differs from how he holds his firearm in the now infamous 're-enactment' video. At 1:18:00 Oscar confirms that he was not holding the firearm in a fully extended (but double-handed grip). He says, "Not like that."

Interestingly Oscar also tells us he moved along the left side of the passage in order to maximise his visuals of the bathroom, or as he puts it, "so I could see as much as possible into the bathroom."

But isn't that odd? Wouldn't someone want to remain unseen, or at the very least protected by the wall (and thus moving along it, along the right side), if approaching danger (which was to the right from the perspective of advancing along the passage?

Referring to the toilet, Nel asks Oscar: "Could you see something?"
Oscar answers: "I could see a little bit of light. If someone were to come out, I'd be able to see their silhouette."

To the OCD reader, put this in an envelope and bury it in your back pocket, because it will be important later:

- *Little bit of light*
- *See their silhouette*

At 1:20:05, as pointed out in *RESURRECTION*, Nel hits the jackpot when he asks this question:

"Can you remember what you shouted?" [as in *exactly* what you shouted]

And Oscar actually answers, "Yes I can." Note the lilting despair haunting his voice.

"What did you shout?"

Now Oscar is in it. For about 15 seconds Oscar is silent. At 1:20: 23 he sighs. This is no ordinary sigh. It is heavy with real emotion. This is an authentic moment. This really happened. At 1:20:24 in a faltering voice, Oscar wails:

"I screamed, I said, "Get the fuck out of my house! [In a high-pitched cry]: Get the fuck out of my house!" [1:20:32] The court – due to Oscar being emotionally overwhelmed – adjourns immediately after this, at 1:20:43. The reader should recall Burger's testimony. We have touched very briefly on what turned out to be excellent witness testimony. Could Burger have mistaken Oscar shouting (it sounds like on one or two occasions) – or was it what he *said* – to the burglar:

Get the fuck out of my house!

For a woman's *terrified screams*? She was *petrified*. It was *reaching a climax*?

Now recall Nel has essentially cross-examined Oscar for only 6 minutes on this particular area (the incident). It's a difficult process, because whenever he touches on it, he touches a nerve. The important issue to remember, for now, is *the nerve was real*. Also, Oscar telling the court exactly what he said, we get a clue of what his voice *could have* sounded like.

Next, we'll look at the following link:

https://www.youtube.com/watch?v=fMsUK8mhGFw

Move the slider to about 0:45 seconds.

Oscar admits that it was a 'traumatic' evening. One assumes he means it was traumatic for him.

The word itself bears closer examination:
- Harrowing
- Hurtful
- Painful
- Distressing
- Shocking

Do those words sum up what it must have been like to shoot one's girlfriend to death? The last two, certainly, but what about the first three. What's 'hurtful' about killing someone, besides that one has acted in a 'hurt-filled' manner. What's 'ainful' about killing someone, besides that one has acted in a pain-filled' manner and inflicted pain on another.

Besides the word 'traumatic' Oscar used the word 'terrified' to describe how he felt that night. As I've speculated in *RESURRECTION*, I have no doubt Oscar *was* terrified. Just not about intruders in his toilet. But if not that, what then?

At about **0:57** seconds Nel shows he's on track, because he asks Oscar isn't the reason he becomes so emotional when recounting the exact words he shouted at an intruder, because, 'isn't that what you shouted at Reeva?' (I.e. 'Get the fuck out of my house!).

At **1:13 seconds** Nel presses the point even further. "I don't understand how you can get emotional now, today, about things [you thought] you shouted at intruders…"

Notice Oscar is somewhat at a loss for words here. He speaks, gathers himself, tries to speak again. Once again admits to being 'traumatised'. Let's reflect again that in the scheme of things, Reeva is dead. He's not sorry, he doesn't regret what he has done. He's simply traumatised. Why would he be traumatised? If it was an honest mistake, a horrible error, sure, it wouldn't be a positive thing to recall. But the overriding feeling ought to be regret. Surely. Not 'feeling traumatised'. This may seem a subtle point, but the reader ought to pay special attention to it. The reason is because within the psychology of the case, and we will not venture much further into that territory here (for now), Oscar clearly places his trauma above Reeva's. It's similar to a car accident victim recalling the trauma of a stubbed toe within the context of one's wife dying in the same accident. A reasonable person would be aware of the hierarchy of hurt and suffering. A reasonable person would defer again and again to the dead, and their injuries, not to one's own (perceived, and thus not necessarily even real) victimhood.

At **1:26** seconds Oscar admits that by 'repeating those exact words' it "reminds me about the night and *what I felt on that evening...morning.*" **1:34**

Indeed.

And by his own account he felt traumatised and terrorised.

What else?

1:00:38 Nel asks what Oscar heard as he approached the toilet door just before he fired at it. Oscar answers: "I'm saying I heard a noise inside the bathroom. And I perceived the noise at that time to be the noise of that door opening...it was a similar type of noise. I didn't have time to think.

At **1:01:48** Oscar: "It sounded...I didn't...my lady I heard a sound come from the toilet which I perceived as being the door opening..."

Traumatised and terrorised. A door opening...
A door opening to what...
People coming to attack me...

Stay on the same clip, but move the slider to **1h04:10**.

This is a bird's eye view over the toilet showing the trajectories of all four bullets Oscar fired. The first bullet is the lowest, or bullet hole A, which struck Reeva in her right hip.

Now listen to Nel's brilliant reasoning. He says that bullet A (the lowest bullet trajectory in the Youtube clip) was aimed towards the toilet. But B, C and D are all aimed to the right. Nel says this is because after suffering the first shot, Reeva fell onto the magazine rack. Oscar then fired in the direction of the magazine rack. In effect, adjusting his aim. Which shows intention.

Just before 1:06:00 Oscar argues: "I would not have been able to hear anyone fall on the magazine rack whilst I was shooting."

Nel points out here that the reasoning (including the falling onto the magazine rack) fits in "100% with Mangena's testimony." That's confidence from the state.

Just before 1:07:00 Oscar in what sounds like a crybaby voice says he did not aim at the door. Nel points out that Oscar's own pathologist, Dixon, that the grouping was 'quite good'.

Oscar disagrees, saying the grouping is "actually quite bad."

Nel points out that Oscar never warned the intruders that he was armed. It seems an almost random point at this stage, except it isn't. Let's focus on these last few minutes now before concluding with this chapter:

1h09:27 – 1h11:35

Nel wants to know: *how would the people/intruder in the toilet get out of your house?*

Oscar answers that they could flee by climbing out the window. Nel asks how they could do that given the window is several metres above the ground (it's a second floor window).

Nel asks, "At the time, you're telling them to get out of your house, how would they get out?"

Oscar answers: "*I wasn't thinking. I was screaming for the person to get out, get out.*" Oscar's voice is noticeably emotional as he admits this.

Nel tells Oscar that *I wasn't thinking* isn't good for his case. Nel emphasises the *reckless* element behind those words. Nel specifically says 'so reckless'. And Nel gives away some of his personal view on what he believes happened by saying, reckless is *the least* one could say about the incident. I believe Nel is onto something here.

Oscar admits, chillingly, that at the time he couldn't think of any others words to say but 'get out'. Oscar also mentions Reeva phoning the police and no doubt, this was under discussion. Yes, Reeva was about to phone the police.

I wasn't thinking. I was screaming for the person to get out, get out.

Nel reminds Oscar one of the ways to get out was to come through the door. "You told the people to get out, but you never gave them a chance to do so."

Oscar answers: "I shouted and screamed for the people to get out…"

"You didn't know who was in the toilet, am I right?"

"I didn't, my Lady."

Nel emphasises Oscar (based on his own version) didn't know how many people were in the toilet, whether they were armed, whether one was a child…

Nel then demonstrates that the door opens outward, in other words, in order to close the door from an open position, a person inside the toilet must reach out (cannot be on the toilet bowl) in order to close it. Nel is emphasising here that someone who is hiding in Oscar's toilet would probably have made a several noises attempting to close the door, *and lock it.*

Next Nel establishes that the defence has a recording of a Oscar screaming in a high pitched voice. Nel asks, "Do you know why the defence has not played the recording to the witnesses, so they could say if that's what they heard or not?"

Let's jump ahead to **1h23:52**

This is a very interesting bit of testimony that Oscar *volunteers*. He tells us that he's never screamed like that before, and adds this vital bit of evidence:

It was after the gunshots had gone off…I ran out onto the balcony…I shouted and screamed for help.

At **1:25:20** Oscar volunteers again. He doesn't like the idea of the 'Burgers' as a couple, and Nel points out that although Burger and Johnson have different last names, they are nevertheless a couple.

Nel at **1:25:40** compliments Oscar, ironically it must be said, for 'having a sense for detail'.

Immediately following 1:26:00 Nel directs the court's attention to the style of discharge. Was it double tap? Or rapid succession

Oscar says: "I fired in very quick succession."
Nel: "How do you know that?"
Oscar: "Because I remember it, my Lady."
Nel: "What do you remember?"
Oscar: "I remember discharging my firearm as quick as I could."

It's quite funny (from a certain perspective) Nel tries to trick Oscar here, because he said, following the voice you heard, it caused you to fire. Oscar, in a plainly distressed tone, objects to what is being put to him. Because yes, it's a form of entrapment.

Nel asks why Oscar stopped firing after four shots, and also, why not fire at the window (someone might be coming up the ladder with a gun).

1:27:30 Oscar answers, tripping over his own words: "I've thought that there was someone in the door, my Lady…"

Nel asks Oscar if he'd considered firing a shot into the shower, as a warning shot. *Incredibly* Oscar answers saying:

"My lady, if I'd fired a shot into the shower it would have ricocheted and possibly hit me."

Nel astutely dives into the next question (and inference): "Firing into that door, in that small toilet, a ricochet of that ammunition would be possible. And it would hit somebody. Am I right?"
Oscar: "That's correct, my Lady."
So you foresaw the possibility that you would hit someone?
Oscar: "That's not what I said my Lady."
What then?
Oscar: "I didn't have time to think."
Nel: "But you thought of not firing into the shower, because there would be a ricochet."
1:29:26 *"I fired where the firearm was pointed where I perceived the danger to be."*

In the final chapter we'll look at why this last seemingly harmless statement says it all.

Sex Kitten?

When we understand that man is the only animal who must create meaning, who must open a wedge into neutral nature, we already understand the essence of love. Love is the problem of an animal who must find life, create a dialogue with nature in order to experience his own being – Ernest Becker

"With great power comes great responsibility." Remember that, from Spiderman? Well, sex, or the desire for it, imbues the desired with power, certainly. And yes, responsibility to manage it well.

Were they…having sex?

http://www.nickvanderleek.com/2014/08/sex-kittens.html

Was Reeva a sex kitten? Was Oscar?

Yes, we will not confine our interrogation on this question to Reeva, we'll be asking it of Oscar too. We will start with Reeva; even so I must emphasise to the reader that I will remain mindful and respectful of the fact that Reeva is no longer here to plead her case herself. But let's try to be honest about answering this question. Once again, her own words are useful, to plead her case. And anyone who has read *Reeva in her own Words* knows (well, *mostly*) the answer to this question.

With Oscar, the *schema* is actually a lot more obvious than it may seem at first. You have a legless man masquerading in full view of a global audience as an able-bodied model, an icon, an inspiration par excellance. He tells us that his artificial legs don't matter. He says they're like putting on shoes. In a world that objectifies its gods, here was a peacock posturing on a global stage, sporting a beautiful, glittering, plastic tail. When you objectify yourself within the confines of the world's shallow spectrums, no matter how gold you gleam, fakery is fakery. Fake eyelashes are fine. A hairpiece, not great but you can get away with it (ask Sean Connery). Plastic surgery can only get you so far. Fake legs? Well, with fakery come lies and deceptions. Legs aren't shoes. And with lies and deceptions comes *The Picture of Dorian Gray*.

http://en.wikipedia.org/wiki/The_Picture_of_Dorian_Gray#Aestheticism_and_duplicity

Wikipedia's description is apt, isn't it:

[The theme is]…Aestheticism and its conceptual relation to living a double life. Throughout the story, the narrative presents aestheticism as an absurd abstraction, which disillusions more than it dignifies the concept of Beauty. Despite Dorian being a hedonist…

Moral duplicity and self-indulgence are evident in Dorian's patronising the opium dens of London. Wilde conflates the images of the upper-class man and lower-class man in Dorian

Gray, a gentleman slumming for strong entertainment in the poor parts of London town. Lord Henry philosophically had earlier said to him that: "Crime belongs exclusively to the lower orders . . . I should fancy that crime was to them what art is to us, simply a method of procuring extraordinary sensations" — implying that Dorian is two men, a refined aesthete and a coarse criminal.

We've touched on this before, but let's face it, in Nature's *schema* there is no place for plastic-tailed peacocks. In the world of Men, there is ample room for artifice, up until a critical threshold. If your peacock can keep up the pretence of a plastic tail, can it also rule the roost if it abuses (or is rumoured to have abused) even a single hen?

In a world that objectifies money and beauty to the extent that ours does, there is little redemption for a man that might reveal himself as a legless boy-man, who cannot stand the sight of blood and screams like a girl. And further, uses these, and his lover's undying love, as a defence for her dying. Because that's what it is: his victimhood, his vulnerability, his lack of masculinity, objectified when he is on trial for murdering his ever-loving girlfriend.

Can society forgive its abusers? They do, all the time. Tiger Woods. Chris Brown. It may be harsh to associate Steve Hofmeyr with these two, but Hofmeyr has had many relationships and children (more than average) and so too, incidentally has our president. So can society forgive (and love) its abusers? Well, the ANC suffered fewer votes this year, but evidently, South African society doesn't care that much about Nkandla, or court cases, or allegations of corruption and poor service delivery. Can society forgive its abusers? Yes, if those abusers, for all their sins, are lovable (or at the very least, affable). Yes, if they are powerful. Yes, if their power is sufficiently authentic and/or meaningful. It might be golf, or music, or political power. But what if it's all talk? All bluster? Think of Mel Gibson. Think of a peacock with a plastic tail?

Why does a peacock's tail even matter? Because a peacock is selling sex. Well, selling itself, its strength, its virility, its bling, its posturing, in order to get sex. That's important in nature, and let's face it, also important in the world of Man. Apparently it's less important in South Africa though:

> http://www.timeslive.co.za/lifestyle/2014/07/22/south-african-men-hard-up-for-sex---only-get-half-world-s-average

> The bottom-line:

> Sex sells.

> Sex buys money.

> Money buys more sex.

> Sex sells.

Make sense? In a world where objectification is a common currency, plenty of treasure rides on those who we objectify as idols. Paris Hilton has made a career out of simply playing the rich, beautiful sex kitten. Leaked sex tapes are part of the charade. That is what celebrity is, it is our worship of perfect gods. It is our desire to be like them, and eventually, to become them (rich and beautiful). In our idolatry, we wish to *be* the gods we worship.

In the *RESURRECTION* narrative and here, in *Revelations*, we've discussed the natural aspect of objectification. But our species is not about reproach when it comes to the unnatural – no, that's too kind a word – the *mischievous* and *counterfeit* objectification in which most of the world seems to wade. It's where we expend a huge amount of resources lying to others. Through avatars. Through charades. Through bullshit marketing. Through empty PR. These are indeed shallow waters. Objectification becomes groundless and pointless when the gods we objectify are frauds to begin with.

One of the most common gods in our social pantheon is the *sex kitten*. It is the default persona most actresses gravitate towards, and it's no accident that the most famous (legendary, iconic) actors and musicians are associated with specifically the 'sex kitten' persona (think of legends such as Marilyn Monroe, Elvis Presley, Dolly Parton, and local 'stars' such as Patricia Lewis, Steve Hofmeyr, and countless others).

The Urban Dictionary describes a sex kitten as:

Usually a young, sweet, cute looking girl, but who ooze's sex appeal and who is most probably <u>a lot less innocent than they look</u>. They are usually very flirty and playful.

Hagen Engler used the word "coquettishness" in his eulogy posted on the Daily Maverick [14 February 2013, 07:28]. In fact Engler's exact words were that Reeva was striking *just the right balance between one-of-the-guys humour and sassy coquettishness.*

But coquettishness is an odd word. Isn't it? I write a great deal and I'm not sure if I have ever used it. As words go, this is quite a big one for what it's trying to say (sexy, basically) so I'm inclined to thinking it's also unusual lexicon for an ex-FHM editor. Point being if I don't know what the word means (exactly), which laddish reader would? Besides Engler I mean? C'mon Merriam-Webster, help us out!

http://www.merriam-webster.com/thesaurus/coquettishness

the attitude or behavior of one who <u>insincerely</u> courts the amorous attentions of others

<such displays of girlish *coquettishness* are really out of place in a business office>

coyness, flirtation, flirtatiousness, **kittenishness**

Related Words: dalliance, play

To be fair to Reeva Rebecca Steenkamp, I don't think one can easily accuse her of insincerity. We see that in her whatsapp messages to Oscar (pretty elaborate statements of intent, right there, pretty sincere) and we see an even clearer picture through her social media, and especially through her Facebook timeline.

In the context of modelling of course, and I've already touched upon this in detail in the foregoing section, objectification is all about insincerity. A posturing peacock isn't appealing to the affections (or aspirations, or brooding ambitions) of a single hen, but to all available females. In the same way, a model in a magazine, or a brand, is selling their wares to all takers. In other words, it's packaged as personal and specific, and that's why it's insincere. Because it's neither personal nor specific. It's advertisimg. It's selling sex for money. To whoever is buying.

So if Reeva can be criticised for anything it is that she courted the admittedly shallow world of celebrity (and brand ambassadorship) that typifies modelling. Does that mean Reeva was shallow or objectifying herself? Yes, and no. I wouldn't say Reeva was shallow, but she did appreciate her talents and wanted to use them. Her beauty, in other words. And there is nothing wrong with that, and she did a fine job, and was doing a fine job, until she lost her life.

So we can say she wasn't shallow or insincere as a person, but we have to concede, that between working as a lawyer, and a bikini model, the latter is a more objectified profession. Is the legal profession a realm for the deep, soul searcher? I studied law in my first year, and have subsequently studied aspects of it (Commercial and Financial). Why did I not become a lawyer? Let's just say the law and justice are not necessarily bed mates. Let's just say that the reputation lawyers have for being *sharks* is not accidental. Let's just say that big money can, and often does, buy a defence. Is the world of the lawyer less shallow than fashion modelling? Tough question. I'm not sure that it is. The law is probably more sophisticated and convoluted – by some margin – than the fashion industry. But both attract shiploads of treasure.

If the theorem for a sex kitten is basically this:

Sex sells.

Sex buys money.

Money buys more sex.

Sex sells.

The theorem, well, the *causa sui* for the rest of us (animal activist, granny, financial planner, writer, and yes, sex kittens too) is something, somewhere within the lines of:

Sex and Death
Love and Death
God and Death

Say what? *Causa sui.* Wikipedia describes it as [denoting] *something which is generated within itself.* Huh? *It relates to the purpose that objects can assign to themselves.*

Is this objectification all over again? No. But objectification is an interesting reference point. An object is simply a thing, and people can ascribe meanings to these things, as they wish. Like money, objectification can be used for good (advertising that you are a doctor or photographer) or bad (in some, if not most social setups (advertising yourself as a hitman, prostitute with STD's or paedophile).

Remember the Ernest Becker quote at the start of this chapter? No? Here it is again:

When we understand that man is the only animal <u>who must create meaning</u>, who must open a wedge into neutral nature, we already understand the essence of love. Love is the problem of <u>an animal who must find life, create a dialogue with nature</u> in order to experience his own being.

In other words, what makes the challenge of being alive uniquely difficult for the human animal is this need for meaning. If it isn't there, we create it. We fathom it out of nothing if we must. The whole business of building brands (and reputations for that matter) is about conjuring something (substance) out of nothing. It's not objectification when there is something to conjure. When what is conjured refers to something. It may be a talent, or a skill, or an internal creativity. Of course when the causa sui, when what is generated is not true (artifice) then there is a real problem, and ultimately an existential crisis.

If your *causa sui* turns is invalidated…ie your God turns out not to exist, your significant partner is cheating on you, the crisis can be extreme. One's entire life can feel extinguished/obsolete etc. This territory was explored at length in RESURRECTION, but here, now, we take that exploration further. Into *causa sui*.

Still not sure what it means? Well, let's look at what *causa sui* isn't:

God as absolutely independent and self-existent by nature, and, consequently, all-perfect <u>without any possibility of change from all eternity</u>, is altogether opposed to the pantheistic concept of absolute or pure being [that] evolves, determines, and realizes itself through all time. – Wikipedia

In other words, a pure being, like God, has no *causa sui*, and does no *causa sui*. Because God is immutable, and perfect, omniscient, omnipotent, omnipresent. But we aren't. We aren't perfect. We aren't any of those things. And as gratifying as it is to believe we were created perfect, here's a revelation: we aren't perfect creatures. We are not even anatomically close to perfect. Many of us have simple aberrations, but the overall system functions pretty damn well. Outwardly it may resemble perfection or at the very least, something close to optimal operations. Of course most of us know our own meaty imperfections all to well.

Mine are, in no particular order:

- Bad teeth (hence several wisdom teeth operations, braces, external braces and gum grafts)
- Imperfect inner ears (hence grommet operations, perforated eardrums)
- Not the best digestive tract (hence spastic colon and the so called 'boesman magie'

- Male pattern baldness (notice all the facebook profile pics wearing headgear of some kind)
- BMI (body mass index, less than ideal)

It's likely if you – the reader – really tried, you might be able to come up with one or two defects too. In other words, no, we are not perfect beings. We are not *actus purus* – *find out more about that here*:

http://en.wikipedia.org/wiki/Actus_purus

See, none of that is us, hence our lives must be based on something else. Well it is, we base our lives on *causa sui*. But does it even matter what system we base our lives on? Hell yes!

Why? Get ready for some Revelation people, and keep an eye on the sky, a few lightning bolts might strike while we venture into this territory. This is a place angels fear to tread, so buckle your seatbelts:

"A person spends years coming into this own, developing his talent, his unique gifts, perfecting his discriminations about the world, broadening and sharpening his appetite, learning to bear the disappointments of life, becoming mature, seasoned – finally a unique creature in nature, standing with some dignity and nobility and transcending the animal condition, no longer a complete reflex, not stamped out of any mould – and then the real tragedy: That it might take sixty years of incredible suffering and effort to make such an individual, and then he is good only for dying." – Ernest Becker discussing Andre Malraux

Let's put it in layman's terms. What is it all about? What is the purpose of life? Why is a peacock doing the thing with his tail to begin with? What is the point? The point is the *causa sui*. My *causa sui* may be the same as yours, or it may be different. But here's the thing. There are not a lot of *causa sui*'s out there. The reasons we ascribe to living are as plentiful (or as sparse) as the themes we come across in fiction, in movies, in music. Franz Kafka once said, "All I am is literature, and I am not able or willing to be anything else." Writers may be able to identify with that, but what about sportsmen, or soldiers, or presidents? Someone else once said that all art, all literature boils down to one theme and one theme only: who am I?

We may think there is more subtlety to life than self discovery. Surely life is about love, betrayal, expansion, growth, attrition, survival, ascendance, competition, circumspection…or is life about God? Or loving and being loved in return? Or giving, and receiving in turn. Is life about accumulating the most we can of everything – happy experiences, love, success?

Whatever your answer to the purpose of life, that's your causa sui. But the chances are your causa sui falls within just a few parameters of living. In other words, your causa sui is your immortality project while alive. Because that is what meaning is, and what meaning does. It is a connotation, a significance, an import or implication…something we ascribe in order to set in motion a dialogue with Nature. You could also call Nature God, but the point is, it is your *causa sui* that imputes meaning. You may have borrowed it from your parents, or society, or a system (economic, social, political or spiritual), and in very rare cases, worked it out on your own, but like it or not, believe it or not, you and me, all of us are not simply walking automatons, we are living according to a programmed code. Our actions are directed by prescribed sets of meaning.

I defer to the likes of Ernest Becker and Jason Silva to describe these immortality projects that operate within our lives (and lifetimes). Hopefully their explanations will help demystify it for the reader (as I sense some cloudiness and confusion hovering between us). So here it is, courtesy Jason Silva:

http://hplusmagazine.com/2009/09/04/immortalism-ernest-becker-and-alan-harrington-overcoming-biological-limitatio/

The mindset of an Immortalist is pretty simple and straightforward: death is an abhorrent imposition on a species able to reflect and care about meaning. Creatures that love and dream and create and yearn for something meaningful, eternal and transcendent should not have to suffer despair, decay, and death. We are the arbiters of value in an otherwise meaningless universe. The fleeting nature of beautiful, transcendent moments feeds the urge for man to scream: "I was here; I felt this and it matters, goddamn it!" In the face of meaningless extinction, it's not surprising that mankind has needed to find a justification for his suffering. Man is the only animal aware of his mortality –- and this awareness causes a tremendous amount of anxiety, anxiety that we have to do something about.

...When I first understood what love was, on a visceral level — that was when I first grasped the concept of death. Death felt real when I pondered losing someone I loved. It was unbearable to imagine that everything and everyone I loved was temporary, even as a young child. Very early on, I comprehended mortality intellectually. I suppose many of us repress this awareness and comfort ourselves with stories, orthodoxies, and songs – but I couldn't. That felt like a cop out.

Not that my life isn't sunny and lusty, packed with fascinating hours. It is. Everybody has the chance to turn his span into an adventure, filled with achievement and love-making. We can dance, skydive, float in space, build marvelous jetliners, travel, drink wine, get high, write poems together, and more. We've never had such a variety of music, art, and dance as today. But when we start to grow a little older –- and when we pause for just a moment –- a faint disquiet begins to intrude on all our scenes.

Alain de Botton, in his book The Art of Travel, *says, "If our lives are dominated by the search for happiness, then perhaps few activities reveal as much about the dynamics of this quest — in all its ardor and paradoxes — than our travels. They express, however inarticulately, an understanding of what life might actually be about, outside the constraints of work and the struggle for survival." I would go further and say that when we travel we are so immersed in the present moment; so fully stimulated by the newness of the here and now – that for a while we step off the moving walkway that carries everyone else towards death. Movies like Richard Linklater's* Before Sunrise *always made me feel this way. It involved two people falling in love while travelling and exploring a new city – and it was intoxicating. That one night tasted like forever. That was a sampler of immortality, and sadly, it ended all too soon.*

Hold on. Am I suggesting *travel* is how we experience life? Yes, it is one way. In fact travelling around the world as Oscar did, and Reeva did (but less), and I have, is a wonderful way to feel alive. Travel of course can also be very lonely, and exhausting. But through our travels (and with international airlines, we can go anywhere today) there is no longer an excuse for not being aware of the size of the world, and the immersive experience that life – and living it a certain way, with movement, and an itinerary – can be. But let's face it, even if life is a journey, unless you're a travel journalist, chances are mere travel isn't going to imbue you, the reader, with the *causa sui* that you're looking for (or resonate with the *causa sui* that you already have). Well if travel isn't what we're supposed to be doing to feel alive, to live with meaning, then what? And what does this have to do with Oscar, Reeva, or a chapter on sex kittens? Wooosa! We're getting there.

The psychologist Ernest Becker wrote in his Pulitzer Prize winning book, The Denial of Death, *that in the face of an acute and agonizing awareness of his mortality, man has developed three main devices to sustain his sanity: the Religious, the Romantic, and the Creative. These illusions act as temporary solutions to the problem of death. Let's take a look at each one of these in turn.*

So there it is. As you go through the passage below, I want you to bear in mind – and try to do this with an excruciating awareness please – for Oscar's *agonizing awareness of his mortality*. Make no mistake, when a man loses his hair and goes bald, he experiences an *agonizing awareness of his mortality*. When a woman finds her hair is turning grey, or she has stopped menstruating, or her breasts are no longer the perky assets of her youth, she experiences an *agonizing awareness of her mortality*. At some stage, we all do. It might be a cut that exposes [gasp] under our translucent tissues is salty, red, bloody stuff, gushing, pipes and tubes and tissues. It might be a rogue heart attack, or a hijacking or a car accident. Any near death experience will do it. Any person close to you who dies, should awaken that sense of your own mortality. It's normal. But what do you with it? Silva suggests all of us respond in one of only three ways. I want you, the reader, to intuit your response, first and foremost, and secondly, Reeva's and Oscar's. It's just a thought experiment, nothing more. Are you ready to embark on yours? Let's go into it together. We start with:

1. The Religious Solution – "God will Save Us"

The Religious Solution has man inventing the concept of God and projecting onto it the power to grant us what we all really want — the ability to bestow eternal life on ourselves and our loved ones, and to be free from disease, decay and death. The belief in an all-powerful God made perfect sense during the dark ages when people lived short, miserable, disease-ridden lives. With no explanation for their suffering, people were better able to bear their hardships by having faith in God and believing that — in the end — their God would "save" them.

However, God never came. Suffering persisted, and people lived and people died. In an age of science and reason, however, the Religious Solution has all but become obsolete. The irrationality of religious dogma has become clear in our modern time of scientific enlightenment, and – rather than alleviating our anxiety – it has only served to exacerbate it. In his book The Immortalist, *Alan Harrington wrote, "Anxiety increases with education. As* we grow more sophisticated, ever more ingenious rationalizations are needed to explain death away." Man still needs something to believe in, it seems.

More than likely, those readers who have stopped reading here, subscribe to the The Religious Solution. They will not like to read that their solution is 'all but…obsolete'. Because they are so invested in this solution, they will not wish to have it (and thus their lives, identities, their very souls) invalidated. Of course, not everyone is fully invested in this *schema* even if they believe they are. Their *causa sui* may in fact be a combination of *schemas*, the hybrid religious and romantic schema is not uncommon.

2. The Romantic Solution – "Love is Eternal"

Enter the Romantic Solution — the second illusion identified by Becker. When we no longer believe in God, we then turn our lovers into gods and goddesses. We idolize them and write pop songs about being saved by their love. For a little while, we feel immortal – like gods beyond time. "Once we realize what the religious solution did, we can see how modern man edged himself into an impossible situation," says Becker. "He still needed to feel heroic… to merge himself with some higher, self-absorbing meaning, in trust and in gratitude…Yet if man no longer had god, how was he to do this?"

The answer to Becker's question is simple. Man did it by turning his beloved into god: "If the love object is divine perfection, then one's own self is elevated by joining one's destiny to it," Becker continues. All our guilt, fear, and even our mortality itself can be "purged in a perfect consummation with perfection itself." And the Oedipus complex can now be understood for what it really is, says Becker, "… another twisting and turning, a groping for the meaning of one's life. If you don't have god in heaven, an invisible dimension that justifies the visible one, then you take what is nearest at hand and work out your problems on that."

The reader may sense Oscar's *causa sui* in the above. Do I need to emphasise where and why? I would like to continue, but briefly:

He still needed to feel heroic…
to merge himself with some higher, self-absorbing meaning, in trust and in gratitude…
Yet if man no longer had god, how was he to do this?
Man did it by turning his beloved into god:
"If the love object is divine perfection,
then one's own self is elevated by joining one's destiny to it."

And what did Oscar say? *I was besotted by her. I loved her more, in the beginning, I think than she loved me. I wanted to show her my world.*

Silva continues:

Harrington offers his own take on the Romantic Solution to demonstrate how romance manifests itself. "Sensuality may turn into a feverish hunt for rebirth," says Harrington. "In carrying on this search, men and women depend increasingly on sexual symbolism. The sexual partner turns into a stand-in for various dream figures, phantasms in a stage-managed RESURRECTION. These figures are all agents of immortality to be conquered or succumbed to many times over, in order that the pilgrim without faith may symbolically die and live again."

The reader may recognise why I have gone to the trouble with these strange sounding titles. RESURRECTION. Recidivism. Revelations. Restitutio. Besides the fact that each has the letters 'R' and 'S' in the title, as a sort of a tribute, these are the symbolic themes we are busy with. And Oscar's life (and Reeva's) was nothing if not symbolic. If they resonate with us it is because our lives are symbolic too. Meaning – *causa sui* – is of significant import to us too. And that's why this case can teach us so much not only about the world, and ourselves, but how the world works, and where our *causa sui* fits in to all of it, not only where, but how, and why it does. Why it must.

When in love, Becker says, "man can forget himself in the delirium of sex, and still be marvelously quickened in the experience." We are temporarily relieved from the drag of "the animality that haunts our victory over decay and death." When in love, we become immortal gods."

Do you see now why the 'Sex Kitten' is such a powerful motif? Not just in narratives, but in the real narratives of our lives. You may not have thought it before, but all of us – at one stage – were sex kittens ourselves. It is that stage either during teenage blossoming or shortly after, perhaps at university, where we reach our maximum attractive potential. We flower with the full ripeness, and deepness, of youth. It is a moment in our lives where death is banished as far from our blood as is conceivable. Sex is in the air. And crisis, for what are we to do with our power, and who should we give it to, or share it with? These are critical, crucial, terrifying decisions. Getting them right, and you can set your ship sailing in the high winds of high living for life. Get them wrong, and you may shipwreck your dreams, and worse, the dreams perhaps of others too, permanently.

I'm going to go out on a limb here – since the chapter is titled 'sex kitten', and the book itself is about *Revelations*, how about this one? Was I once a blonde demigod? You be the judge:

https://www.youtube.com/watch?v=6AWN_-Xcoh0

Yes, youth is a powerful elixir. Perhaps the most powerful, because youth by its very nature is beautiful, and innocent, as long as it isn't naïve, or naively stupid (which, let's face it, it often is). While on the subject of me, if I reflect on the 26 year old me, I remember a sexually inexperienced young man who loved deeply and due to my convictions on the one hand, and my innocence on the other, was pretty much a sitting duck for the relationship that came along that I decided was 'meant to be'. Like Oscar, I too had lost my mother at a young age (17), and my father, a good guy, is a sort of absent figure (for whatever reason).

Is love at the age of 26 under these circumstances a big deal? You better believe it. If you're a sex kitten (or you kid yourself that you are) and you're targeting sex kittens, because that's what you feel you deserve, and it turns out, well, that might not, or you might need to adjust your expectations, at that age, that's a pretty devastating blow. It's pretty devastating at any age, just ask Demi Moore, or ~~Kirk Douglas~~ Seal,

http://www.dailymail.co.uk/tvshowbiz/article-2195909/Heidi-Klum-mends-broken-heart-help-tattooed-security-guard-intimate-family-holiday.html

or Mel Gibson.

http://www.dailymail.co.uk/tvshowbiz/article-2563560/Mel-Gibsons-ex-Oksana-Grigorieva-files-bankruptcy-legal-debts-just-years-turning-15m-custody-settlement.html

Can Moore's Seal's and Gibson's partners – while they were happily ensconcenced in their respective relationships – could they be called, 'sex kittens'? Ashton Kutcher? Heidi Klum? Oksana Grigorieva?

But no relationship can bear the burden of godhood. Eventually, our gods/lovers reveal their clay feet. It is, as someone once said, the "mortal collision between heaven and halitosis." For Ernest Becker, the reason is clear: "It is right at the heart of the paradox of man. Sex is of the body and the body is of death. Let us linger on this for a moment because it is so central to the failure of romantic love as the solution to human problems and is so much a part of modern man's frustrations."

This is the revelation we all come to in a romantic relationship when sex is revealed to represent "species consciousness" –= a mere process of reproduction in service of propagation, rather than in the service of "man as a special cosmic hero with special gifts for the universe..." Man is revealed to be a mere link in the chain, with no lasting purpose or significance. Passionate love then tends to transition into housekeeping love — boredom and routine coupled with the impossible standards we have for our lovers collides in a flurry of disappointment, and perfection begins to show its cracks.

This is why most marriages end in divorce and why love doesn't ever quite seem to last forever.

Hmmmm. Who could imagine such a roundabout route could bring us face to face with that toilet door? Yes, I know, you were wondering what I was smoking, what all this *causa sui* stuff was about. It's a big fucking deal. And the peacock is fully fucking aware of the stakes. We may laugh at it, we may think it's a lot of effort into a tail, but it's a big fucking deal. That tail determines whether Mr Peacock gets to have a family or not, and who gets to be part of that family? Will it be a *dud* hen or a *Marilyn Monroe* (sex kitten) hen?

Did Oscar wish to be…*a special cosmic hero with special gifts for the universe*

Did Reeva discover with Oscar's imminent departure to Brazil, then Manchester, then Italy, that there was… *no lasting purpose or significance*.

And his idea of buying a huge mansion, a huge empty glass house for her while he was a world away, was it the same thing with Warren all over again: *Passionate love [tending] to transition into housekeeping love — boredom and routine coupled with the impossible standards we have for our lovers colliding in a flurry of disappointment.*

And yes, when a man has no legs, and a woman has her own career to consider *perfection begins to show its cracks.*

Although we have probably found our answers to Oscar and Reeva (above) let's consider one more, the third and last possibility. According to Silva there's also:

3. The Creative Solution – "My Art will Last Forever"

At this point in his analysis, Becker identifies the last illusion man has devised — the Creative Solution. He explains our urge to leave a legacy – to create a great work of art that has lasting impact and value, something that carries our signature and lives on after we're gone. "This is the artist's way of scribbling 'Kilroy was here' on the wall of the final and irrevocable oblivion through which he must one day pass," Harrington explains. This is quite touching and clever, and not surprising, but ultimately it fails where it counts: you still die.

The absurdity and ache of our condition can be summed up by the opening line from the award-winning 2006 documentary Flight From Death *narrated by Gabriel Byrne, "To have emerged from nothing; to have a name, consciousness of self, deep inner feeling; an excruciating yearning for life and self-expression. And with all this; yet to die. Human beings find themselves in quite the predicament. With our minds we have the capacity ponder the infinite, seemingly capable of anything, yet we're housed in a heart-pumping, breath-gasping, decaying body. We are godly, yet creaturely."*

And so is Oscar. Godlike. Yet a dwarfman with stumps rather than legs. A legless man that can hardly walk without artificial help, who then pretends his prosthesis give him no artificial advantage over able-bodied athletes.

Neil Engee, in his essay "Laughing at Death," amplifies this theme, "The dread of death is terrifyingly magnified when we consider the possibility that our life and death could be insignificant in a meaningless indifferent universe. <u>Participation in the transcending cultural drama lends us meaning and enables us to keep such dark concerns out of mind, unconscious, suppressed by the security blanket of social verities enfolding us in comforting embrace.</u>"

There are other ways we hide from mortality in contemporary life. "The disco has become an electric art form," Harrington rails. "We loosen our anxieties with the help of enormous guitars in a temple of fragmentation." These assaults on our senses all have one purpose, "to smash the separateness of everyone present; to expose feeling and break through thinking; to make us live, in the phrase of Alan Watts, 'a perpetual uncalculated life in the present'... all this too amounts to one more attempt to hide from the end; a sort of electronic Buddhism in place of sequential perception."

But celebrity is another. It is a contract between the *cause célèbre* and society. There's voyeurism and inspiration for as long as the pretense of uncalculated living is maintained. This applies equally to the model and the athlete, and equally to the 'coquettish bikini model sex kitten' as the 'sauve ladies man, the charming Olympic Champion bad boy.'

It would be easy to stop here, and say that we have solved our mystery. Part of the mystery of Reeva and Oscar's *causa sui* is solved, sure, but what about our own? What about the mystery of our own lives? What about our own *causa sui*? And what about trying to find deeper *Revelations* in ourselves? Given what happened to Reeva, and Oscar, surely we ought to see whether this rabbit goes, not so? Well, let's have a look:

The Immortalist Solution – "Overcoming Biological Limitations"

The Immortalist Solution is simply this: the time has come for man to get over his cosmic inferiority complex. To rise above his condition – and to use technology to extend himself beyond his biological limitations. "We must never forget we are cosmic revolutionaries, not stooges conscripted to advance a natural order that kills everybody," says Harrington.

While Ernest Becker identified our need for heroism and our extensive attempts to satisfy it symbolically, Alan Harrington proposes that we move definitively to engineer salvation in the real world. He proposes that we move directly to physically overcome death itself, "Spend the money, higher the scientists and hunt down death like an outlaw." Where some cry heresy and gasp in protest at the pretense of "playing god," Harrington simply states, "The truth is, of course, that death should no more be considered an acceptable part of life than smallpox or polio, both of which we have managed to bring under control without denouncing ourselves as pretentious."

Harrington also suggests that what must be eliminated from the human drama is, "the inevitability of death as a result and natural end of the aging process." He is speaking of the inescapable parabolic arching from birth to death, "being alive now, ungoverned by span, cycle or inevitability. ...Civilized man's project will no longer be, as Freud suggested, to recover his lost childhood, but rather to create the adult equivalent: an immortal present free from the fear of aging and death," Harrington continues.

Harrington also rails against any philosophy that teaches complacency. "All philosophical systems insofar as they teach us sportingly to accept extinction are a waste of time," he writes. "The wisdom of philosophers may nearly always be found trying to blanket our program to conquer death." He critiques men that propose surrendering to the "eternal now," stating, "Alan Watts and Norman O. Brown write passionately, with intimidating erudition, about the unimportance of erudition. Supremely self-conscious and egocentric men advance themselves, their systems and anti-systems, never stop talking, all the while insisting that the mind should be retracted, the intellect forsaken, and that everyone should instead worship the sensuous present."

The Immortalist point of view can be summarized as a project that uses technology to "Individualize eternity, to stabilize the forms and identities through which the energy of conscious life passes."

Curiously, we see Oscar has gained 'a second life' so to speak, thanks to the cosmic technologies Harrington references here. Biological limitations are exactly what Oscar was able to overcome. He overcame them to such an extent, and so magnificently, for a while he seemed superhuman. And thus he was able to live a life far larger than that of a mere disabled person. He was granted the special privilege to run alongside able-bodied runners, and pretend to be like them, even better, pretend to be better than the best able-bodied athletes in the world. But that's not the technology Harrington is talking about. Harrington is talking about defying death. Oscar has been preoccupied with defying social death (which is anonymity).

This is hardly a stretch for human beings, says Harrington: "We have long since gone beyond the moon, touched down on mars, harnessed nuclear energy, artificially reproduced DNA, and now have the biochemical means to control birth; why should death itself, 'the last enemy,' be considered beyond conquest?"

Once again, to quote Harrington, "Salvation belongs to medical engineering and nothing else; man's fate depends first on the proper management of his technical proficiency; we can only engineer our freedom from death, not pray for it. The beautiful device of tragedy ending in helplessness has become outmoded in our absurd time, no longer desirable and not to be glamorized. The art that embellishes death with visual beauty and celebrates it in music belongs to other centuries. Anything that celebrates or bemoans our helplessness has gone as far as it can. We are done teaching accommodation to death and granting it static finality as the 'human condition'."

In closing, I want to leave you with this biting and eloquent passage I read somewhere on the Internet:

"There is nothing about death that is less than abominable. I am forever bewildered by the placating palaver wasted in efforts to quell this irrational horror. The cessation of all that is, the chasm that devours every memory, every fleeting intellection, every redeeming fragment of meaning and love and lust and friendship and hunger and hopeless vitality, and reduces it all to the inconceivable cosmic ash of nothing—That is my enemy."

Let's look at that last part again, because it's important:

the chasm that devours every memory, every fleeting intellection, every redeeming fragment of meaning

and love and lust and friendship and hunger and hopeless vitality,

and reduces it all to the inconceivable cosmic ash of nothing

—That is my enemy

What is the 'chasm'? It is death, or the threat of something that extinguishes life. We'll deal with this 'chasm' in the last chapter. But first, Glass Houses. What's that saying about people who lives in glass houses…?

Glass Houses

Freud tells us to blame our parents for all the shortcomings of our life, Marx tells us to blame the upper class of our society. But the only one to blame is oneself. – Joseph Campbell

Right now it's 17:12 on 28 July 2014. I haven't been able to do any work on my PC because the system has been compromised, and not for the first time. From what I have been able to establish, at least five folders have been removed from my PC (personal computer). I called a technician and asked

a) Whether this was possible (remotely)
b) How it was possible

I was pretty surprised – and alarmed – because I thought my several sets of antivirus software (including Microsoft Essentials), and AVG, were sufficient. No, says my PC expert friend. I have to install software that sets up a firewall. I thought AVG does that.

No, he says, it doesn't. Your PC is vulnerable to external sabotage. And so it has been.

To date, 5 folders have been deleted off my system. The first was a folder label Oscar Pistorius File. I knew that one was gone because I suddenly had no folder marked 'O' when I tried to save an image. I then created two new files, and cleverly (I thought) labelled these MTB and Triathlon Africa, thinking a sleuth wouldn't bother with them. Both those folders have been removed. This morning, the same day an article analysing *RESURRECTION* appeared on the shelves (via People magazine), written by Rod MacKenzie (safely holed up in New Zealand), when I received an email asking me to invoice for an article recently published, my *Invoices* folder appeared to be missing too. I did a search of the computer just to make sure. Yes, the folder is gone, with quite a lot of private information. Editors, sums for content and of course, my personal home address, tax number and banking details.

That's four. I thought four was it, until I checked for what is arguably my most important folder, the one where I save the original drafts of my fiction manuscript. I've been working on that for two years, although, in truth, I started that manuscript in High School (std 8), lost it, recovered it, then lost it again. In 2013 I took the brave step of trying to recover it from memory. I see the folder labelled *Bloodline*, that's fifth folder I am aware of, is also gone.

So that's three Oscar related folders, and then two folders are strategic (and of very personal) importance to me. Would a random virus be *that* selective in getting its teeth into my work? Doubtful. *Bloodline* certainly has no value to an outsider, in the same way that any unpublished fiction has arguably little or no value. Does it have value to me? Of course it does.

So do I take this latest invasion into my privacy, and personal security, personally? You bet I do. Am I intimidated by it? You bet I am. Wouldn't you be? Do I know who is behind it? I'm pretty sure I do

I do think there may be a real strategy to neutralise rogue elements. And yes, I do think Oscar is still very much invested in protecting his brand. As recently as 12 July he was posting brand enhancing bible verses on his own twitter page, to neutralise the fallout from his bar brawl (the story broke on Sunday night the 13th). Why does he wish to protect a brand that seems to have no inherent value, I don't know. Perhaps he knows something I don't. Perhaps he knows (or believes, or is betting) that an acquittal is a certainty. Or an appeal can be won. In terms of an acquittal, the reader should remember there are also two assessors to consider, besides Masipa herself. And there's no doubt the Pistorius Dynasty have fingers in many pies, and a great deal of influence through vast swaths of Pretoria.

What's that saying about people who lives in glass houses...?

People in glass houses shouldn't throw stones.

With the global media glare on you, should be heading out to a bar and making scene? Well, only if you want to add the unfair media glare to your portfolio of slights. I'm also not sure if it behoves someone, about to face the closing arguments in their own murder trial, to counter the ramblings of some nondescript freelancer. Whether via some service or set of personnel. I don't know. What I do know is the basic rule of thumb:

When you find yourself in a hole, stop digging.

I will cover the incident in detail in the last chapter, but I think the foregoing provides a useful premise to the following section. If you are arguing, and you consciously arm yourself, and you consciously (knowingly) kill someone in an estate-type complex, what would give you the confidence to do that (ie not just throw stones, fire bullets) and feel you can probably get away with it?

Because I think we need to ask that question. In *RESURRECTION* I provided a possible Motive. Before we get to the Method, we have to ponder:

If he did it consciously, intentionally, deliberately, and even in a premeditated fashion, why did he do it, unless he thought he could cover himself, hedge the downside. I have to admit, when I saw those first photos on the morning of 14 February 2013, and I saw Oscar dressed in a tracksuit, with a grey hoody pulled over his head, something didn't sit right with me. Intuitively I mean.

Author's note: *It is now 12:03 on 29/07/2014 and I have just finished downloading and installing a powerful new firewall. Despite numerous reboots, no additional files seem to have gone missing. A direct email on 28/07/2014 seems to have done the trick.*

Where were we? Oh yes, the hoody. I had a sense of disquiet about it, because intuitively I knew how Oscar is all about presenting a certain persona to the public, to the media, to all his salivating sycophants. So why the disquiet? Because there was something…subtly…inappropriate about it.

What do I mean? Well, in the movies, even the bad guys have a cool factor. The bad ass dudes, are somehow still attractive in a badass way. Think of Jason Statham. Vin Diesel. Darth Vader. When I saw Oscar sporting a gangster-style tracksuit I thought it was just too dressed up. You shoot someone to death and you're still going to find time to look the part? No tear stained face, bloodshot eyes, and desperate, begging pleas of "I'm sorry!" Because someone who desperately loves someone and then kills their partner by accident is nothing but self-effacing. But who goes out into public after shooting someone to death, has the presence of mind to dress in fairly hip ganger style, hires a crack PR team, and then hauls a newspaper over the coals a few months later for daring to insinuate he (Oscar) had been rude to a few car salesmen?

Did Oscar's behaviour after the incident change, or did he seem to – sort've yes, ja, kind've – want to continue as per normal? Well, we know he continued training regardless. He was flirting up a storm within weeks, regardless. He was cleaning up his twitterfeed and presumably other digital trails. And hiding in a cupboard because he couldn't sleep at night.

And, making movies with his sister as a prop. He was using his uncle's mansion as studio. And then, at a critical moment, this private video, this vital piece of evidence manufactured by the defence (highly privileged information, and thus highly sensitive) was suddenly broadcast to a worldwide audience. Talk about making your mansion into a glass house!

If we go back to 14 February 2013, 286 Bushwillow Street, 1am, 2am, 3am…what we find is right across the house, evidence of struggle. We find a pair of jeans outside. The front door unlocked. Evidence of struggle in the bedroom and in the bathroom. I won't go over these in detail again, but the point is, there was a protracted period of 'unrest' on 13 and 14 February. There was screaming and banging. It was, in a word, chaotic.

If Reeva wasn't merely killed, but murdered, Oscar would have been all too clear that there was an orgy of evidence to explain. Explaining what happened inside 286 Bushwillows was a relatively simple matter, he could make up any story (in this scenario). But outside of 286 was a whole different ball game. How to neutralise the annoying neighbours? How to make safe potentially damning testimony from nosy parkers? Simple: you make the estate manager your first port of call, and isn't that pretty much what Oscar did? In spite of his own testimony, where he said he shouted at Reeva again and again to call the police, did *Oscar* call the police? No. Despite Oscar pleading with Stipp and the Stander's to get Reeva to hospital, *is there any evidence* that Oscar called for an ambulance himself? Is there? Yes, there is a 66 second recording. But where is the recording? The paramedic told Oscar not to wait, but get Reeva to hospital immediately? So where is that 66 second recording?

But who do we know for certain he did call? The estate manager.

Speaking about what he knew of the shooting, Stander said: "I received a phone call round about 3.19am from Mr Pistorius. And he said on the call 'Johan please, please, please come to house. I shot Reeva. I thought she was an intruder. Please, please, please come quick'."

Now, three things bother me about Stander on the scene.

1. Why did he take his daughter to a potential murder scene where a young woman had been shot and was bleeding to death? What sort of father takes his daughter into a situation like that?
2. Why were there black plastic refuse bags under Reeva's head?
3. Why was Oscar – based on Stander's testimony – 'relieved' to see them?

There are a few more questions to ask, for example, how come Stander didn't notice the jeans lying outside (or his daughter for that matter). Didn't even care to mention it.

Juror13 **provides a possible reason:** *because the jeans were beneath the bathroom window, which is on the back side of the house. It was dark outside and they never went in to his back yard. They would not have seen those jeans.*

How come Stander goes to the scene but feels he should wait outside? And how come by the time Stipp arrives the ambulance still has not been called, apparently by anyone. The questions in this paragraph are speculative, whereas the three questions posed above, I think, are somewhat less so. Hence we'll examine them in more detail. But first, let's go back to what actually happened when Stander arrived at 286 Bushwillow Street, close to 3:25am on 14 February 2013:

Stander said when he got up, his daughter Carice came through to his room to say she'd heard screams -- Stander's wife told her it must have come from Pistorius' house, as he'd just called to say he shot Reeva.

Stander and his daughter drove by car to Pistorius's house and parked on the street outside.

So the inference we can make from this is that Stander may have intended to go [by himself] to Oscar, but because his wife and child had also been awakened, whatever he arranged with Oscar over the phone, that may have subsequently changed when Carice entered his bedroom. It may be irrelevant, but I am interested to know how far Stander's house is from Oscar's and why they drove there, rather than walked/or ran. But when you check (thanks *Juror13*)

http://juror13lw.files.wordpress.com/2014/03/op-neighborhood.jpg

the two houses are clearly quite far apart, and the road that connects them is somewhat convoluted. Great graphic, it's only missing the Stipps.

Juror13: *Their houses are actually pretty close. On a normal day, they could probably do that walk in only a few minutes. In an emergency, they would definitely hop in to a car.*

Yes, but it *was* an emergency, wasn't it?

Now, let's face it, if Oscar really wanted to get Reeva to the hospital, why wouldn't he take his *own* car and drive at breakneck speed as he was in the habit of doing? Was Stander's car faster? Doubtful. Was Oscar's car in the garage? No. But what we do know is that Stander stopped his car *in the road*. Was that in order to receive her body and quickly drive off?

When they approached the front door, they found it slightly open.

Not merely unlocked, *ajar*. Come inside so I don't have to be seen outside? For someone who has just mistaken someone in their home for a burglar, this is an interesting scenario. If true, an armed and emotional and beside-himself Oscar might 'accidentally' shoot *another* additional intruder, not so? What if, at 3:25am – it's still dark at the time of the morning – with the door left open, a random passerby could have entered the house, which is now a *crime scene*, through the open door? This business of Oscar running up and down stairs while Reeva is breathing her last makes no sense. No reasonable man would abandon, even for a moment, someone breathing their last breaths. They would not move. They would stay still and treasure those last moments of life. If, of course, the shooting had been accidental. If it had been intentional, well then you'd expect a lot of running around, perhaps picking up items of clothes, putting a bag of toiletries in the bathroom, placing her overnight back (packed, yes) on a chair beside her bed.

Carice entered the house first. As she pushed the door wider, the two of them saw Pistorius descending the stairs carrying Steenkamp. They noticed she had a head wound.

"When Mr Pistorius saw us there was relief in his face," Stander testified.

I don't know about that. Even in Oscar's *schema*, if he truly cared about saving Reeva, seeing the Stander's would not have changed that. Because she was still dying! Who has time to feel relief while someone is dying? It doesn't make any sense. If anything makes sense, if Oscar felt he had allies in the father, or daughter, or both, then their arrival, first on the scene would have been a relief. I'm not convinced. What was the plan? That Stander would rush away with Reeva's body? If it was, why would Oscar be *relieved* to see Carice with the estate manager? Surely that alone would be a sign that the plan (if there was one) was no longer workable. There's another possibility too. Perhaps Oscar vocalised it, saying:

"I am so glad to see you!" Or: "I am so relieved you're here, please help me...etc."

When Pistorius reached the bottom of the stairs, Carice asked him to put Steenkamp down.

This may seem an incidental factoid, but what we get is Oscar purposefully carrying, moving the injured/dying/dead Reeva, and Carice telling him to stop. Not her father. From this there is some merit to the assumption that Oscar didn't expect Carice to be there as well, when Stander arrived.

Stander said Pistorius was crying and asked them to take Steenkamp to hospital by car.

Pistorius wanted them to take Reeva somewhere by car. Is that what he had arranged with the estate manager over the phone? Remember, Oscar's pattern when he was in trouble (ie shooting the gun at Tasha's, his 'zombie stopper' remark at the firing range, firing through the roof of the car near Modderfontein', and many other incidents) was to cover it up. Denial and subterfuge. His persona as a disabled man was about covering up his disability. So, having just shot Reeva, wasn't his *automatic response* to do the same? Get her body elsewhere, and then – if he possibly could – cover it up with Stander. Was that the plan? If it was, Carice was the spoiler.

"We tried to calm Mr Pistorius down. He was broken. He was screaming, he was crying, he was praying."

Was he helping Reeva?

Stander himself, by that stage during his testimony, became tearful.

"He was torn apart. Broken. Desperate. Pleading.... And his commitment to save the young lady's life... How he begged her to stay with him, how he begged God to keep her alive," Stander said, weeping.

Oldwadge told him to take his time.

Taking Stander's account, and I do not mean to sound scornful or unsympathetic, but it sounds like plenty of sound and fury from Oscar, but what was he actually doing? Pleading, begging, crying – we've got that. But was he doing anything constructive to help the dying girl? Isn't screaming and going *te kere* highly inappropriate when someone right beside you is hanging onto dear life by a thread. Does one not try to preserve that thread? So why didn't Oscar?

Stander then said that while he was on the phone trying to call for an ambulance when neighbour Johan Stipp arrived and introduced himself as a doctor.

Stipp entered ....

What do we get from this? When Stipp arrived an ambulance had not yet been called. Let's recall that no one called Stipp, he came of his own volition. And what does he find? Stander is standing outside, talking on his phone. He says he was *trying* to call for an ambulance, which suggests he failed, he didn't call the ambulance. He may, and this is speculation, he may have been speaking to someone else. Who knows? What's very interesting is that Stander is standing outside. The dying girl is inside, and so is his daughter. And it is Stipp – seeing Oscar jog up and down the stairs a few minutes later – who ponders the safety of the situation. Where is the gun? Why did Stander not think his own daughter's life could be endangered? Could Stander have had motives of his own? If he helps Oscar, there might be something in it for him… What about that?

Stipp entered to see if he could help and told Stander to phone 082 911. Stander managed to get through to paramedics at 3:27am and was busy on the call when Stipp, who had ascertained that Steenkamp was dead, came outside and explained to paramedics how to get to the house.

So there we have it. Reeva was shot at around 03:15-17 and it took at least ten minutes for anyone to phone an ambulance. Stipp even had to give Stander the number. Ten minutes is an awfully long time to be kicking and screaming besides someone who is slowly dying. It is a long time for someone driving to a crime scene, and standing outside in the garden, and not making a call. Well, not to an ambulance. And as we hear again and again, Oscar was insisting *they take Reeva to hospital*.

What's interesting in this psychology is yes, you do take someone to hospital, and you should, if they are badly injured. But there are two exceptions at least.

1. You don't move a body that has critical injuries, such as massive haemorrhaging. And Reeva was losing buckets of blood. We see clearly from the toilet that there was a lot of blood, and there was a heck of a lot of blood in the toilet bowl itself. Did Oscar do anything to stem this blood flow? No, he had to be asked. Her almost amputated arm was what upset Carice the most

2. If an ambulance is on its way, it would be quicker to get medical attention by waiting for it to arrive, than to start driving to a hospital. Yet it seems, this is what Oscar intended. Not to wait.

The ambulance arrived quickly and paramedics declared Steenkamp dead.

How quickly? Exactly what time did they arrive? Roux introduces a photo of the Netcare 911 ambulance's arrival at Silver Woods Estate at 03:41 on 14 Feburary. That's roughly 24 – 26 minutes that passed by after Reeva was shot. In the scheme of things, that's not *terribly* long. The question we must ask is this:

- Did the ambulance arrive as a result of Oscar's 66 second call at around 03:17?

- Or did the ambulance take 14 minutes to arrive (including a delay at the gate, and to find them) after Stander called at 03:27.

In other words, did the ambulance take 14 minutes or 24 minutes to get there?

Stander said Stipp told him he had heard four shots, silence and screaming and another four shots.

People who live in glass house should not throw stones. Celebrities, who lives in celebrity bubbles, should not fire a series of bullets through a locked door, killing someone, and expect to be forgiven for an 'accident'.

http://www.enca.com/south-africa/oscar-trial-estate-manager-weeps-he-testifies

So we've dealt with possibly suspicious behaviour in the time it took to call an ambulance. And the sense behind calling the estate manager first. We won't go into the black garbage bags here, but that will be touched on again in the last chapter. What we do need to ask, bearing in mind the theme of this chapter is:

Why did Oscar's domestic worker and those neighbours closest to him not see or hear anything of any importance?

Who are Oscar's immediate neighbours? Have a look:

http://juror13lw.files.wordpress.com/2014/03/op-neighborhood.jpg

Have a look at the Stipp's direct line of sight – from their bedroom to Oscar's house at this link:

http://www.nickvanderleek.com/2014/08/glasses-houses.html

Before we move on, a few comments on Stander and 'the ambulance situation' courtesy of *Juror13:*

The ambulance situation is a VERY tricky one to figure out. Literally everybody gave different testimonies on the stand so it's very difficult to say by what means the ambulance arrived, as well as who is actually telling the truth. I have listed summaries of the testimonies below.

1. *Oscar called Netcare at 3:20. Nobody from Netcare testified, so all we have is Oscar's statement that the ambulance company told him to bring her to the hospital himself.*

2. *Then we have Dr. Stipp's testimony (summarized): After Dr. Stipp had been inside the house, and saw that Reeva was deceased, he went outside and asked Mr. Stander if the ambulance was on their way. Mr. Stander said no, he hadn't called them yet so Dr. Stipp called the hospital emergency department and asked them to send an ambulance. They told him he had to call an emergency number, not them directly, so Mr. Stander called an emergency number. Dr. Stipp spoke to the dispatcher, explained the injuries, and they proceeded to send out an ambulance.*

3. *And next, we have Baba's testimony (summarized):*

Baba was so shocked by what he was seeing that he couldn't think for a few moments. How could everything be "fine" when Oscar was carrying a badly mutilated, bleeding woman down the stairs. When Mr. Stander said "Oscar", Baba kind of snapped out of his shock. Carice was inside and Mr. Stander was standing in the doorway (it almost sounded like he was blocking Baba's entrance).
<u>Mr. Stander told Baba to go call police and the ambulance.</u> [my emphasis] He also gave the guards instructions to <u>make sure that no cars were parked at Oscar's house</u>[my emphasis]. Baba never went in to OP's house that morning. Baba stated that he went outside and made the calls.

4. *And then finally, we have Johan Stander's testimony (summarized):*

<u>Carice parked the car in the street</u> [my emphasis] *and they rushed to the front door; Carice walking in front. The door was slightly open and there was a light on. Carice pushed the door open and they saw Oscar coming down the stairs with Reeva in his arms. Mr. Stander could see that Reeva had a head wound. ...While Mr. Stander ...was out trying to call the ambulance, Stander says he asked Dr. Stipp to go inside and see if he could assist. He also asked Stipp for the number to an ambulance because he couldn't get a hold of them. Stipp gave him the number 082911. As Dr. Stipp was walking to go in the house, he turned around and said to Mr. Stander "I'm actually a Radiologist" and then carried on walking. (Both Stander and OP really tried to throw Stipp under the bus during testimony, which was totally shitty considering this guy came over to the house on his own accord to try to assist during a scary, violent situation. Instead of a thank you, he gets shat on by OP and his crew.)*

Stander then says he phoned 082911. He managed to get through. While he was still speaking on the phone, Stipp came back out. <u>Stander states that he said to Stipp he was having a hard time explaining to the people on the phone where to come. How is that possible? He has lived in the estate since 2009. I find it odd that he had difficulty explaining how to get to the estate. So Stipp then took the phone and spoke to them.</u> [My emphasis]

Most importantly, they all gave very different testimony. If we were to believe all, then Oscar, Baba, Stipp & Stander ALL called for an ambulance. Somebody is not telling the truth here. The most bizarre differences in testimony were between Stipp & Stander.

Stipp went out of his way to help that night and both OP and Stander made him sound like a bit of a bumbling fool in their testimonies. And on top of that, nobody from OP's side (Stander, family, etc) bothered to tell the police that Stipp was even there that night. STIPP had to approach the police on his own two days later since nobody ever contacted him.

If I've alluded to the possibility that Stander's actions are…a little strange, and *Juror13* independently reinforces this. What stands out especially is observation from *Juror13*:

I find it odd that he [Stander, who has lived in the estate for 4 years] *had difficulty explaining how to get to the estate. So Stipp then took the phone and spoke to them.*

Now we're going to fly through the next section. In January/February 2013 Oscar was preparing to buy a new house, and from the images we've seen

http://www.samachar.com/pistorius-bought-luxury-house-to-move-into-with-steenkamp-says-friend-ohfadMeifee.html

it was a far bigger, more palatial, and yes, *glassy* version of his Silver Woods cottage.

According to the local estate agency Firzt, the property has <u>four ensuite bedrooms</u>, a large dining room, <u>family room</u>, study, breakfast room, outside patio, <u>four garages</u>, a lap pool, another patio with a barbecue area and a big garden. The house is about four years old, spanning about 750 sq metres on 2,000 sq metres of land.

Looks like a home for a man fixing to start a family, right? All it needs is a babymaker.

Ricardo, who recently sold the house for the same price of about 9m rand, added: "He seemed like a nice guy. He didn't say why he was buying the house. He just wanted to move to Sandton. Everything seemed fine at the time of the negotiations. When I heard the whole situation, I was shocked."

He just wanted to move to Sandton. There's some serious intent from Oscar. He buys a house in Sandton in order to be closer to Reeva. Think about that for a second. You haven't even moved in together, the relationship is barely on the 3.5 month mark, and you're buying a 'let's live happily ever after together here' home. Some big moves. And how does Reeva respond? How does Reeva feel about her price parking nearer to her stomping ground, when Reeva herself was moving (again) into a small apartment in Janaury 2013? Well, obviously she's impressed. But she must also be a little alarmed by the speed at which the fastest man with no legs operates when it comes to romance. This speed – in terms of flirting, has also come up time and again in the media:

http://www.timeslive.co.za/local/2014/07/20/partying-oscar-hit-on-reeva-double-just-52-days-after-shooting-girlfriend

Pistorius took to the dance floor and kept asking the blonde beauty to accompany him to another party, several guests said this week.

He grabbed her hand to dance and flirted, giving up only after all his advances were rejected.

http://www.news24.com/SouthAfrica/News/Oscar-was-flirting-on-night-out-20130415

A woman who attended the party last Saturday said: "He was drinking shooters and he was flirtatious. He didn't seem like someone [who had] lost the love of his life."

Another person said: "I can't believe he showed his face in public, carrying on as if nothing's happened".

http://www.sundaystandard.info/article.php?NewsID=20593&GroupID=5

"Is Oscar Pistorius pathologically stupid or could there be some other excuse for his behaviour?" Can we simply put this behaviour down to poor judgement or is this incident just another example of the aggressive behaviour and poor impulse control?"

Oscar is – by no stretch of the imagination – stupid. A family does not set up a dynasty by being not very smart, and let's recall, Oscar was singlehandedly creating his own self-styled Dynasty when it all went south. Yes, he was about to buy a R9 million mansion, and there was talk of his driving a R3 million McLaren (which may not have been much more than talk). Even so, this has nothing to do with stupidity. Is there another excuse for his behaviour? Laurie Pieters-James, I think so. In fact, I wouldn't be surprised if Oscar intentionally went out to create these scenes in order to garner some press. WAell, some bad boy press; the sauve, free wheeling, playboy bachelor (yes, still available..) is out there, and he knows how to have fun. He's not a victim. He's just suffered a setback.

Is it possible that these scenes were *also* carefully planned? Let's recall each one seemed to require an explanation to the press from his PR spokesperson (Burgess). So, isn't it possible all this was about making sure that Oscar's *Don Juan* flag

http://en.wikipedia.org/wiki/Don_Juan#Don_Juan_legend

remain flying? It's hard to say for sure, but given that so much of Oscar's life was calculated, it's hard not to imagine seeking out a scenario as fraught with danger as clubbing is (all those able bodied limbs kicking out in the dark, waiting to trip him up) – so it's tough to imagine it wasn't part of some larger design, or framework. Remember, according to Oscar himself, he preferred to spend Valentine's night quietly at home, rather than with friends. That's maybe that's how he rolls, right?

So…what happened at the VIP room on 12 July 2014?

Reports are that murder accused, paralympian Oscar Pistorius, who killed his girlfriend Reeva Steenkamp, was downing tequila shots, and socialising with known violent offenders. It is alleged that he had scantily-clad women sitting on his lap prior to the fight that led to him being asked to leave the VIP Room nightclub on Saturday night.

On Twitter, @aleshavr tweeted "@OscarPistorius how abt a pic of those underdressed... i mean underprivilaged women u had on ur lap at VIPRoom on Sun morn jst b4 u tweeted"

Sometimes, when you live in a glass house, you want to be seen to be doing certain things. Don't you? It's a little like when the Queen is in residence at a particular castle, a flag is raised to say, "Her majesty is home, take note." Well, isn't that what all this has been about? The Oscar show is still in town people, get your tickets. The court case is just a side show, the real show is still steaming ahead…

The original object of his affection, how did she respond to the idea of being queen of his castle? Well, in typical Reeva style, with grace, with kindness and with a sense of humor:

On 23 January, Steenkamp wrote to Pistorius: *"It will be just fine. It's a lot of money but that's just it. Money. It's a beautiful house that you will make (?) little home. And if u can't pay for it anymore one day and I can't help you either then we run away to the eastern country and live in exile from the banks. Ill bake to make money and ill still look after u ok.*

"That's the worst thing that can happen here. The best thing that will happen is that you will get your house and live happily ever after. Don't let the formalities in between confuse you."

It's sweet but it's not clear (yet) whether Reeva sees herself as part of his game of thrones. She reassures him, yes, that she will be there for him, she will support him (as she supports her parents, and animal welfare), but she also says, in no uncertain terms:

The best thing that will happen is that you will get your house and live happily ever after.

Not we, *you.*

Sultans of Spin

I think it was Nietzsche who said, "Be careful lest in casting out the devils you cast out the best thing that's in you." – Joseph Campbell

How can you reveal the truth if those to whom you are speaking (or writing) don't want to hear? No, those aren't my words. They belong to a *little troll. Fucking Walsh. Fucking little troll.* Say what?!

Professor Tim Noakes recently gave a speech on what a balanced diet *actually* is. Because, well, what it is… in 2014 we still don't seem to know what we should be eating. We've nailed the perfect petfoods for healthy dogs and cats, we know exactly what to feed poultry, and livestock, exotic parrots and the odd leguan, but when it comes to the naked ape, we're dumbfounded. We're just not *quite* sure how we are wired. Apparently. Because people are complicated right?

I sat in the front row with my camera, taking notes, while Prof Noakes made his presentation to an audience of medical students, practitioners and professors. I needn't have bothered. Well, that's a bit harsh. I did learn a few things. But I have interviewed the learned professor a few times on the same topic, and also another investigative reporter, Gary Taubes, who broached the high protein/low carb lifestyle – as an idea – as long ago as 2002. Takes us South Africans a while to catch on, it seems. I've been writing about it, in several publications, since 2012. Is it important? Sure. Do we get it? Not so sure. Why not:

How can you reveal the truth if those to whom you are speaking (or writing) don't want to hear?

While the content of Prof Noakes' speech is undoubtedly compelling, what I found unexpectedly fascinating was how it was relevant to this narrative. I intuited that the Oscar shenanigans are actually going on all the time, everywhere. It's going on in our homes, and when you take out the garbage. Sound familiar?

http://youtu.be/Doofg9m5w_Q?t=1m29s

You see it when you look at your window. *When you turn on your television. When you go to church. When you pay your taxes.*

Morpheus: Is the world that has been pulled over your eyes to blind you from the truth.

If the Oscar narrative hasn't convinced you that is:
 a) Happening and
 b) Happening all around us

then *Revelations* must succeed where *RESURRECTION* has failed.

This chapter aims to address this question. The truth is being hidden from us. Purposefully. By design. By calculated actions and omissions. Is it a *conspiracy*? Is the peacock competing with other peacocks involved in any kind of conspiracy? Well, if a conspiracy is a *scheme* towards a certain end, then yes, all peacocks conspire to get hens. And they're pretty obvious about it too. In the world of Men the *schema* is obvious, but a lot more substle. Ten thousand shades of gray subtle. And why are all these schemes in play? Well, to the extent that the fox can find its way into the henhouse, he can – let's just say, our society is rigged in much the same way Nature is rigged.

Winner takes all.

Ask Lance.
Ask Oscar.
Ask Tiger.

So what do investigative journalists have to do with that? Actually, everything. If you're Lance Armstrong, and you've built an empire by riding a bicycle, but all those millions (or a substantial fraction) are ill-gotten gains, then you have to defend those secrets. Against whom? Those lone wolves that drift and roam within the media. There aren't many of them, it's true. But there are enough of them. And when the shroud that blankets the world is dark enough, that's when you see the real stars. And that's what investigative reporters do.

It applies to sport, to business, to politics, to celebrity. Even nutrition. Massive amounts of money are based on selling a lie, or selling a *scheme*. Does the minty stuff in toothpaste actually whiten our teeth? No. What does it do? It gives a sense of a clean mouth. Does it clean the mouth? No. So when you buy toothpaste, does that minty stuff do any of the stuff toothpaste is really supposed to be doing? Like fight plaque, clean or whiten your teeth? Not really.

I've studied advertising and worked in advertising, and I can tell you, it's all about selling a scheme. It's about bullshitting. What is the best story that will get your product to sell. How can be it be used to infiltrate the mind down paths of least resistance. These days products are sold not so much on functionality, but on feelings. The associations they have with ego, and aspiration, and belonging, and identity. When you buy a certain car, or deodorant, does that make you The Man, or does it simply make you feel like you might be? It's selling you a few plastic peacock tail feathers, not much else.

It is a revolutionary feeling when you see a man with integrity, and conscience, and honesty, a real champion, a man who really cares about the science, and about the implications of our knowledge, when he recommends that medical professionals read a book by an investigative journalist. No, not a doctor. Yes, Professor Noakes recommended, as prescribed reading for today's next generation of doctors, a book by an investigative journalist. We'll get to that in a moment. During the same presentation, Noakes highlighted that quote (at the top of this paragraph) from *another* investigative journalist: David Walsh. Ever heard of him?

No? Well if you haven't you'll be making *someone's* day. David Walsh is the Sunday Times (UK) reporter who exposed Armstrong. Well, tried to anyway. Walsh was vindicated in large part thanks to Armstrong's ex-teammate Tyler Hamilton breaking pro-cycling's *omerta*, or code of silence. So when Armstrong finally returned from a ~~sabbatical extensive hiding~~ vacation in Hawaii, he went onto Oprah to do his confessional (and the customary remorseful sniff) . And so his arch-nemesis, Walsh was asked by BBC News if that – Armstrong's confession – was, well, good enough.

Walsh told BBC News: "There is a legal issue in that the Sunday Times was sued by Lance Amstrong, in a sense he won even though there was an out-of-court settlement. The Times paid £300,000 [about R5.38 million in adjusted pounds] *towards his costs. They had £600,000* [R10.77 million]*of their own costs. They are seeking to recoup that money and they have every entitlement."*

"Remember the Sunday Times was the only newspaper who consistently asked questions about a guy who was probably the biggest cheat sport has ever known. Now to be penalised for asking those questions is just reprehensible and hopefully the Sunday Times will get its money back.

"On a personal level I don't want any apology from Lance Armstrong or any kind of explanation, because <u>I was a journalist being paid to do what I did. It was my job</u>[emphasis mine], *I'm not looking for any thanks from anybody. Any concern I have is for the sources who told the truth and were vilified for it."*

Walsh was heavily criticised by Armstrong over his years covering cycling. Once asked about Walsh in an interview by American writer Daniel Coyle, Amstrong said: "I just hate the guy. He's a little troll. Fucking Walsh. Fucking little troll."

In the interview with Doyle, Armstrong went on to say that he hoped he was someone that people in the US looked up to. But he said: "You know what? They don't even know who David Walsh is. And they never will. And in 20 years, nobody is going to remember him. Nobody."

Well. I remember him. So does Noakes.

But do you see the contempt? The arrogance, from Lance? Here's some more context:

In an agreed statement in 2006, the paper said: "The Sunday Times has confirmed to Mr Armstrong that it never intended to accuse him of being guilty of taking any performance-enhancing drugs and sincerely apologised for any such impression.

"Mr Armstrong has always vigorously opposed drugs in sport and appreciates the Sunday Times' efforts to also address the problem."

<u>*Walsh first raised questions about Armstrong in 1999*</u>*, when made a comeback after life-threatening testicular cancer and made an extraordinary break from the pack in a mountain stage during that year's Tour de France.*[Imagine if Walsh had been taken seriously in '99? There wouldn't be a 7 year blank space where there is currently no official winner from 1999-2005 – i.e. the entire Armstrong oligarchy of the Tour de France].

The Sunday Times journalist said on Friday [January 2013] *that Armstrong needed to name those who had helped him and criticised Winfrey for not going far enough.*

He said it was "reprehensible" that Armstrong had sued the paper in a bid to hide the truth.

Walsh said he did not think Oprah went far enough in her questioning of Armstrong. "My feeling is that the interview was fine in as far as it went, but it did not go nearly far enough, and even in as far as it went, I was particularly disappointed that he didn't admit what might be called the hospital room admission from 1996," Walsh told the BBC.

The hospital room is a famous scene from the Armstrong *mythos*, where in the contect of an imminent operation, a surgeon asked Lance, in front of other riders, and some their wives (including Frankie and Bertsy Andreu), whether Lance was using any steroids. This is an important question to answer honestly, if you are about to be anaesthetised. And so, Lance did. But he underestimated the resolve of Betsy Andreu, a staunch Catholic, when it came to protecting his secrets. And the rest is history. If that's something you're interested in, be sure to download the audiobook version of Tyler Hamilton's The Secret Race, it's a doozy. For my money, one of the best books on sport ever written, and it did win an award.

Interestingly, The Secret Race, by ex world #1 pro rider, Tyler Hamilton, whom I have also interviewed, reads like…not merely a confessional…but it is the Holy Grail for disillusioned cycling fans. And I have to admit, despite the deception, despite the dishonesty, it's not as though these sportsmen don't have guts, or talent. The whole thing, as I wrote for a men's magazine at a time, reads like a Shakespearean tragedy.

Hamilton told me, and says in his book, that telling the truth "feels *so* good." He seems like a good guy. I'm sure he is. But he did live a lie for a very long time, and went to extraordinary lengths to protect this lie. And it's hard to miss that when Hamilton did tell the truth, he had been subpoenaed to testify before a grand jury. Well, the jury got more than they bargained for. And while Hamilton was at it, he got his book deal. Pro Cycling has ostracised him, for life, but he walked away with something to show for it, and – having been a pariah – could draw an appreciative crowd here and there (as he did at the Discovery Vitality Summit in Sandton, in 2013).

The point being, there are dozens, hundreds, thousands, tens of thousands of role-players invested in these deceptions. It's massive. And that's just pro-cycling. Sticking to a narrative means everybody profits, except those suffering from conscience anxiety, and there are a few exceptions. Pro-riders, I mean, who would rather not dope because:

    a) It's illegal (officially at any rate)
    b) It's harmful
    c) It's expensive

Hamilton said he paid his crooked doctor (Fuentes) $50 000 a year to take care of his bud. That's half a million Rand from one cyclist. Are there incentives to keeping secrets in cycling? Of course there are. Are there incentives to keeping secrets in the Global Fast Food business,

http://www.foxnews.com/health/2014/02/03/lack-of-regulation-of-fast-food-fueling-obesity-epidemic-study-says/

in the energy markets,

http://www.miningmx.com/news/energy/Sasol-slapped-with-another-cartel-fine.htm

http://www.engineeringnews.co.za/article/sasol-to-pay-r111m-for-polypropylene-collusion-contests-excessive-pricing-charge-2011-02-28

http://www.independent.co.uk/news/uk/home-news/all-in-it-together-big-six-energy-chiefs-feel-heat-from-mps-8911466.html

amongst South Africa's bread suppliers...

http://www.moneyweb.co.za/moneyweb-industrials/tiger-brands-admits-to-bread-pricefixing-pays-fine

How about milk?

http://www.iol.co.za/news/south-africa/milk-producers-less-than-lily-white-1.387575#.U9fXMBCSxOg

Banks?

http://www.thewire.com/global/2013/12/eu-banks-collusion/355765/
http://www.ibtimes.com/top-banks-investigated-collusion-derivatives-1153911

South African Banks?

http://mg.co.za/article/2014-03-06-banks-bear-brunt-of-gold-fix-blame
http://africanbank.investoreports.com/african-bank-fine-verges-on-overkill/
http://www.ideate.co.za/2008/01/17/collusion-and-price-fixing-at-the-banks/
http://www.vaaltriangleinfo.co.za/general/consumer_articles/finance/bank_charges_1a.htm

Property markets?

http://www.property24.com/articles/bedfordview-retail-collusion/13283

Automakers?

http://www.nytimes.com/2013/09/27/business/9-auto-parts-makers-plead-guilty-to-fixing-prices.html?pagewanted=all&_r=0
http://mobile.reuters.com/article/worldNews/idUSBRE95C1AY20130613?i=6

Okay, what about South African automakers:

http://www.just-auto.com/news/automakers-accused-of-price-fixing_id73984.aspx
http://www.autonews.com/article/20040506/REG/405060708/s.-africa-automakers-deny-charges-of-price-fixing

How about major retailers, like Pick 'n Pay, Checkers?

http://mg.co.za/article/2010-12-31-sa-grocers-cleared-of-price-collusion

Confectionary?

http://www.confectionerynews.com/Regulation-Safety/US-chocolate-price-fixing-suit-against-Mars-Nestle-and-Hershey-melts

Cigarettes?

http://www.economist.com/node/687703

http://faculty.quinnipiac.edu/charm/CHARM%20proceedings/CHARM%20article%20archive%20pdf%20format/Volume%2010%202001/155%20solow.pdf

Alcohol?

http://www.who.int/bulletin/volumes/90/1/11-091413/en/
https://wagner.nyu.edu/files/faculty/publications/Liquor_Paper_Draft_4.pdf

Collusion is *everywhere*. At one stage there was a story about local *bicycle merchants* that were colluding

http://mg.co.za/article/2011-04-01-cyclists-go-shopping-online

with each other to fix prices. Why does everyone do it? Money. To make more. To make better profits. Who benefits? They do. Is there a loser? There always is. It's usually us.

So, could there be collusion in the media?

http://www.cnn.com/2013/10/24/world/europe/uk-phone-hacking-scandal-fast-facts/

What about mobile phone operators?

http://www.bdlive.co.za/business/technology/2013/10/10/cell-c-takes-bigger-rivals-to-competition-commission

http://www.dailymail.co.uk/news/article-153211/Phone-networks-fined-20m-price-fixing-con.html

Construction companies?

http://www.biznews.com/thought-leaders/2014/07/bad-news-construction-companies-govt-seeks-fresh-collusion-price-fixing-fines/

http://www.sacommercialpropnews.co.za/business-specialties/property-construction-development/6225-construction-collusion-hurts-south-africa.html

With Oscar Pistorius we're talking about a son of South Africa, and a darling of South Africa's media. There wasn't any collusion in Oscar's world, was there? I mean, nothing like what we saw with Armstrong. No media colluding – by going along with, and letting someone else – set the pace, set the standards, and 'control the narrative'. That wasn't – isn't – happening here, right? Because collusion…is one of those conspiracy theory things. It's paranoia. Right?

South Africa's media – struggling to weather the contractions to their various bottomlines – couldn't be colluding amongst each other to draw the Oscar Pistorius story out – could they? Because this is a content goldmine, let's face it the longer *everyone* draws out the story (and everyone drawing out a story is collusion) the longer you:

a) Get to tell the story
b) More money you make out of telling the story

In other words, News now becomes SoapStories. You never really cut to the chase, because you need a full quota of episodes for each series, and then you go about series 1,2,3,4,5 etc. You can only do that, if you never really get to the point. I thought that was *the point* of news, personally, but never having studied journalism, and since I'm not a qualified journalist, I'm no expert. If we use Smallville as an analogy though, the premise of Smallville is Clark's trauma of emergence…iow his *becoming* Superman. I think there are ten series, and so what the writers must not do, is have Clark don his Red, White Yellow and Blue outfit, and fly off into the sunset. Because although that *is the point*, getting to the point would kill the soap, kill the drama, kill – yes – the calculated narrative.

Another version of this is any romantic comedy, like Who's The Boss, or Sex in the City, or Dharma and Greg, or Friends, which shows the luckless exploits of singles…trying to emerge, trying to find a partner. How do you kill that narrative? By having them get married. Because that's how that story ends. It's the point of the story, but in order to perpetuate your *schema*, you need to never get to the point.

That may be good for entertainment television (and I'm not sure if it is, I'm not even sure if it is good storytelling) but it's certainly not good for news. Which is meant to be in the public interest. Which is why this trial is televised. The original deal with news, and newspapers, and media, was to serve the public interest. To protect and to serve. Not exploit. Not manipulate. Not…try to survive by fair or foul means. Serve.

Which is why, it seems to me, there may be an agenda at play to draw out Oscar's story as slowly as possible, sort of hedging that Oscar is…not that bad. Possibly innocent. And depressed. Is that the story? Is this that thing called 'Editorial Independence' and 'balanced', 'educated' and 'non-sensationalist' reporting? In other words, no analysis of what is said in court. But a brawl in a bar is worthy of huge headlines. And a lookalike ex-girlfriend. Is 'balanced', 'educated' and 'non-sensationalist' reporting really happening in South Africa's newspapers, because when last I looked our number one newspapers and magazines were/are tabloid publications. In other words, sensationalist reporting. And after all that, the serious book deals (from the same journalists selling the soap).

Would we (the public) rather read about Oscar's depression or an analysis of the case? Unanswered questions? Do we want insightful, investigative stories that expose the truth and…I'm not sure…the kind've stuff reporting is actually *supposed to be* or do we want to be titillated. Do we want 'News' as 'Porn'? News of brawls and being drunk and what swear words were used? Sadly, most people do want and will sign up for that. Is it in the public interest, or is it simply a case that the public are interested?

Oscar is a quintessentially South African story, so when I look at how South African media houses are handing it, yes, I frown. What is going on in our local media houses? I recently asked someone – another journalist – why Hagen Engler's Daily Maverick piece was a non-story – despite being published at 07:28 on February 14, 2013 and the response was (obviously confidential):

Gosh - that was very fast of Hagen.

He used to be an editor at Media 24 so I'm not too sure that they'd go there [to interrogate the ethics of it] . *He did know Reevs well and I think all of her friends knew from about 6h45am that morning (I know I did, before it was on Twitter). It's just very interesting he'd write something before most of the world even knew, I agree.*

This chapter, lest we forget, is titled *Sultans of Spin*. So I've put it out there, on twitter: *has SA media done a good job of covering the Oscar trial*?

When someone said something…not positive…they were accused of 'casting stones'. Someone else asked, 'Is having an opinion casting a stone?' One reporter said, 'A good reporter reports, and doesn't give their opinion?' Maybe when Lois Lane was a reporter, not in the post Oprah age. Now there are comedy shows entirely dedicated to tearing the news apart, and to making fun of the fakery that is politics (especially in the US). All the time, TV news channels are dedicated to fathoming the stories behind the stories. Experts are interviewed in order to get their opinion, their analysis on possible patterns, or trends. But news is not about opinion? The entire concept of news is opinion. One person's news is someone else's:

report, announcement, story, account;

(news) item, article, news flash, newscast, headlines, press release, communication, communiqué, bulletin;
> message, dispatch, statement, intelligence;
> disclosure, revelation, word, talk, notice, intimation, the latest, gossip, tittle-tattle, narration, rumour, scandal, exposé;
> *informal* scoop;
> *literary* tidings;
> *archaic* advices
> "colleagues were stunned by the news of his death"

Did you get: *message, intimation* and *exposé* somewhere in there? How about *revelation, account* and *narration*?

An SMS message from someone you care about, saying they've arrived home safely, is important news to you. An intimation that someone is about to divorce you, or your president hinting that he may go to war, or from an investigative reporter that a certain cyclist may be doping – these are potentially *critical* sources of information. A tip from a trader. A leak from a whistleblower. These can change or shape our lives. An exposé on a company or syndicate that is bankrupting gullible citizens can save you your pension, or if you miss it, you can cost you your life savings, and with it, your retirement. So is news only good news if it is educational, non-sensational and balanced? What is balanced?

One journalist used these exact three words to describe how good the coverage of the Oscar Pistorius Murder Trial has been in South Africa. Yes, 'balanced', 'educated' and 'non-sensationalist'. But not insightful, investigative, exposing the truth or…I'm not sure…the kind've stuff reporting is actually *supposed* to be.

I apologise if this offends some people, but Jacques Steenkamp's book *The Griekwastad Murders* which I reviewed at one point, is the sort of riveting first person reporting good writing needs to be. It is well researched, factual, and insightful and you know what, *something* else. There's a little bit of personal, firsthand comment thrown in there.

Charne Kemp's book covering the same topic is measured, descriptive but impersonal, factual but flowery and as a result of its 3rd person detachment, I couldn't even get halfway. I gave the book away and the person I gave it to told me they gave up reading it after about 25 pages.

Kemp's book is clearly 'balanced', 'educated' and 'non-sensationalist'. Is it interesting? Does she share her own personal insights? Does she add to the narrative that's in the news? She's a reporter, so she ought to have – like Jacques Steenkamp – a treasure trove of firsthand encounters, and meaty stories (background stuff) she could dig out. But she doesn't. She describes the sights between Upington and Kimberley. And the 'stilte' on the farm. But that's not why I am reading a book about a youngster who shot his family to death. If I want to read a poetic book about the South African landscape I might try Olive Schreiner, or Isak Dinesen. When I read a story about a potential killer, I want to know what happened. I want to know the reporter or writer knows more than I do. I want to learn something, and – and this part is almost unvoiced – I want some need in me, that's driving all this agitated collecting of information, I want that to be satisfied. A good writer knows how to resonate with this need.

Is it a need to question the validity of our systems? To question the veracity of what people are saying (at face value). Is it a subtle (or not so subtle) sense of outrage? It might be all of these things.

One of the things that I didn't expect, in analysing and investigating and researching this case, is the…lack of skill…I think is the best way to describe it, of the media, in reporting a legal process. No one, or very few, seem to know what to do. Do you simply tweet the case? Can you express an opinion or are the sacred commands, uttered in unison across SA newsrooms in these cases:

- Thy shalt not judge
- Thy shalt not express an opinion
- Thy shalt not think about the case

In other words, please, please PLEASE do not think! Innocent until proven guilty, it is *not* our place to judge – just report the news. Please DON'T think about the case! PLEASE!

What do you get when you have news no one thinks about? Generic information. What do you get when you have a book with no insights, no personal investment? No passion, just reporting? You get cardboard writing. It's boring. It's very boring. In South Africa there's a website called News24.com. I hope I am not bursting any bubbles when I say this, but I don't need any more news than that. I only need one news website. So why would I go to IOL.co.za or Timelive.co.za or any other local news site if I am going to read the same vanilla news? Answer? I'm not.

So hang on, who are these reporters and editors saying thy shalt report the news, the whole news, and nothing but the news, and let your sub help you! Who are they? I'm not sure but if you don't want a job, if you want your publication to fizzle and become invisible, then carry on, make it indistinguishable from everything else that is online. Carry on doing what everyone else is doing and see where that gets you. Or, think. Even better, think *different*!

But it seems editors are afraid to think outside of the box, in case it doesn't make business sense. I think, sad to say, this countries journos watch…dare I say it…*too much television*. I've been told I'm an idiot for speaking such bunkum, but I got a second opinion from an editor I hardly know, but who knows the law, and knows publishing. What does [this person] think of SA media's coverage of the Oscar trial?

[We] editors have had a lot of amusement watching and reading the news on Oscar and other high-profile cases.
They really get it tangled, and throw in expressions from American law, because they've watched too many USA television shows. Which further confuses the public! And some of our local soapies really get the procedural law wrong when they put one of their characters as an accused in a criminal trial.

Look at guys like Walsh, and Noakes, and Noah. Remember Jobs? Mandela? Homer (Simpson)? Mrs Doubtfire? They were all vilified. How about Edward Snowden?

http://www.news24.com/World/News/Snowden-a-recluse-one-year-on-from-asylum-20140731

Key quote: *Accused by Washington of espionage and stealing state documents, Snowden travelled to Moscow via Hong Kong after revealing the true extent of <u>global US electronic surveillance</u>. ..."Snowden has become <u>a symbol of the struggle for freedom, and that's useful for Russia</u>. Today, that's one of the strongest arguments [Russia] could put to the international community" as relations with the West deteriorate, he said.*

How does Prof Noakes respond to this? He tweeted some time ago:

Galileo like Darwin was vilified for contesting religious beliefs. Today vilification occurs whenever livelihoods are threatened.

Livelihoods. Orientations. And yes, Schemes.

How does it feel, when you're the interrogator of truth, and there's *Revelation*?

"It's been fantastic that people want to hear the truth now, because for so long, the one thing people didn't want to hear was the truth, it's come full circle," [David Walsh] said.

"[The] UCI didn't want to catch Armstrong; sponsors didn't want to catch him, the Tour de France company didn't want to. His team, the doctors, everyone was covering up for him.
"I didn't feel like: 'Oh, this is affecting your integrity.' I mean people thought that I was wrong, but I felt I was getting it right and I didn't care what other people thought, I cared that I was doing the right thing."

Walsh's inquiry uncovered one of the most sophisticated doping schemes in sporting history and led to the downfall of a man previously considered by many to be one of the greatest athletes of all time. But in Walsh's opinion, Lance Armstrong's biggest crime was not doping or in fact the legacy he built on false pretences.
"<u>His greatest crime was the bullying and the way he set out to destroy people's lives</u>," he said.
"Many people have doped, but not many people have gone to <u>the lengths he went to protect his lie</u>."

Noakes again, via twitter: *David Walsh perceived truth - his gut feeling - and wrote about it <u>http://amzn.to/X6HJxd</u> . He was vilified by many for 14 years. Seek truth.*

Armstrong sued Walsh and his employer, successfully silencing his major critic using UK defamation laws which are so plaintiff-friendly that they have in recent years given rise to the phenomenon of <u>libel tourism</u>.

Last week, in an interview with Oprah Winfrey, Armstrong finally admitted to cheating, and also issued a qualified apology to Walsh after repeated prompting.
'I would apologise to David,' the disgraced former cyclist said.
Walsh joined Breakfast *this morning to discuss the confession, and said although Winfrey did a good job, Armstrong's first attempt at truth-telling was something of a dress rehearsal for the <u>revelations to come</u>.*

http://www.port.ac.uk/uopnews/2013/03/07/the-truth-always-outs/

I'm not sure whether my research into this Oscar Pistorius Murder Trial has made me more cynical (or simply busier) but for the first time this year I missed most of the Tour de France. Yes, part of the…disappointment…of the Tour was Froome (born in Kenya, raised in South Africa, went to school in Bloemfontein and Johannesburg) – dropping out. And then Contador. And of course, Daryl Impey dropping out before the Tour had even started.

http://www.darylimpey.com/News/DisplayNewsItem.aspx?niid=34129

Daryl, whom I interviewed for Tour de France, has been completed silent on twitter since July 2nd, 2014 [as of today's writing, July 31 2014]. Am I personally disappointed about these 'allegations' of doping. Of course I am. Zapiro sums up the vibe with this cartoon:

http://www.zapiro.com/cartoon/123015-070726indep

That was 2007. It's 7 years later, have things changed? Because Impey's statement reads scarily close to Hamilton's (and every other doper's) initial, strenuous denials. During this years tour, I loved those incredible opening scenes, narrated by Phil Liggett and Paul Sherwin, through Yorkshire. I have met Phil and covered a bicycle race with him (we shared the same media bus) and I have incredible respect for him. He *is* the voice of cycling. But he is also a media person of sorts, and so is Sherwin (who, incidentally, owns a goldmine in Africa).

One can't help noticing that year after year, Phil and Paul narrate this race (yes, with its castles, its beatific scenery, and let's not forget the romping, psychedelic colours of the Tour de France Cyclopede) but fail to interrogate one singular aspect of it. Through the 7 years of Armstrong's oligarchy…not mentioned. Was Impey's failure to turn up mentioned? If so, I missed it. So we examine every other aspect, all the other stats, from the age of castles, to the number of teeth on a chainring, but we don't examine the authenticity of the race itself?

I understand Phil and Paul are simply doing their jobs. And that there are rules. And that business is business. But it's become harder for me (and I think many others) to take certain things at face value. Because you can't. Collusion is everywhere. And if we accept that, then we must legalise collusion. So why don't we legalise collusion? Because it isn't fair. It doesn't serve the common good.

I mention the Tour de France not to take pot shots at Phil or Paul, I look forward to their commentary and I still do watch the Tour, but I mention it to show how prevalent this problem is, and how difficult it is. It reminds me to some extent of the dilemma of multinational companies. What do I mean? You can't go to war, if you're the USA, or any NATO ally, if your business interests are in the country you intend to invade. You might call these business interests an alliance, or you might call it collusion. You might even call it capitalism. But the point is, underlying, unstated, strategic relationships are what drive the power setups in Nature. Human and animal. Oscar and Impala.

We're talking about *Sultans of Spin*. Is spin restricted to the media? To journalists? Or do we get spin from politicians, presidents, CEO's, just about anyone and everyone angling for more power?

When you keep asking questions about collusion, you have to take that debate even further, beyond bread, and the Tour de France, and ask:

a) Is there collusion between church and state?
b) Between the state and the criminal underworld?
c) Between the criminal underworld and the church?
d) Between business and the church?
e) Between business and politics?

Well, what do you think?

It's one thing to have an opinion, an intuition, it's another to investigate it. Few people do. But we have google. So why don't we? Just as the media are used as a tool for ill, they also leave a trail of breadcrumbs for those good men (and women) who might wish to do something, to resurrect the reins of control we as society ought to exert over ourselves. Can societies not be self aware, organic, self determining organisms? With social media, surely we can vote immediately on those things we care about, and so enforce an immediate consensus. RT's are votes. So why not use them for the greater good, to exert political and social determinism, rather than for mere entertainment?

If you think these are small matters, think again.

I recently asked a freelance journalist friend of mine if he had emailed Hagen Engler about our question….did he really post that article at 07:28? We debated it and then I suggested, since Engler hadn't answered me, why didn't my friend ask him. A pure and simple yes/no would suffice. Did you, or did you not, post your article at 07:28? Yes? Or no?

But another Oscar (Wilde in fact) tells us "The truth is rarely pure and never simple." So why don't we gloss over those questions compiled (casually, one might suppose), above.

Collusion between church and state? Who cares if the political party you support is in power, and the religion you support, is having it's heyday. If these forces are with you (church and state) who could possibly be against you? Well, the church and state. Do you *really* think the church and state have your interests at heart? Or do they – yes, church and state – have their own interests at heart?

The answer, when we're asking about interests, is everyone has their own interests at heart. You do. The postman does. So does the president. There are very few saints in the world, very few altruists. Mandela is one. A singular hero. Quick, can you name another? I'm not sure if I can. Branson perhaps, and he's a businessman. He's not got his own interests at heart? Of course he does.

Some may even say that altruism, in the raw Christian-sense, is unnatural. That self-interest is, in fact, Natural. Self preservation is…hard wired into us for survival. In fact it's even recognised in the common law. You are allowed to kill someone else in self defence. You're even allowed to protect your self, and kill another, if you mistakenly (reasonably though) believe there's a credible threat to your life (even though, in the scheme of things, there wasn't).

We can give the church and state a little credit for having their own self interest, can't we? After all, everyone needs an incentive. Well, the thing with the state and the church is they are both organs of society. Society wants them there to improve society. To serve society. I'm not going to go into the tedium of how governments serve themselves, or how corrupt the church is in all its permutations. Both are so well known they're clichés. Corrupt politicians and the moral monsters that some men of the cloth turn out to be, are well known. But if you need reminding, a topical reminder, from today, of the moral bankruptcy around the world (in terms of church and state) there's this:

Collusion (and corruption) in the Church: http://allafrica.com/stories/201407311134.html

http://www.patheos.com/blogs/frankschaeffer/2013/09/american-religious-right-and-russian-orthodox-leaders-are-colluding-in-putins-persecution-of-gay-people/

(South Africa has countless examples of 'miracle' practising charlatans, the Sowetan has dozens of examples.)

Collusion by the State:

http://www.theguardian.com/world/2013/feb/05/ireland-magdalene-laundry-system-apology

Collusion between Church and State:
http://www.independent.co.uk/news/uk/crime/church-and-state-colluded-to-free-ira-bomber-priest-2061168.html

These may seem like small matters, but they aren't. So allow me to shock you. Ready? If you think collusion between church and state is sort've okay (especially if you subscribe to both parties), here's a quick illustration why it isn't okay. Nazi Germany and the Catholic Church. Talk about *Sultans of Spin*! The post WWII perception that Hitler was an atheist muddies the truth of why and how Hitler, Germany's Father and Saviour, was able to dupe millions of good German's into jumping into a full scale world war, hot on the heels of the First World War. How do you get people to sign up, enthusiastically for World War? You make it a Holy War. You call yourself God's Chosen people, and you declare land (that actually isn't yours) part of your divine inheritance (as in, your right to something, given to you by God, but *begotten* via the state and the church). Am I exaggerating?

http://www.independent.co.uk/news/world/europe/religion-rome-and-the-reich-the-vaticans-other-dirty-secret-479043.html

http://en.wikipedia.org/wiki/Pope_Pius_XII_and_the_Holocaust

http://en.wikipedia.org/wiki/Hitler's_Pope

But that was the Second World War. What about, closer to home? Like, South Africa? Well, Apartheid was a system that involved very clear, and very well known collusion between the church (specifically the NG Church) and the state (the National Party, who in those days were the Fathers of Apartheid).

http://www.h-net.org/reviews/showrev.php?id=4730

http://countrystudies.us/south-africa/53.htm

http://overcomingapartheid.msu.edu/sidebar.php?id=65-258-6

Interestingly, in today's ANC government, especially before it's time to vote, suddenly there's plenty of association by political leaders about voting for the ANC and earning your ticket to heaven. By inference of course. Nelson Mandela (who I'm not certain was a Christian) is in heaven we're told, and having an ANC card and voting ANC will count in your favour went you encounter Saint Paul at the Pearly Gates. Church and state.

We could go through the rest, collusion between:

- the state and the criminal underworld
- the criminal underworld and the church
- business and the church
- business and politic

–But I'm not going to. The point is collusion is relevant, collusion is popular, collusion is widespread and it is real. Does it really matter though? So what if a few companies or individuals benefit, kudos to them for taking the initiative, right? Actually, it's not easy to overstate the deleterious impacts of collusion. That's a big word that means 'very bad'. Yes, it's hard to overstate those impacts and how profoundly damaging they are to our lives.

A few days ago I was discussing my personal experiences of crime (the topic of the next chapter) with some friends of mine in New Zealand. We spoke for over 100 minutes on Skype, and the last half hour was all about crime. One of the points that came up was Mandela. And my friend in New Zealand (a friend of a friend really) made the offhand remark that Mandela's 'sainthood' is overstated, that Mandela is really a flawed person just like everyone else. I understood what he was getting at, but since I am researching Mandela myself (as part of a separate project to these eBooks) I felt – intuitively – that this person's 'version' of Mandela was seriously out of whack. So I interrogated him on it. He admitted that he saw Mandela basically as a terrorist, someone who may have done a lot of good, but…still…a terrorist. I was shocked and disappointed at this admission. Shocked because I had once been indoctrinated in exactly the same 'pure and simple' truth, and surprised because my friend still carried the same indoctrination – in New Zealand *nogal* – for the past 20 years or more.

So I turned to the media for help. I asked him if he's ever read *The Long Walk to Freedom*, as I did circa 1995. When I read that book, which is essentially a firsthand account from the man himself, I realised how I had been *bullshitted* – I'm sorry there is no more appropriate word – by my own parents, by authority figures in my life, by the political milieu. In other words, I was only able to break through this collusion of lies (and untruths, inaccuracies, impressions) once I had gotten the story straight from the source. When I did, I was blown away by the man himself, and my respect for Mr Mandela has remained undimmed ever since. Hence I ~~admonished~~ advised my New Zealand friend to interrogate his ~~prejudicial~~ ideas. I told him, as a South African, or ex-South African, he should do himself a favour, because in the end it is an affirming story about a truly great man, and so, he owes himself to honour that, and being part of that. I am not sure if I convinced him, but what I do know was that *Long Walk to Freedom* changed my mind fundamentally, and it only happened because I found the truth out myself, getting it directly (well, via the book) from its source.

http://en.wikipedia.org/wiki/Long_Walk_to_Freedom

I also mentioned *Invictus*, the film based on the novel, *Playing the Enemy* by John Carlin (Carlin is currently researching his own book on Oscar, and has read my research on Reeva and Oscar) – but my New Zealand friend said he could half remember that he had watched *Invictus*. "And?" I pressed. He said he didn't feel his impression of Mandela changed or needed to change having watched that film, and maintained that Mandela is a flawed person just like the rest of us. Do you see the strength, the absolute power of a *schema* that has been reinforced via years of collusion, through many pillars of society, to establish a false narrative? Do you see how hard it is to displace it? Do you see that what collusion does is it perpetuates ignorance, deception and dishonesty.

There is also another kind of collusion, where we cannot blame our parents, or church, we cannot blame our schools or the government, we cannot blame corporations or the media. We can only blame ourselves. It is when we collude amongst ourselves, to hide the truth. It is when we are ashamed to admit our own mistakes to ourselves, and to the world. Because it makes us uncomfortable. Because, well, we might have to learn from them. Because it means we aren't perfect, and neither can we be seen (by others) as perfect. What am I ~~talking~~ writing about? And what does *any* of this have to do with Oscar? Plenty. It has plenty to do with Oscar.

Earlier this afternoon I was discussing a particular aspect of the case, the incident itself, the mechanisms and forces involved, if you must know. I asked my listener to glance at the wooden door behind him, as I tried to make my point. And then I noticed something odd. You see, I wanted to put him in Oscar's shoes (as I do), and so I needed him to look at a door and intuit, with me, a few point of logic. But *he didn't want to look at the door*. Eventually, perhaps saying it for the third or fourth time, I said, "X, look at the door…" And that's when he stopped me. He said, gently but firmly, that his wife was (is?) a close friend of Oscar's. And…actually…they would prefer not to talk (or perhaps think?) about the trial.

I have to say I got a shock. One has to realise that Oscar had an enormous impact on a lot of people, and also has friends across South Africa. Unknowingly I had come across one of them. One realises one must treat this case with sensitivity. Whether one is right or wrong, whether one's ideas are on track or off, we are still dealing with a real person. Who killed (rightly or wrongly) another real person. My point is that this clearly articulated code (of silence, of denial) is part of how society colludes. And when they do that, what happens? We collectively fail to interrogate the truth, and thus, we fail to learn from it.

Why do friends of Oscar not wish to talk about it? Surely, when he was triumphing in London in 2012 one would make sure everyone knows – and sees – one's personal support for Oscar. So why not when the hero is – possibly – about to be stripped of his hero status? Because we'd have to admit then that we may have been wrong.

More remains to be written along this line of thought, but I will cut it short. Although this book is titled *Revelations* I am limited by how much I can expose because of my relationships with certain people. Although I have privileged, sensitive information, it doesn't necessarily mean I will use it. I have not used all the information at my disposal to make my point, but I have used most of it. Am I involved in collusion, by keeping these 'secrets'. Maybe. Overall, I am honouring the trust and relationships not necessarily of particular people, but the relationships they have with *others*. It may be wives, or friends, or sources, as the case may be. The truth is never pure, and it is never simple. But, if we ask questions and attempt to answer them, we ought to get the gist of it.

Note to the reader: The next ten pages are devoted to expanding on the *Sultans of Spin* theme by exploring Biblical motifs. If this is a bridge too far for you, scroll down to the last paragraph before just before the start of the next section, which is *Crime in South Africa – up close and personal.* For those readers who elect to join me on this excursion through time and space, Noddy Badges will be provided. **End of Note.**

Still with me? We're interrogating the *Sultans of Spin.* If we're serious about interrogating our allegiance to the truth, then we need to take this next step. I've mentioned self-interest as something that is designed into us a vital mechanism for survival. But there's an attendant mechanism too. If self interest is an evolved trait (it protects us), then why can't *society* act in its own self interest as well?

We are social creatures, people, and we are protected from harm firstly by our own efforts at securing our self-interest, but also via our collaborations with a group, to protect our self interest (as well as those of the group). Social animals tend to be pretty successful. Think of elephants compared to rhinos, lions compared to leopards, springbok compared to duiker, hyena compared to a jackal. Even social insects do pretty well. Compare the success and level of organisation of bees, wasps and termites versus, say, a spider, mosquito or praying mantis, all of whom go solo.

Our allegiance to truth depends to some extent on GroupThink, this is true, and GroupThink depends so some extent on the individual (and co-opted) learning of individuals. How do we learn though? When we recognise mistakes. Groups tend to like to hold onto the power structures and status quos, hence groups certainly don't like the instability that ensues from admitting (as a group) that it was wrong. Think about the discomfort when groups must admit the Holocaust happened, and Apartheid. Awkward!

In the same way we do not like to interrogate many other GroupThink projects, such as our belief systems. Is there a God? Is there life after death? Is one religion more authentic than another? How many Christian Jews are there in Israel? Just as in the Oscar Pistorius trial, most people rush to judgement rather than making a serious effort (on their own) to investigate these questions. And yes, it takes courage to do so. And once risks very real isolation, alienation and ostracism if one does so. But one can also gain a sense of personal liberation and job through this revelatory process.

Let's touch on the most uncomfortable topic of all now. Not the church per se, but Christianity. This book is not called *Revelations* for nothing, so *let's get biblical*.

Christianity and Oscar

Are you a Christian? Do you think you know your bible? Let's test that. Because Christianity plays an important role in Oscar's narrative. Christianity is a great reinforce not only of GroupThink but of taking things on faith. In other words, believing things spoken without evidence. In fact the less evidence the better, as this demonstrates how great our faith is. A familiar refrain in the Oscar trial has been, 'You weren't there so you shouldn't judge.' Or, 'it's not our place to judge'. I've already interrogated the lunacy of these axioms a few times, so I won't be doing that here. I will be interrogating the validity of some of the most conventional ideas we have about the world, and God, and one of the most famous bible stories ever told. I do so to illustrate how widespread and detrimental our ignorance and our prejudices actually are. To who? To ourselves? To the credibility of the whole human story, and all the human projects underway, including and especially our own personal efforts at Immortalism.

If Oscar had Christian inclinations, Reeva did too. She describes herself on twitter as ' a child of God'. Oscar too, he tells us, has been praying a lot, and we see his family, present daily (almost without exception) during the unravelling of the trial, muttering behind him. It looks like it might be prayers.

Thousands of people still support Oscar. Thousands, probably tens of thousands, perhaps even more, believe in his innocence. And it's easy to see people supporting Oscar out of a sense of Christian solidarity. Here, forgiveness of sin (instant, unconditional, uninformed forgiveness) forms an integral part of this GroupThink. And what's obvious is Oscar's Christian family (uncles, aunts, cousins, siblings) are all automatically part of this Christian-centric camaraderie. For them forgiveness was also (so it appears) instantaneous. One wonders if they are in court simply to appeal to a higher power than the judge, or does it matter what is actually revealed in court? It looks like a few of Oscar's cousins were playing the role of bodyguards in those first few days when we saw him walking to court. (Later, some may have noted, the long walk to court became a lot shorter, as he was dropped near the front entrance).

Oscar's visits to court have attracted all manner of supporters. Many of these have been women, who want to show the world their generosity of spirit, and are happy to hand out balloons and hugs, and make sure the world sees their public displays of support. And love. And admiration.

One pastor even felt it necessary to visit the Pistorius family from the USA to pray for them (and enjoy some press while he was at it). It's hard to tell why this particular pastor didn't feel the need to counsel Reeva's mother, or Reeva's side of the family. But let's face it, religion has a defacto collusion hard wired into it. Either you're part of the group, or you're out. Either you're good, you're included, you're saved, you're part of the group, or you're not.

Since this chapter is devoted to *Sultans of Spin*, and the absolute experts in this field (of knowing what to say, what people need to hear, how words can inspire and change lives) are your spiritual leaders, I *must* devote a few pages to dealing with this highly influential brotherhood.

I am obviously aware that to discuss religion is like walking on ~~hot coals~~ glass. But I'm going to play a trick on the reader, who likely, has particular and varied idiosyncratic beliefs and sensitivities I ought to be wary of. In order to do that, I will try to tread carefully around the topic, and then tiptoe my way back into it. That way I may be able to sneak in through the back door, rather than be turned away at the front door (as so many Hari Krishnas, Mormoms and Seventh Day Adventists often are). How I aim to do that, how I plan to trick you, is I'll get to this testy topic via another topic. It's one we are all – well, *most* of us one imagines – are enthusiastic about. Cinema.

Recently a film was released with a biblical theme. The bible story (and the film) are actually both based on a myth, known as the *Epic of Gilgamesh*. What I found intriguing was the calibre of actors , Sir Anthony Hopkins, Russell Crowe, Emma Watson and Jennifer Connelly that signed up for Darren Aronofsky's epic. Unfortunately, as this review contends, it is *an epic of embellishments*.

http://www.nola.com/movies/index.ssf/2014/07/noah_director_darren_aronofsky.html

The reviewer gives the film 2 out of 5 stars, for the same man who made *The Wrestler* and *Black Swan*. *The Wrestler* was condemned as "anti-Iranian" in many Iranian newspapers and websites because Mickey Rourke violently breaks in half a pole (sporting an Iranian flag) across his knee. 'Facts' 13 and 21 are worth looking at here:

http://thoughtcatalog.com/nico-lang/2012/12/25-little-known-facts-about-black-swan/

Aronofsky said of his spiritual beliefs in 2014, "I think I definitely believe." Yes, it looks like it. And his beliefs seem clearly…Jewish. Well, Noah is an Old Testament story, so we may accept it – superficially – as a Jewish story.

Well, except that it isn't.

Wait a minute. Can't we accept that a story written a long time ago, set in the vicinity of the Jewish homeland is…Jewish? Well, one *can*. Does it matter that Jerusalem is over 1220km (about a 14 hour drive) from Baghdad? In other words, do we mind talking about something that happened in Cape Town when it really happened somewhere in Zimbabwe or Mozambique? I mean, it doesn't *really* matter where exactly something happens, right? It's still Southern Africa?

Look, if you don't want the truth, and you want the story of the flood to be a Jewish story, just say so, then we can ignore a few facts. Like this one:

Wikipedia: The term "Sumerian" is the common name given to the ancient non-Semitic inhabitants of Mesopotamia, Sumer, by the Semitic Akkadians.

The Sumerians wrote the Epic of Gilgamesh.

The Sumerians were non-Semitic people – in other words, *not* Jews.

And these non-Jewish people wrote an epic myth. And they lived in a place called Mesopotamia.

Is Mesopotamia, like, Israel? Where is Mesopotamia? Have a look.

http://en.wikipedia.org/wiki/Mesopotamia

Does Mesopotamia look like Israel? Well, does Mozambique look like the Western Cape? If you live in Poland or Texas you might say *same ol' same ol', it's southern Africa somewhere, no biggie*. But actually there is a world of difference between the Western Cape and Mozambique. In the same way, the Middle East may seem to us just one endless similar desert landscape – but it's not. Iraq is not Israel. Jews and non-Semitics people are not the same, in the same way Bushmen and Bantu people are distinctly different. In the same way that the English and Afrikaner, and French and Germans, and Americans and Mexicans are different.

The interesting thing, when we ask questions (when we're simply curious, rather than prejudiced, and sure of our answers) is what we can learn. For example, while a few caves north of Johannesburg are widely considered the cradle of humankind, the seemingly unremarkable strip of land between two rivers at the annexure of three continents (Africa, Asia and Europe), the Tigris and Euphrates, is considered a cradle of civilisation.

At various times, there have been a few cradles. Egypt (along the Nile) may be considered another, Greece another, and Rome another, and Brittania yet another…and there are many more besides. When we speak of time it's easy to become confused. So let's make it simpler. Right now, the year 2014 is part of the 21st century. A century is 100 years, so 21 x 100 years is 2100. We're accustomed to thinking a lot about the last two days, less about the last two weeks, less about the last two years, very little about the last two decades (unless we're talking music) and we seldom discuss the last two hundred years, unless we're dealing with economic ideas such as industrialisation, or climate change, or population growth. Rarely, if ever, do we think back two thousand years, and almost without exception, when we do, it is within a Biblical context. Or perhaps to glance at the Romans, or the Greeks. Looking further back than that is anathema.

That's an odd relic of the time we live in. We seem to think 2000 years is enough context to tell us who we are. Actually, it isn't. Does the average person even know where and how the systems we use today even came from? Do we assume they came from Rome? Most people don't know, because most people don't ask. Most people don't ask because they assume the *bible tells me so*. Does the bible explain the invention of the wheel, or how the alphabet (in which the bible is expressed) came into being? No. Shouldn't we know the answers to these basic questions though?

I think so. And when you – the reader – follow this short thought experiment to its conclusion, I hope you will experience some kind of revelation. Even if it is in the basic psychology that *being curious* is good. *Being curious* is useful. Asking questions is more helpful at finding answers than assuming we know everything. We don't like uncertainty, so we don't like to acknowledge what we don't know. But as long as we do that, we can't learn anything.

I touched on time, allow me a chance to touch on it again. Right now it's the 21st century. It's now the time of the American civilisation (or world power). Once upon a time, a long time ago, far far away, there was a civilisation called the Sumerians. They were a world power in their time, and in that time, world powers didn't last 50 years, or a 100 years, they often lasted 10 or 20 centuries. The Egyptian empire, sprang up at around the same time as the Sumerian empire and incidentally, developed their own writing style, which we call hieroglyphs today – a sort of picture-word alphabet. The Sumerian civilisation started up in the 31st century BC, that's more than 5000 years ago. There wasn't much left of that empire by the 18th century BC. Sumeria was a kingdom of southern Mesopotamia, and it basically got supplanted by a northerly kingdom, the Akkadians. These were Semitic (similar to Jewish people). Although the Akkadian language also went extinct, Sumerian continued to used as a sacred, scientific, ceremonial and literary language until as late as the 1st Century AD. In other words, the Sumerian language and writing system had a 3000 year lifespan. English, by contrast has been around 500 years or less.

http://en.wikipedia.org/wiki/History_of_the_English_language#Old_English_.E2.80.93_from_the_mid-5th_century_to_the_mid-11th_century

But why would a language continue to be used after the civilisation that spawned it had long since disappeared? Simple (but also not so simple). There was a common appreciation of the value of the knowledge, and culture, painstakingly pieced together through the ages and bequeathed through this particular language, and civilisation. That's also why Latin is still used today, especially in court rooms, and also in medical and biological nomenclature, amongst many other surviving applications.

The words *sub judice*, are Latin.

http://www.oxforddictionaries.com/definition/english/sub-judice

But there are literally hundreds if not thousands of Latin terms we use in a legal and colloquial context, because they found their place in our world in Rome, and have remained useful ever since.

Think of:

Via
Veto
Versus
Vice versa
Subpoena
Pro rata
Pro bono
Persona non grata
Nota Bene (NB)
In situ

Lingua Franca
In extremis
In absentia
Et cet era

And in terms of the Oscar case:

Error in persona
In camera (which actually means, in the chamber, not literally 'camera')

The merits of this case really revolve around:

    1. Dolus directus, or direct intent. It was your goal to kill someone.

    2. Dolus eventualis, or knowing the *possible* result of your action will kill someone and recklessly going through with it anyway. It's akin to what the Americans refer to as second-degree murder.

    3. Dolus indirectus, or indirect intent. When a person's death is a substantially certain outcome of your action, such as committing arson and knowing factory workers will die as a result.

For more terms, go here:

http://en.wikipedia.org/wiki/List_of_legal_Latin_terms

So we can see just how widespread, useful and popular Latin is, a language that exists even though the Roman Empire that birthed it is long since turned to dust and ruin. Now, to put English into perspective next to Sumerian, the English of Shakespeare's era (that's the early 17th century) is barely comprehensible to today's high school students. The Latin we know today (those terms quoted above) come from Classic Latin, in other words, until the time of Julius Caesar (or 44BC or 1st century BC). In other words, those terms we use without really thinking about them are roughly 2000 years old. Sumerian writing was used for 3000 years. Sumerian is the longest used writing system in history.

Now, can we say we've enjoyed *modern* English for 300 years at most? Perhaps we can. Consider a language that was used for literature, science, celebrations and in sacred ceremonies for 3000 years! And then what happened? After 1AD it was forgotten. 1900 years passed until someone started asking questions, and a group of Assyriologists began deciphering inscriptions and finding answers. They even discovered two separate arithmetic systems, a decimal system (units of ten) and a second, the sexagesimal system (based on 60 units) which survives in the modern era as units of time (seconds and minutes) and trigonometry (360 degrees).

Just imagine where the English language will be (or perhaps the Chinese language) after 2700 years of internet use, texting, and hopefully, eBooks like the one you're holding (and consumed, ironically enough on a *tablet*, by some).

So I hope if I have conveyed anything I've conveyed that many civilisations come and go, but some are quite significant. Like the Romans. Like the civilisations that gave rise to the English languages (the Saxons, the Britons, the Angles). And the Sumerians. Do we know much about them? Most of us probably know more about the heritage of another ancient people, the Semites (the Jews of today). But the Sumerians were really special too. Really special. Why?

Because here, in a cradle ensconced between two rivers, we got our start on some of the basics. Like agriculture. With agriculture we were able to transition from hunter gatherers (in other words, nomads) and start up something pretty revolutionary for its time – farms. And then villages. And since people were parked in a certain space for a length of time, they had time – for the first time – to really fiddle and work things out, and *invent* things. And so we moved out of the Stone Age into the Bronze Age. The first plough was probably a bronze attached to a rope, and dragged behind a donkey. But as they got better at planting crops, and harvesting them, and paying attention to what worked and what didn't, they started thinking. They needed jars to hold seeds, so they started pottery. And that led to other inventions. Like the wheel. It actually started with the potter's wheel, and then some genius realised a wheel would also work for other things, like a barrow, and wagons.

And with wheels wheeling around the newly tilled lands, these farmers, the world's first started to pay attention to how the change of the moon and stars heralded seasons, and fluctuations in the weather. They studied the wheeling stars overhead and named some of the brightest in The Milky Way. And yes, in the very same place – Mesopotamia (a Greek word meaning 'between rivers) – our species finally found the time to figure out writing. And an alphabet. And arithmetic. And astronomy. And the first differentiated military. The first known codified legal and administrative systems, complete with courts, jails, and government records. The human story was on a roll!

According to Wikipedia:

the first true city-states arose in Sumer, roughly contemporaneously with similar entities in what are now Syria and Lebanon. Several centuries after the invention of cuneiform, the use of writing expanded beyond debt/payment certificates and inventory lists to be applied for the first time, about 2600 BC, to messages and mail delivery, history, legend, mathematics, astronomical records, and other pursuits. Conjointly with the spread of writing, the first formal schools were established, usually under the auspices of a city-state's primary temple.

Finally, the Sumerians ushered in domestication with
intensive agriculture and irrigation. Emmer wheat, barley, sheep, and cattle were foremost among the species cultivated and raised for the first time on a grand scale.

And at the end of all that, the *Epic of Gilgamesh*, which is considered the *first ever* Literature work.

It may seem now that the Sumerians discovered everything. They discovered a lot, and they gave the human story a real shot in the arm, and it was much needed after the devastations and depredations of the previous Ice Ages (which almost wiped us out). But we still had a long way to go. The invention of stirrups, of course was huge, as that allowed men to ride – and stay on top – of horses, and uses them as cavalry. That came from elsewhere, so did the revolutionary Viking ships, and gunpowder, and steam engines, printing machines, flying machines, electricity, light bulbs and everything else.

How many of us knew the true import of the Sumerians?

Note: If you'd like even more background, visit these links:

http://en.wikipedia.org/wiki/Sumer#Legacy

http://history-world.org/sumeria.htm

http://www.ancientscripts.com/sumerian.html

Of course if we assume the Flood Story is 'a Jewish story' we extinguish all the above history and context (which is part of the whole of the Human Story), and we eviscerate a part of ourselves. When we study something as simple as the Epic of Gilgamesh we're offered a keyhole's view into history. Yes, we exchange one massive legacy for a smaller human story that is associated with one particular group. The point is, it seems almost like sacrilege to do so. To ignore 3000 years of the vital, crucial, wonderful human story that we all belong to.

But, for the sake of argument, let's assume Noah's Ark *is* an original story, and that Aronofsky is right to put a Jewish 'spin' on it (as Sultans do). What do we get?

Embellishments yes, but what sort of embellishments, and why? Why embellish one of the greatest stories ever told? And why would you want to embellish a story of 'Biblical' proportions. Biblical proportions are by definition enormous, so why would a colossal story need to be further embellished?

http://www.thefreedictionary.com/biblical

I have no idea, but that is what Aronofsky does. In other words, he plays at being a Sultan of Spin, within a cinematic *mythos*, yes, but he also fucks up a story for reasons unknown, and perhaps unknowable. For example he introduces 'The Watchers', bizarre rock-like monsters who help ancient man build the Earth. These alien-like beings stumble clumsily along, like a sort of rocky avalanche in broad human form. Even though they are made of rock, their eyes glow yellow. According to Aronofsky, these creatures were angles, creatures of light that crashed down to Earth when god cast them down, and when they hit the Earth, they melted the rocks, and these rocks then coalesced around them, to form a molten – and then later – an epidermis of solid rock.

But it gets even dodgier than that. A young girl is introduced, Emma Watson, who has sex with one of Noah's sons shortly before the flood (as in a few hours before) and then gives birth two twin daughters whilst aboard. What happened to 40 days and 40 nights? A normal pregnancy last 9 months, so Arnofsky is not only toying with the *dramatis personae* (besides Watson he also includes a stowaway), but messing with time, and the laws of nature (I'm not sure how creatures made of light and rock can actually function, scientifically speaking. What would they eat?)

The tragic thing is *Noah* really has its moments. But then Arnofsky adds his own fluff and he ruins it. He takes a very well known version, one many trust and understand, and he sort of adjusts it – one imagines – to make it more palpable to modern audiences. Except he fails dismally. All his little additions irk terribly. So why does he do it? Well, he wants an incredible story to seem not only more credible, but more dramatic. Maybe he can't explain (to himself) how Noah could build such an enormous vessel himself, so he cheats. Unfortunately, when you ask a question and you invoke aliens, you're in trouble.

What Arnofsky has done is fuck around with Myopoeic thought, which is a hypothetical stage of human thought preceding modern thought. It was a time when humanity didn't think in generalisations but saw each event as an act of will – in other words, an act from some personal being. As a result, the ancients created myths. Myths is a way of portraying events as acts of gods or spirits.

Mythopoeic means myth making, and yes, these guys were also 'Sultans of Spin'. It was a way of expressing oneself symbolically, but people sort of gathered what you were trying to say, and the idea that powerful beings were running the show somehow made it all easier to understand, and less certain. But was it spin? Absolutely. So here we see that inherent to the human narrative, inherent, in fact to storytelling, to language, is 'spinning' things into a version that isn't quite accurate to reality. Gilgamesh was supposed to *be a demigod of superhuman strength who built the city walls of Uruk to defend his people from external threats, and travelled to meet the sage Utnapishtim, who had survived the Great Deluge. He is usually described as two-thirds god and one third man.*

Some – more inclined to melodrama – might call this an approximate description of Oscar. Oscar has been an inspiration, an icon, a 'demigod?' Does his speed (on his carbon fibre legs) and his good looks – is that sufficient to make him two-thirds god and one third man? For some, it may be sufficient.

Has human thinking really changed so much since the Sumerian civilisation? If we're still using words in our courtrooms from 2000 words ago (terms that we literally pluck out of history so we can understand and rely on the different – tried and tested – legal versions of guilt), how much has our thinking changed? The answer, a lot and not at all. Mythopoeic thought is concrete and personifying, whilst modern thought is abstract, and a lot more personal.

http://en.wikipedia.org/wiki/Mythopoeic_thought

http://en.wikipedia.org/wiki/Mythopoeic_thought#The_loss_of_mythopoeic_thought

The God of the psalmists and the prophets was not in nature. He transcended nature — and transcended, likewise, the realm of mythopoeic thought. Moreover, they didn't see the divine as a will within nature: for them, the divine will was a force or law behind all natural events.

This is a subtle difference. In other words, if you're in the Gilgamesh psychology, the God of the flood is sort've the same thing. It's all happening at ground level. The moods and emotions happening on the ground cause things to be unleashed in the world. Okay? The Jewish version is a little more sophisticated. Now it puts God above the world, and thus, separated, God pulls the strings then decides how it's all going to play out. God is in heaven – in the heavens – but he's not the stars themselves. This may seem like a bizarre psychology to even raise here, but the reader will – in the final chapter) how and why and where Oscar seems to use both in his version, and also, we'll learn why we are so easily deceived by it.

In other words, my assessment is that Oscar's version of the incident – like Aronofsky – places some unnecessary (and thus, unlikely) 'spin' on his story, but more than that, Oscar places himself in the story, and outside of it. Confused? Good! More *Revelations* will come later! Two more questions before we wrap up:

1. **What is the moral lesson of the Flood?**

I'm not sure the moral lesson, if there is one, is very clear. One of the more disturbing lessons is that the flood shows God as a capricious, jealous, moody sort of being who occasionally acts excessively, and then apologises.

If that's the lesson, I'm not buying. Is the *real* lesson here that if society loses its centre, society as a whole will be destroyed (or will destroy itself)? By centre we mean moral centre. If its centre is corrupted, the entire system faces collapse. Systemic collapse. That means what we've seen in the past, again and again, as the collapse of civilisations will happen to ours too. And think about that for a second. In a very real sense we're living in a time of a Global Civilisation. So a collapse might be global too. But how could that happen? Well why do civilisations collapse? Because of our moral malaise, our distractions, our dalliances, our dishonesty, we may lose sight of what really matters. We may be unable eventually to tell truth from lies, and thus critical questions will go unanswered. There may be important questions that science might be able to answer, and provide solutions for, but our beliefs, and feelings, and collusions, might cloud these sufficiently that we never get to them. Energy for example. Are we solving the energy problem, in our lives? Questions regarding resources, and climate, and the impacts of both of these on unchecked population expansion – are we ahead of the curve on these questions, or falling behind. I hear the term denial a lot. And there are some publications that have a policy not to publish stories on climate change because it isn't good for business. Like certain 'business' publications.

What is the lesson of the Flood? That we if don't pay attention, we could lose everything.

2. **What is the moral lesson of the Oscar trial?**

Let's examine a summary of the story of Icarus and then Gilgamesh (which, let's face it, you still don't know!) to answer this question.

From Wikipedia: *Icarus' father warns him first of complacency and then of* **hubris**, *asking that he fly neither too low nor too high, because the sea's dampness would clog or the sun's heat would melt his wings. Icarus ignored instructions not to fly too close to the sun, and the melting wax caused him to fall into the sea where he drowned.*

So Icarus has a tragic theme of failed ambition.

http://en.wikipedia.org/wiki/Icarus

Now it's the turn of Gilgamesh, king of **Uruk**.

From Wikipedia: *Gilgamesh, two-thirds god and one-third man, is oppressing his people, who cry out to the gods for help. For the young women of Uruk this oppression takes the form of a droit du seigneur — or "lord's right" to sleep with brides on their wedding night. For* *the young men it is conjectured that Gilgamesh exhausts them through games, tests of strength, or perhaps forced labour on building projects. The gods respond to the people's pleas by creating an equal to Gilgamesh who will be able to stop his oppression. This is the primitive man, **Enkidu**, who is covered in hair and lives in the wild with the animals.*

I'm not sure if you see Oscar in there. I think I can. And the equal that comes along, who is perhaps even more than his equal, is Reeva.

How can you reveal the truth if those to whom you are speaking (or writing) don't want to hear?

The moral of the Flood is the same moral we see in Icarus, but Icarus, ironically – like the Noah *mythos* – also uses the classic themes of sea and sun to tell an all too human story. The same thing that is true of Gilgamesh, and Noah and Icarus is true of Oscar. It's about being reined in (excuse the pun).

The *Sultans of Spin* create fogs and clouds; they muddy the world with their schemes and their collusion. Is Oscar a *Sultan of Spin*? What do you think? When life is at its bleakest, when justice seems furthest from view, when all about is noise and nonsense – only when it is dark enough can you see the stars. But you must open your eyes, and look up, to see them.

Crime in South Africa – up close and personal

The world is a dangerous place to live; not because of the people who are evil, but because of the people who don't do anything about it. – Albert Einstein

If the world is a dangerous place, some places are more dangerous than others. South Africa is one of them. There's a popular, highly rated television series, 1000 ways to die. In South Africa you can take your pick between being murdered (but not before being raped and tortured), dying in a car wreck or catching a killer disease like AIDS.

In this section I will provide the official statistics before providing a more personal – and firsthand view – of how these statistics actually bear out in the real world. In other words, I'll give you a peek into my life, within this theme, this framework of crime, and we can then reflect on just how dangerous crime may – or may not be – in the rainbow nation. So let's start with the stats.

In 2013 there were 16 259 murders in South Africa, that's 45 murder a day (more than 2 per hour). That's the equivalent of a Grey College-sized high school, every single pupil, in every classroom wiped out, sixteen times over during the course of a year.

There were also roughly the same number of attempted murders in 2013. Our murder rate is about 31 per 100 000. South Africa's murder rate is 4 and a half times higher than the global average (6.9 murders per 100 000). Put in another way – if you doubled the global murder rate, and doubled that figure again, our murder rate would still be higher.

In terms of aggravated robberies (200/100 000) there were also more than 60 000 street, or public robberies in 2013, around 18 000 home burglaries and more than 16 000 business break ins.

Common residential burglaries reached 262 113 in 2013, which is an average of 720 household burglaries every day in South Africa. In Bloemfontein, one of South Africa's smaller cities, an estimated 40 burglaries take place each day.

http://africacheck.org/factsheets/factsheet-south-africas-official-crime-statistics-for-201213/

As if being murdered wasn't bad enough, South Africa's death toll due to car wrecks is in the high 20's/10 000, virtually matching our world leading murder numbers, murder for murder. So in addition to 45 murders daily, there are also around 40 or more fatal car accidents each day. More ominous still, there are no records for road accidents for 2012 or 2013. Most South Africans are familiar with the 1000+ fatalities over the festive season (essentially the month of December). What they don't realise is there are 1000+ fatalities *every other month* as well.

For more information, stats and graphs, visit these links:

http://www.arrivealive.co.za/documents/Presentations/FINAL%20Swedish%20Embassy%20Presentation%205%2012%202013.pdf

http://mg.co.za/article/2013-05-23-south-africa-ranked-worst-in-global-road-safety-report

Rape is an even uglier picture. Official statistics are 144 rapes a day, that's six cases every hour. Based on research conducted on women in Gauteng, only one in 25 women report being raped. When we extrapolating these figures it appears there may be 3600 rapes every day in South Africa.

http://www.iol.co.za/news/crime-courts/up-to-3-600-rapes-in-sa-every-day-1.1466429

Being raped in South Africa is a death sentence in itself, because South Africa has the world's largest HIV population, with an estimated 5.6 million people living with AIDS. Our infection rate per capita, despite the outdated stats at the below link, have recently overtaken Lesotho.

http://en.wikipedia.org/?title=List_of_countries_by_HIV/AIDS_adult_prevalence_rate

Before we leave these grim statistics behind, the reader may be interested to note that official annual deaths due to HIV/Aids are were over 17 000 per year in 2011, according to StatsSA. I'm not sure which stats to believe because this article puts the death rate due to AIDS at 250 000 (yes, a quarter of a million) in 2013.

http://allafrica.com/stories/201407230801.html

If we assume StatsSA's figures are accurate, and I'm not sure we can, but if we do, then HIV is only the 7th ranked cause of death, ahead of murders. The top 6 are:

6. Intestinal infectious diseases (19 376)
5. Diabetes (20 171)
4. 'Other forms' of heart disease (23 564)
3. Cerebrovascular disease (25 732)
2. Influenza and pneumonia (33 381)
1. Tuberculosis (54 112) – that's 965 cases per 100 000 South Africans, or more than 6 times the global average of 160.

Up close and personal

In order to wade into this subject, I'll start by providing an excerpt from an email dated July 16 2014. The time of writing now, is August 1, so yes, the email, from a friend's wife in Johannesburg is about two weeks ago. She told me her she was enthusiastically reading *Reeva in her own Words* and *RECIDIVIST ACTS*, and I asked them to review it.

I will do the review, things are a bit hectic now, we had another armed robbery yesterday (we are all fine thank God) but I'm just busier than usual.

On July 30 (two days ago) I sent a follow-up email asking how things were going. She answered:

We are all good tx. What happened two weeks back was similar to my hold up 2/3 yrs ago ...which was also in july(I find crime picks up in winter) thankfully the children and I were not home this time!

3 armed men came in broad daylight and broke our main gate with a pick axe, and then held [the domestic worker] *up- asking where our safe was. I was on my way home from* [X] *(I was delayed in 3 occasions thanks to my guardian angel) when my gardener (the*[domestic worker's] *son) called me to alert me- he was hiding on the garden - and so I called security and we arrived home together 2 min later. There was a bmw waiting outside my house, I took a pic of the reg no and then he drove off slowly when security vehicle arrived, he must have warned the guys inside and so they fled and jumped over the back wall via swimming pool, clearing our elec fence, and jumped over the neighbours unelectrified wall. The BMW fetched them two blocks down- according to onlookers.*

In my robbery 2/3 yrs back, it was the same story - broad day light, broke our gate, 3 armed guys looking for our safe, and they had a pick up car nearby.

I asked for her advice, how should one respond in a situation like this?

What to do: stay calm, keep your hands visible, dont argue or try be smart, just give them what they want so they can leave! And pray! After all,
This is Crazy SA, but we still love it here....

Her husband sent me this email on the same day (June 30):

Hi Nick,
Must say crime is quite bad at the moment. Two incidents where I or my family have been involved. One last week, one this morning...

Last week: 3 armed guys with a pick up vehicle basically bent the arm of our front gate with a pick-axe at mid-day/1pm. They forced their way in, around the back of the house in into the kitchen which is open as result of maid working. Fortunately the gardener saw them, hid in the garden and phoned [my wife]. [My wife] *immediately phoned* [a security company] *and they arrived very quickly. The armed robbers had balaclava's on and requested the maid show them the safe. We have one, but its empty and stands open - it was put in by previous owners and we have never used it. Any case, they took maid upstairs and kept asking for safe and jewellery. Looked in our cupboards in main bedroom. Seemed when* [the security company] *arrived they got tipped off - maid said they were phoned and bailed, left everything - only took my cuflinks. Ran out the back door, over the wall and into garden next door and escaped. Next door guy doesn't have an electric fence, so they just jumped the fence. Fortunately* [my wife] *and kids weren't home and gardener phoned immediately.*

This morning I was the subject of an attempted bike-jacking... Yip. Rode with bunch but me and a friend dropped off a bit around the bottom of [a suburb in Johannesburg]. *Guys walking on the pavement (couldn't really see them and lots walking to work) suddenly stepped into the road and the one guy grabbed my arm while riding and I hit the ground. Fell quite badly on my hip and elbow. Got up quickly and they wanted to attack me. A car came by and I jumped into the middle of the road to stop the car. My mate by then also turned around and shouted at them. So they ran away. Fortunately all ok, just bruised and sore. Not a great experience. They could've had knives and they were ready to attack. Think they were a bit surprised I got up so quickly. They probably wanted me to fall and lay on the ground and just make off with the bike... Any case, I am quite fortunate and blessed to be ok.*

So, as I said above, I am a bit disillusioned with the country at the moment and although I don't want to leave I have to ask questions about me and my families safety.

There are many more stories in jhb about crime and at the moment I think its the worst I have ever experienced.

My response:

Sorry to hear about it. I think it is because of so many many unemployed, and more and more becoming unemployed. I was horrified to read in today's paper unemployment is 35% in the Free State. That's 1/3. Heard somewhere there are 40 break-ins every day in Bloemfontein. 40.

If I could leave, I would. If you can, go!

His response:

I agree. Think that unemployment is a big driver and on top of that an uneducated youth and a massive one. Its a big problem.
Any case, its not that easy to pack up and leave, but one has to consider all options. Staying fit is a challenge and has been tough since I broke my hand. I actually have had two good weeks getting back into some shape and now this happened. Not great. I am quite sore and will def have to take a few days off. Also, quite nervous about my next ride... So not a good space to be in at the moment.

So there's the first revelation, or disclosure. If I could, yes, I would prefer *not* to live in South Africa. Why, because I don't feel safe here. Because crime is enough of a concern on a daily basis that I think it seriously diminishes the otherwise fairly good quality of living South Africa provides.

Earlier this week, I had long discussion, over Skype, with friends in New Zealand. [I mentioned that in the previous chapter, remember, I said I admonished the husband for his cynical views on Mandela, and told him he should read *Long Walk to Freedom* etc]. Towards the end of the discussion I brought up David Bain. This is a case similar to the Griekwastad murders, except several orders of magnitude worse. Readers who have found the Oscar case food for thought should make an effort to investigate the David Bain case.

http://en.wikipedia.org/wiki/David_Bain

I have also done an extensive analysis on my website, so feel free to use the site's search function and type in 'David Bain' at the top left of www.nickvanderleek.com.

What was interesting was in the few minutes of discussion I had with my New Zealand friends, (who had also paid fleeting attention to it) I was able to shift their perception of the case quite substantially. This is what happens when we're curious, when we ask questions and investigate them (Google is a powerful tool) and we simply pay attention to all the details.

We then discussed crime in South Africa and versus crime in New Zealand. What was interesting, was what emerged. When I asked my friends in smoke free New Zealand whether they slept soundly at night, they answered (surprisingly), "No." They described a pretty bleak gang culture, fuelled by drugs one images, and the friend also indicated that his employees 'hate' him. It's not personal of course, it's simply a case that when someone in his position (at a particular mine in New Zealand) gives an instruction, some people have to work more and let's face it, miners are not the cream of the crop.

We then compared notes to our experiences in the South African Defence Force (SADF). Today it is known as the South African National Defence Force. In 1990 I was in the Air Force, at Valhalla in Pretoria, and he was in the army at Tempe in Bloemfontein. At that time Apartheid was still going strong in South Africa, and military service was compulsory.

I was appalled – and I told him this – by the cross-section of white South Africans I encountered at Valhalla. And I had been lumped with university graduates, even though I had just matriculated, so these guys were at least – one may have anticipated – a tier or two above the bottom of the South African society's barrel. In other words, these troops *weren't* the bottom of the barrel, if I can be as un-PC as that. Despite this, we had to place chains through the sleeves of our shirts, and the legs of our trousers, and secure these with locks, to make sure our laundry wasn't stolen off the washing line. Socks unfortunately couldn't be secured. Nor could one's mattresses be locked anywhere. Yes, that's right.

Each recruit was given two pairs of blues and browns, and a bed, mattress, cupboard etc. Yet some, in their wisdom, felt it necessary to steal – yes – even mattresses from their fellow recruits. Why? To do what with? To use where? I have no idea. Perhaps an extra shirt nicked off a clothing line could be given to a brother as souvenir. But a lot of stealing went on, and in the end I think I lost an entire set of blues. I went away for a weekend and returned to find my metal cupboard (or *kas*) bent open on the one side, and my *balsak* (literally 'ball bag') had been removed and basically emptied. That was 1990 and I actually had a novel (well, piles of paperwork, meticulously handwritten and typed during my last two years of high school) also stolen out of the *balsak*.

That was what I cared about. And a few photos of a girl I was infatuated with at the time. I didn't really care about the clothes or anything else missing. The thief/thieves probably didn't expect this, but I put up posters all over the place, offering a reward for the safe return on my papers. A few agonising days later a locker was discovered in the dormitory right beside ours, where all my papers had basically been stuffed inside. What I remember feeling was…well…a sense of personal injury, because the guys in these two particular dorms sort of knew each other and hung out together, so it was actually an inside job. In other words, it wasn't a complete stranger taking a chance, it was someone you hung out with, and ate beside in the mess hall, and watched television with, who, when you went away for the weekend, took his opportunity and saw what sort of booty he could get his hands on. It made me sad. I guess not everyone can be trusted.

So although I recovered my novel, a few t-shirts and some photos of my surfer girl, I did lose a whole set of blues. I was wearing the other set during the weekend pass, so fortunately I at least had that. And two sets of browns. I never replaced the stolen blues. Blues didn't matter as much because I was in MCU (Mobile Communications Unit) and although we tended to hang out with the high ranking officers (conveying their orders) we tended to run (or be flown, or driven) around with our radios and our data transmitters, wearing browns most of the time. We only wore blues to parades really, and in some circumstances outside of base.

The epilogue to this episode is that I did eventually have *all my remaining military clothing* (boots, both sets of browns, blues, flight cap etc) stolen from a cupboard, during a month spent living on my father's farm. But I've never been called back to do 'camps', and compulsory national service has since been abandoned, (it's now voluntary) so I've never needed them since.

And this is what I discussed with my New Zealand friends in a 100 minute long Skype. Then conversation turned to crime, *in general*, in South Africa.

"Crime is far worse though in Johannesburg, than Cape Town."

"Not in my experience. And I don't think that's true statistically speaking either."

Yes, I can be a bit anal about certain details. But am I right? Let's ask questions, and then check for the answers shall we…

Let's start with Jeremy Clarkson, a criminal ~~mastermind~~ expert if ever there was one:

"Honestly? Johannesburg is Milton Keynes with thunderstorms. You go out. You have a lovely ostrich. You drink some delicious wine and you walk back to your hotel, all warm and comfy. It's the least frightening place on earth. So why does every single person there wrap themselves up in razor wire and fit their cars with flame-throwers and speak of how many times they've been killed that day? What are they trying to prove?"

Times writer and blogger Jackie May writes: *The reason, he says, we tarnish our city is that we want to save the lions in Kruger Park from refugees – "At present, it's estimated that there are 2,000 lions in the Kruger National Park and studies suggest 90% have feline Aids. Some vets suggest the epidemic was started by lions eating the lungs of diseased buffalos. But there are growing claims from experts in the field that, actually, refugees are the biggest problem."*

That comes from here, by the way,

http://blogs.timeslive.co.za/minor/2009/03/jeremy-clarkson-says-joburg-is-safe-and-were-softies/

the original article is locked behind a pay wall now, and I won't be shelling out R20 to share it with you, much as I would like to. Now, Clarkson may not be the wittiest mechanic in the world (or maybe he is), but he's not *altogether wrong* on this one. Johannesburg is not South Africa's most dangerous city. Note the article below was published March 5, 2015:

http://businesstech.co.za/news/general/53824/south-africas-most-violent-city/

I hope you went there because it's an important read. The *Sultans of Spin* have certainly done their work, haven't they? What a job to undo it. Because when we ask a simple question and try to answer it – using curiosity (not assumption) as our guide, what we come up with is the rather startling revelation that South Africa's (SSSSSSSHHH) most violent city is *Cape Town*, not Johannesburg. And Nelson Mandela Bay (Port Elizabeth), not Johannesburg, is South Africa's *second* most violent city. And third is *Durban*. Johannesburg, despite its fearsome reputation for crime, is fourth. Cape Town, despite its clever PR campaigns, is a gangland. Cape Town is in fact the 20th most dangerous city in the world! Who knew?

Well, I guess I sort of knew. But I have to provide some additional context here. I've lived in three of those four (aforementioned) cities and I personally experienced Cape Town as a lot more criminally active than Johannesburg.

Let me share a few anecdotes about my days in Cape Town with you now. I'll try to be brief:

Hout Bay is basically on the opposite side of Table Mountain as Cape Town. That's where I was as a young law student on holiday in 1991. It's a beautiful harbour, and *Hout* is an Dutch word for 'wood' and its forest certainly add to its loveliness. But the Bay is slowly being carved into townhouse developments and living space for squatters. In equal measure. I am not sure which is worse. I remember an area behind my grandmother's going up in flames on Boxing Day, with gas canisters shooting up in the air like rockets (hot enough to heat one's forearm, as one stood, watching, from an upstairs balcony). Since the squatters had set up shack in a wooded area, tall bluegum giants were also set alight. These trees contain highly flammable aromatic oil, and the crack of bark as they exploded alternated with the gas canisters detonating, one after the other. Since those early fires, land was set aside for them, my grandmother's house was razed to build yet another townhouse development, and rich and poor have been jostling it out in Hout Bay ever since.

In 1999 I made a stop in Hout Bay –

a) To try to recover from the world's worst divorce (I wasn't married but as breakups go, this was epic, and I *felt* like I had been) and

b) Getting ready to jump back across the pond, and set things up in Scotland (and Aberdeen, of all places).

I wanted to travel, but also save some money so I could start on a good wicket (financially) when I was back in South Africa.

When I returned in 2000 I finished off my degree and did a postgraduate in marketing at AAA Advertising School in the same year. I spent the first few months in Hout Bay, and moved out shortly after a burglary. It wasn't so much a burglary as my aunt hiring someone – one of those squatters – out of a sense of Christian charity, and basically allowing one of these chaps run of the house while he basically picked off items of value at his leisure. I think my uncle lost valuable camera equipment, but a lot had been pilfered when we finally figured it out, and I unfortunately lost thousands of Rands in overseas clothing (which is a lot better than what our shops sell) and some excellent cycling gear and trisuits (Speedo, Zed-team etc), bought in the best sports shops in Edinburgh, London and Bristol. Once that was zipped I wasn't too keen on living in Hout Bay any more, so I moved to the city bowl. I stayed in Oranjezicht, and there my car was stolen (for the first time) but fortunately recovered, I think in Langa, or Gugulethu.

I remember the policemen saying that often cars are stolen simply to get the thief a drive home, and then they dump the vehicle. So I was fortunate to get it back. A few months later I was in Flower Road, around the corner, having dinner with some friends. We heard a noise, looked out the third storey window and saw my vehicle moving backwards down the road.

"NICK! NICK! YOUR CAR IS BEING STOLEN DON'T JUST SIT THERE DO SOMETHING!"

I explained with more than a wry smile that the gearlock was on, which secures the gearshift (and is virtually unbreakable) so it was impossible to drive the car in any direction except backwards. Which is what the thief did until it wasn't really working out for him. He stopped the car, got out, ran away, prompting laughter from us. I finished my dinner, fetched the vehicle (it had simply been reversed 100 metres and then abandoned) and parked it in the same place.

Later in the same year, I had engine problems with that vehicle. Basically when I was driving when I looked in the rear-view mirror I thought there was a veld fire. The car was smoking very badly. I took it to a mechanic situated very close to Cape Town's Houses of Parliament. Due to commitments at AAA I wasn't able to fetch the vehicle immediately once it had been fixed, so they parked it in the road opposite the garage. Eventually I got another call from them, saying Parliament would be in session soon, and the road needed to be cleared of all parked cars (for security reasons) and so, could I come and fetch mine. And by the way, some *bergies* (Cape Town slang for local tramps, or vagabonds) had turned the car into a sort of campsite (one of the windows was broken, and the door wouldn't lock, so it was easy to break into.)

When I arrived I found a sort of laager had been created using the car and a number of large plastic waste containers. "Errr…do you mind if I…take my car back?"

"Hold on. Ons dinge is binne." (Our things are inside).

More than one *bergie* it seemed, were basically using the car as a base, to stow their clothes and a few other things, and a base of operations for sleeping and hanging out. I handed one of them a big black plastic bag filled with clothes and paraphernalia, and they removed their other incidentals out of the cubbyhole. Then I drove off, noting a very, shall we say, *lived in* aroma in the upholstery.

A few months later, having moved to a neighbouring suburb, Vredehoek, with a girl (but not a girlfriend), but nevertheless a very good friend, I suffered probably the worst burglary ever. I was on my last or second last day interning at The Jupiter Drawing Room, it was the very last work I had to do in my year at AAA, and I returned to find virtually all my clothes gone. If I had any leftover clothes from the first burglary, this one completed the job, and also took the clothes I'd slowly assembled to replace the last lost wardrobe, some neat threads from YDA and that sort of thing. Fortunately I had my notebook computer with me that day (which I had spent 6 months saving up for in the UK, instead of travelling), otherwise I would have lost that too.

All I know is I went to Wimbledon, returned to South Africa, had my Wimbledon sweater stolen, when I went back to the UK, I went back to Wimbledon (more to buy a new sweater than for the tennis) and that sweater was subsequently stolen too. So, that's kind've frustrating. I think I ought to start shopping for clothes closer to home from now on, right?

There's more to say about my encounters with crime in Cape Town, but some of it is…a lot more sensitive, and a lot more personal. I think it's sufficient to illustrate in the few months and not many years I lived there my car was stolen twice, taken over by vagabonds, and I suffered two pretty painful thefts of my entire wardrobe. Given that the clothing was bought overseas definitely made it worse. And did I mention the girl I lived with, none of her outfits were touched. The thief obviously, like me, had damn good fashion sense (or, was simply a man looking to look better plying his criminal trade, walking the streets of Cape Town).

Jokes aside, drugs and gangs and intractable poverty are the unholy triumvirate behind Cape Town's world class crime numbers. And, not to labour the point or anything, but crime in Cape Town is actually more than the crime in Johannesburg and Pretoria *combined*. In fact:

Cape Town residents are almost twice (1.8 times) more likely to be murdered than Johannesburg residents.

http://africacheck.org/2013/09/19/where-murder-happens-in-sa/#sthash.yImkr9aF.dpuf

http://gctca.org.za/substance-abuse-is-fuelling-most-of-our-violent-crime/

Before we move along that black artery that connects Cape Town to Johannesburg (the N1), let's do a quick stopover in Bloemfontein, the dead-end *dorp* where I was born, and grew up, and couldn't wait to get the hell out of as a student.

All I want to say about Bloem is to reiterate what I said in that email, to my friend in Johannesburg, and what I pointed out earlier in this section. Common residential burglaries reached 262 113 in 2013, which is an average of 720 household burglaries every day in South Africa. In Bloemfontein, one of South Africa's smaller cities, an estimated 40 burglaries take place each day.

40 burglaries a day – is that a lot?

Well let's say this, as a student at the Free State University where I started studying law, it was pretty routine parking your car outside, in the road, at night. But during my student years I probably had about half a dozen break-ins, targeting my car radio. I solved that one buy buying one of those removable radios, which was subsequently updated with a radio's whose face you removed. Today though, you won't find *any* cars parked in the streets at night. Moreover, while I used to cycle to school, it's unheard of that kids today generally do that, certainly not nearly as much as we used to. It's not safe not only due to higher traffic volumes, but because kids on the street simply aren't safe.

Because we live in South Africa, and we have collectively adapted our behaviour to each painful jab criminals have made against us, I'm not sure if we realise the freedoms we have given up. Do we see them? Because it's quite obvious in the suburbs, in the way people lock themselves up behind enormous walls, in the way people become recluses in their own homes.

A friend of mine recently visited me from Scotland, and she remarked how odd it was that no vehicles are parked in the street, because this is the norm through the United Kingdom and the rest of Europe. I used to live in London and Edinburgh myself, and it's common to see residential suburbs at night, jammed with cars. Another difference is pedestrian activity and public transport. There's unfortunately a reason why electric vehicles (which have much shorter ranges than conventional gas guzzlers), and public transport is likely to *sukkel* (struggle)in South Africa, and never really take off. Can you guess the reason? Security.

Electric Vehicles, with their far higher chances of leaving drivers stranded, are simply to risky for the South African scenario. Hybrids yes. Public transport is another pickle. In order to embrace public transport South Africans will have to leave their vehicles at home, or at some parking setup, unattended for several hours. They must also feel safe enough to walk from their point of arrival to wherever they're going. Do they? If the companies that arrange public transport can guarantee security, then certainly, public transport has a chance. But I am, not sure if there are any guarantees in South Africa.

Before we leave Bloem, some local letters and comment (if you can't read Afrikaans skip this section, as there is only minimal translation **in bold below**):

Hoewel die inbrake by wonings in Navalsig, een van die minder gegoede woonbuurte in die Rosestad, afgeneem het, loop inwoners hier steeds erger onder misdaad deur as in ander woonbuurte.
Volgens die jongste misdaadstatistieke wat verlede week deur die polisie bekend gemaak is, is daar tussen April 2011 en Maart vanjaar [thus, over a period of a year] *230 inbrake by huise*

in Navalsig aangemeld.
Daar was vir dié tydperk in Navalsig, wat 'n bevolking van 11218 het, 205 huisbrake vir elke 10000 inwoners.[**There were 205 break-ins for every 10 000 residents**].
Bayswater (170) is volgende op inbrekers se lys, gevolg deur Bloemspruit (139) en Bainsvlei (130).
Ds. Jannie Smith, voorsitter van die Navalsig-gemeenskapspolisiëringsforum (GPF), sê inbrake in dié woonbuurt is 'n groot probleem.
Volgens Smith is armoede, dwelms en prostitusie aan die een kant die grootste oorsaak van huisbrake.[**Poverty, drugs and prostitution are given as the main reasons for this ongoing criminality.**]
"Dit is gewoonlik mense wat weens dwelmgebruik inbreek om hul verslawing te befonds.
"Omdat Navalsig ook so 'n arm gebied is, is dit 'n manier vir mense om kos op die tafel te sit."
Hy sê die padwerke in Andries Pretoriusstraat en straatligte wat nie werk nie, dra ook by tot die vlaag inbrake in die woonbuurt.
Die meeste inbrake vind op Woensdae en Donderdae plaas wanneer mense by die werk is. Smith sê inwoners moet deel van die forum en netwerke word om te verhoed dat hulle die slagoffers van misdaad word.[**Most break-ins are on weekdays when people are at work. People should form networks, and stay informed on what is happening in their neighbourhoods**].
"Mense raak eers betrokke as hulle slagoffers was.[**People only get involved once they've become victims of crime. Before that they think it doesn't affect them.**] Voor dit dink hulle dit raak hulle nie. Hulle moet eerder vroegtydig betrokke raak en saam planne maak in die stryd teen misdaad."
   Source : Volksblad

   BRIEWE /**Letters**

Baie inbrake in stad se eens veilige woonbuurte /**Many break-ins in the city's once safe suburbs**

Gister se hoofberig, "Boewe laat Bfn sidder", het my gedagtes teruggeneem na Kersfees 2012.
My seun en sy gesin het die 23ste Desember by ons gekuier toe sy selfoon wys dat die alarms by sy huis in Bainsvlei afgaan. Eers die deur by sy braaiarea. Hul hond kry toe die skuld, want daar woed 'n storm in Bainsvlei.
Minute daarna gaan die voordeur se alarm af. Skoondogter besef dadelik daar is fout. My seun bel die buurman om te kyk of hy iets sien.
Die volgende oomblik gaan sy selfoon weer af. Die rowers is nou in hul huis. Hy, skoondogter, die alarm-maatskappy en buurman jaag na die huis. Buurman sien toe die wit Mercedes wegjaag en sit dit agterna in die gietende reën.
Toe hulle by die huis kom, is die kluis uit die muur geruk en so ook die alarmstelsel.
Kersdag maak ek vroeg ete sodat die kinders voor donker terug kan wees by hul huis. Hulle besluit toe om 'n ompad te ry en te kyk of hulle nie dalk die kluis iewers sien lê nie. En sowaar, in die veld kry hulle die kluis en al hul gewere!
Natuurlik is ons bekommerd oor hul veiligheid. Ons bly dan in Hillsboro, een van die

*veiligste gedeeltes in die stad en het so pas ook ons erf met 'n muur omhein. Hoe dan anders?
'n Paar dae later, terwyl my dogter by die huis in haar kantoor sit en werk en die huiswerker
staan en stryk, spring die rowers oor die muur, ontglip hulle en steel my juwele.
Selektiewe diewe! Net die duurste is goed genoeg vir hulle.
Dieselfde modus operandus as by buurvrou en 'n kollega. Goud en silwer wil hul hê; die
goedkoper juwele los hulle.
Nou bly net een ding oor: elektriese heining.* **[Now there is only one way left to secure our
property – electrified perimeter fencing].**
*Die afgelope twee weke is by buurman en sy bure en by buurman oorkant die straat, asook by
ander kennisse ingebreek.
Vandeesmaand sal Hillsboro, die eens veilige woonbuurt, seker die buurt wees met die
meeste inbrake, terwyl ons toekyk hoe elektriese heinings, lemmetjiesdraad, mure ensovoorts
opgerig word om ons self te beskerm teen die vlaag misdaad.*

*Annetjie du Randt
Bloemfontein*

http://ahibloemfontein.co.za/nuusbriewe/jul_2011.htm

Here's a blog post, September 29 2006:

http://www.nickvanderleek.com/search?q=wild+coast+pistol+whipped

Note the highlighted text:

While the world worries about civil war in Iraq, an invisible war of attrition is taking place in South Africa.

Robberies, especially those involving businesses situated in big shopping malls, have increased 32%. This means in the year 2005-2006 there have been at least 1000 more robberies than in the previous year. Cash in transit heists have increased even more: 74.1%. Bank robberies have also increased 1.7%.

Meanwhile, the headline in today's local newspaper reads: **'SA becoming safer and safer'**. *The Minister of Safety and Security, Mr. Charles Nqakula, has described the future security situation in South Africa as* **'rosy'**. *He has also referred to current trends in crime as having reached a 'turning point'.*

Meanwhile, 18 545 South Africans were murdered in the period from April 2005 to March 2006. This is an almost unnoticeable shift from the previous figure for the previous year: 18 793. Hijackings have also increased by 3.1%.

Recently TV news and newspapers have focused on a particularly heinous crime: two youths murdered a 4 year old girl by stuffing her underwear deep into her throat cavity. They also raped her babysitter. A third man stood guard outside while these crimes were being

committed. Today the judge, Gerhardus Hattingh sentenced the youths to numerous years in prison, but **expressed regret that he was not able to mete out a death sentence which he said he felt was more appropriate. He referred to elite sectors of the community as being 'permissively tolerant' of deplorable crime levels. He said the lack of a more stringent penalty amounted to the sanctioning of many of the atrocious acts committed daily.**

The Free State is the province where I live. It has one of the smallest populations of all the provinces, at just **2.7 million**. Although the region is generally considered to be safe, at least comparably safer than most other regions, at least **1000 people per year are murdered here**. To put this figure in perspective, consider that **the Netherlands, with 12 million people, loses less than 200* people a year to homicide.**

What is my personal experience? A week ago my girlfriend's car window was smashed open and her car radio was damaged in the process of attempting to remove it. The car was parked in an enclosed area, surrounded by high metal fencing with sharp projections on the end. The car was also parked about 7 meters away from the nearest bedroom.
What about accommodation? I am moving to another part of the city, and finally decided on a small studio. When I showed my girlfriend where I'd be moving to she immediately recognized the place. She said a friend of hers had stayed there and had lost her microwave, in fact everything, in a burglary.

In the last few years I've had my car stolen, so has my father, so has my girlfriend. **My father and sister, while on holiday on the Wild Coast, were pistol whipped and robbed. The story appeared in a local newspaper.**

Many South Africans shrug when these statistics or anecdotes are recounted, possibly because they feel nothing much can be done. The people in charge are even worse. When calls are made to address crime, people like Nqakula insist that things 'aren't that bad'.

On the positive side, the president and high ranking business leaders have begun to pour millions into an initiative called Business Against Crime. I'd like to see more squad cars patrolling the neighborhood. I can't say I've ever seen a policecar cruising around at night, making sure everything is in order. There are plenty of security companies, but all they can do is react when the alarms go off. By then, it's usually too late.

So it's likely that for as long as extreme inequalities persist in South Africa (where the very rich try to fence themselves off from the very poor) there will be a continuation of this invisible conflict, this war of attrition of the wealthy.

*198 to be exact

Unemployment in the Free State, as I've mentioned earlier, is the highest of all South Africa's provinces, at 34%. That's one in three people that are unemployed. There are unfortunately clear signs and symptoms that the Free State economy is stuttering, under maladministration, but also due to simpler things, such as the failure to stimulate jobs. Some of these signs include:

- The persistent water crisis and shortages plaguing Bloemfontein's northern suburbs. Water pumps have broken with such regularity that many Bloemfontein residents have had to use their swimming pools as reservoirs, for example for washing, and to flush their toilets.
- The recent cancellation of the OFM classic, the Free State's cycle challenge that's the equivalent of the Cape Argus or Johannesburg's 94.7 bicycle race. The marketing manager of OFM (the main sponsor) cited 'economic reasons' for the discontinuation of their sponsorship. 4000 cyclists is also a disappointing figure when compared to the iconic Argus in the Mother City race and the 94.7, both of which attract 4 to 6 times as many cyclists.
- The imminent depart of Adriaan Strauss captain of the local Toyota Cheetah franchise (to the Blue Bulls) has caused a local uproar. Strauss maintains that he was not offered an extension on his contract, which is another way of saying, his employer (or sponsor) could not afford to. The poaching of local rugby players, many of them ex-Grey College players, to other wealthier franchises is a regular theme. Many of the Sharks players, for example, are former Free Staters, with the Du Plessis brothers being prime examples
- The closure of Bloemfontein's railway station can be seen as playing an instrumental role in limiting Bloemfontein's ability to act as a central rail hub for the country's freight at a time when road transport (via truck) is becoming less viable. Reopening this hub, and in fact, revitalising the country's rail system, and redeveloping all this lost infrastructure, could alone absorb many thousands of jobs for South Africa's unemployed and downtrodden
- Finally, the Free State is farming country. With the murder of farmers at 30 per 100 000, threats to nationalise (or redistribute) farms, along with increased inputs (especially fuel and electricity) tens of thousands of rural Free State farmworkers have been put out of work. As a result, this happens:

Farms are dying, TimesLive, 1 August 2014:
http://www.timeslive.co.za/thetimes/2014/08/01/farms-are-dying

Werkverliese skrikwekkend - veral in landbou [Job losses shocking, especially in agriculture]; 73 000 landbouposte verdwyn in 'n jaar, 39 000 in 'n kwartaal 30 July, 2014:

http://www.volksblad.com/sake/2014-07-30-werkverliese-skrikwekkend-veral-in-landbou

VS en NK dorpe dra die Hartland [Free State and Northern Cape towns carry the Heartland], 10 October 2013:

http://www.volksblad.com/opinie/2013-10-10-hoofartikel-vs-en-nk-dorpe-dra-die-hartland

But these jobs are not lost because the land is not productive. On the contrary, in Farmer's Weekly, May 28, 2014:

> *South African maize farmers are expecting the biggest maize crop since 1981, according to the National Crop Estimates Committee (CEC).*
> http://www.farmersweekly.co.za/news.aspx?id=58212&h=Record-maize-crop-expected-

In conclusion, and this refers specifically to the Free State, if you want to tackle crime you have to tackle poverty, if you want to tackle poverty you have to tackle unemployment, and if you want to tackle unemployment, one of the ways to do it, is to kick-start infrastructure projects that are massive employers, such as

1. renewable energy operations (this is happening),
2. railways (always underway) and
3. sustainable rural employment (but in this area, despite rising demand for food, the reverse is happening, often due to political mischief and meddling).

Right, I think we've dealt with the Free State! Shall we move on?

The Road to Parys

About three quarters of the way to Johannesburg, travelling from Bloemfontein, on the N1 you reach the Vaal toll plaza. It was there that a policeman ordered me to remove my license plates. They were outdated number plates, the numbers were correct, but the plates – the design – had to be renewed, if that makes sense. Now, sensing that riding with no plates was a greater contravention, I explained to the officer that I would have them changed. He insisted that I remove them then and there. Because the number plates were actually attached (with screws) to the bumper at one end, I was reluctant to do so. I then called a police station and asked if this was 'normal/legal' behaviour. The officer told me it was unusual, but if a traffic policeman insisted, he should give me a receipt of some kind. Because I called another police station, the officer got angry and told me I was refusing to co-operated, he was impounding my car and I would spend the weekend in jail.

He then sent for a *vangwa,* which is converted pick-up truck with a canopy on the back, it's windows are meshed over, and it is typically used for transporting prisoners. I said I'd be happy to drive my own car to the police station at Parys and hand myself in there, which, both sets of officers seemed okay with. Once there, a number of officers jeered and made a lot of intimidating remarks. While I was being processed (reminded on several occasions that I'd be in jail over the weekend etc and wouldn't get my car back) I noticed a few phone numbers on the wall above my head. I then called one of them. The station commander. I informed him of the situation, he told me not to sign anything, and said I had been 'unlawfully arrested' and that I should remain calm, he was on his way.

I asked the officer who had arrested/was arresting me, for his name. By law a policeman is supposed to wear a name badge. He wasn't. He wouldn't give me his name. I then tried to take photos of the officers who were essentially colluding in their scheme, and of course, then all hell broke loose. I was allowed to leave once the commander arrived, who was also most upset about the cellphone images. Once he was satisfied these had been erased I was free to go (with my license plates still attached).

Given the above anecdote, which may seem harmless, or even funny, note the contents of this article, and note the date.

http://www.iol.co.za/news/crime-courts/police-throttled-him-until-he-collapsed-1.1728859#.U9uinhCSxOg

Yes, August 1, 2014. This is happening now. In police stations.

Let's move on to Johannesburg

Like everyone else, when I moved to Johannesburg from Bloemfontein in mid-2007 to take up a job in the newsroom at a large media house in Rosebank, my impression of Johannesburg was hijackings and traffic jams. I have to say, Johannesburg is a surprisingly great city to live in. The climate is moderate, probably better by some margin than both Bloemfontein and Cape Town, and perhaps the city with the best climate in the world.

I also thought I'd be intimidated by the cities highways and urban sprawl, and I was, but far less than I imagined. A nice surprised was joining up with a cycling club (the Illovo Group?) and moving like a twinkling Christmas tree through Houghton's leafy streets, through Befordview and so on. I had no idea that was even possible. As it turns out, if you wake up early enough, Johannesburg is a wonderful haunt for serious cyclists, and I loved it. We even cycled once from Houghton, via Montecasino, to Sun City (yes, around 180km, and a 3:30am start). But, I digress.

Although I lived in Johannesburg for a fairly short time, just short of three years, I can't say I experienced too much crime. Not a single break in to my car. And nothing else stolen. The same friends I mention at the start of this section, though, had a close call with an intruder literally in their bedroom. If you add it up that's at least three serious break-ins in roughly three or four years. In other words, quite a lot.

Now, although I wasn't a victim of crime per se, I was a victim of ... Well, here's what happened.

What happened was I was renting a lovely upstairs loft studio in the Northern Suburbs. The first incident involved a break in at the residence adjoining mine. So if I was occupying the Loft, the house Proper, the mansion in other words, that was the section that was targeted. By three attackers, if memory serves. I can't recall if I saw something through my window, or if a panic button had been pushed, alerting a security company, but for whatever reason, I went downstairs and into the garden and looked through the window into her bedroom.

I think I was accompanied by a security guard, and he would have wanted access to the property, and that's what alerted me to something being – possibly – wrong. When I 9we?) looked through the bedroom window I saw things lying on the floor – blankets, clothes, her handbag. I immediately knew something was wrong, because I'd been in her home before, and it was extremely neat.

I went around trying to get in, and we were able to get in through a pair of doors linking the outside garden to her bedroom. They were closed, but unlocked. Once inside it became glaringly obvious that something untoward had happened. I noticed a piece of cheese that looked like it had been half eaten lying somewhere in her bedroom. No chance of her doing that either. So we walked around, trying to find her. Again, I can't recall how I heard her, what the particular sound was, but I followed it to a safe, I turned the key and there she was. [It was a large safe, about the size of small toilet].

When I opened the heavy safe door, the old lady (my landlady) was inside, crouched over, her face had been beaten to a plum-purple pulp. She was, understandably both traumatised and miserably grateful. Then she noticed a remote lying on a table, and she cried, "Oh it was him." Meaning, her garden boy, a Zimbabwean whom she had recently fired (whilst still in possession of access control to her property). I think she fired his wife at the same time, so the couple couldn't have been too happy.

Yes, I felt badly for the old lady, but I also felt relieved I hadn't been attacked. But then things took a turn for the worse.

Surburbia or Disturbia?

How it started was my girlfriend lost her job in Bloemfontein and came to stay with me for a few days. By that stage things with the old lady had…deteriorated considerably. For starters, she had rented out virtually the whole mansion, for something like R14 000 a month, to an engineer, if I recall. Meanwhile, she had started squatting in a room beside the pool with a Jacuzzi inside. She'd placed a board over the tub area, fashioned it into a makeshift bed, and was using the swimming pool area for washing (and bathing). The swimming pool area was below my window, and it was sort've my section of the property, but I didn't make a big thing of it. I did notice more of her things cluttering the garden downstairs, and then the garage, and then things got more and more out of hand. Because my girlfriend was staying over, she caught the landlady coming into my place to use the refrigerator, make tea and basically making herself at home. Once again, in the beginning I guess I felt sorry for her, and didn't really know what to do. What solution was there?

But things came to head when I my girlfriend and discussed safety, and we decided it was best if we parked her car in my garage (which was long, and could just squeeze in two cars, and hers was a compact Corsa). Rather than leave it outside. Problem was, the garage by now was cluttered with junk. Two refrigerators, a washing machine, piles of rolled up Persian carpets and paraphernalia, boxes and boxes piled to the ceiling, there was even a boat stuffed in there somewhere. It was so bad eventually I could barely get my car into the garage, and once in, I could barely get out.

The critical thing that happened was I eventually said to the old lady, she'd need to move some of her stuff out of the garage so my girlfriend could fit her car in. Of course, the old lady threw her toys, and insisted my girlfriend leave. I told her, quite firmly, that she couldn't dictate those sort of terms, my girlfriend was visiting me, it was the first time she had ever done so for any length of time. And I said although I understood her circumstances weren't great, and I was trying to make things easier for her, she also had to respect my rights to the free use of a property I was paying to use.

But she didn't agree.

So I said I would make space myself for my girlfriend's car, if she didn't. And so that's what I did. What followed was she went to the local police station and opened a case of *Malicious Damage to Property*. I won't go into the details, except to say I didn't damage any of the items I moved. She specifically sought R3000 I think for her 'damaged refrigerator.' Well, I hadn't damaged it. Ironically enough, on the morning I was supposed to appear in court, there was a power failure in Johannesburg, and so I needed help lifting the heavy garage door. I went over and asked the neighbour (the engineer renting the mansion section). I made the remark that I had a case against me for damage to property, and pointed to the offending object in the garage.

"That refrigerator?" he asked.

"Ja, she said I damaged it. That's what this is all about. I'm supposed to go to court now."

"That refrigerator has been working all week. A sachet of milk fell over, and milk had dribbled through the door and onto the paving, so I mentioned it to her."

"She says when I moved it there I broke it."

"When I opened the door, the light came on, it was functioning."

"But why would you open her refrigerator?" I asked.

"To find out where the milk was leaking from."

I asked him if he would put it down in writing. And I would collect it as a sort of affidavit if I needed it. I then went to the police station, as I had arranged to follow one of the vehicles to court (since I wasn't sure where it was). When I arrived I was told I was to be arrested, fingerprinted, booked into a cell etc). I explained that I was there to go to court. In any event, my watch, pens, belt, shoes (presumably I might hang myself or attempt to garrotte someone else?) even my yellow Livestrong bracelet (which I still believed in, and never took off, in those days) was removed, so I could be processed for jail.

Jail Time and Injustice

Corrine Whitman: *I'm very sorry for your distress, I wish I could help you with your problem but I simply cannot.*
Isabella Fields El-Ibrahimi: *My problem? My problem?*
Senator Hawkins: [overlapping] *Young lady, if you just leave your name and information*
...
Isabella Fields El-Ibrahimi: *You have my name. You have my home address, you have my phone number, you have everything! You have my husband!*
[they look at each other and begin to leave]
Isabella Fields El-Ibrahimi: *Please don't walk away from me! Just tell me where he is!*
Guard: [restraining her] *Ma'am.*
Isabella Fields El-Ibrahimi: *JUST TELL ME HE'S OKAY!*

Yep, I was a jailbird once. An ex-con. A wanted felon. A member of the Shawshank Redemption. If you thought I couldn't *just* be a journalist, or a scribe, up, you'd be right. In another life I was a kingpin of the underworld, an emperor standing on the dirty Underbelly of South Africa's criminal trade. For a time, this was *my* world!

It's true. I'd watched dozens of prison flicks as a kid, and secretly memorised the slang. Secretly, yes, I'd *always known* the prison lingo* from all those jailbird flicks would come in handy one day. And now it was finally here. My time had come to use this uncommon education. So when I stepped into the cage I didn't waste any time. No-one wants to *dance on the blacktop* while you're in the cage. But you can't expect not to have your *chin checked*. So I stepped inside, looked each of them in the eye, and seized my chance right off the bat, telling my cellmates I was in for a *bum beef*, but at least I wouldn't be inside *All Day*. I'd ask, careful not to *dip too much into the Kool Aid*, which officers were *Bugs*, and who were *Ducks*. They'd tell me about *Buck Rogers Time*, and whose *Cadillac* was whose. I'd find out who could *hold their Mud*, and who I could get *in the car with* [not, not the *Cadillac*, the *other* car]. And who was the *Juice Card* around here. And no, I didn't have any cigarettes in my *Keister*. Not with so many *Bugs* and *Cowboys* dressed like *Ninja Turtles*. I'd need the straight up on who the *Prison Wolves* were, the *Rabbits* and who was selling *Wolf Tickets*. Nobody wants *back door parole*, and neither did I. So I'd need to get an in on who had the *shank* around here, and who was in for a *Three Knee Deep*.

But I didn't make that speech, I just blinked. Big eyes in a pale face. Was I afraid? I was pretty close to shitting myself. I soon found myself, watchless, beltless and practically legless, in a stark little concrete cell with no bed, instead there was just a folded blanket lying on the floor, which I'd have to share, at very close quarters, with three other prisoners. One was a suspected murderer; the other was accused of some other offence, drunk driving or hijacking. I can't remember what the third one did. Instead of a crime dog, bad ass, big shot bullshit speech, all I did was crack a joke when I arrived. And then I sat down on the floor, to protect my ass. I said something along the lines of:

"I guess all of us are really innocent right?"

The tragic part is I soon started to believe that. Maybe I'm gullible, or naïve, but although I was only in that cell with them, sweating bullets, for about 40 minutes, my *clot catcher* really went out to those prisoners. The suspected murderer told me he was the neighbour of someone who had been killed. He had been asked to report to a police station to explain what had happened and when he had turned up, he had been arrested on sight. Now, if someone had really murdered someone else, would they really turn up at a police station and make a statement? I doubt it.

The hijacker guy was actually injured, and dressed in a hospital gown. Secretly I was relieved about this, as it meant two possible thugs to fight off when they tried to sodomise me, rather than three. Two, if I couldn't *ride with* them, well, maybe I might have a fighting chance.

See, the other guy'd been in some sort of car accident, and from what I gathered from him, the police wanted him to confess that he was the driver. He said he wasn't, and from what I gathered, was being refused visitors (or something) until he signed what they wanted him to sign. In any event, I ended up feeling camaraderie with these guys, and sympathy, whilst I was slowly developing a growing terror for the pigs.

I said as much here:

http://www.nickvanderleek.com/2009/04/glimpse-of-prison-life.html

I don't know if they expected a bribe, but I was eventually released and giving a document which was a warning to appear in court. As this was going down, I noticed a white dude was handling the black prisoner, and a black officer was in charge of shaking me down. The white dude, from where I was standing, was saying some pretty scary stuff. The hijacker dude had been let out of his cell to sign something, and was claiming bitterly about not being able to have visitors.

Next I was told, "We're releasing you with this warning, you have to appear in court tomorrow." And so the next day I bypassed the cop shop, I found my own way there, with my girlfriend in tow, and with the affidavit from the neighbour explaining the damned refrigerator had been working all along, and the case was thrown out.

Good thing it was, because instead of going to work, I chased from the courthouse in Hillbrow straight to Montecasino, where I interviewed Gavin Hood. Hood had just directed X-Men Origins, Wolverine, and I was really hoping jail wouldn't prevent me from talking to him. It is, still to date, one of the best interviews I think I've ever been in. The funny part is half way through it he started interviewing me. Somehow in the middle of discussing *Wolverine* we got to talking about *Rendition* a flick he made about someone who is wrongfully arrested, tortured and imprisoned. The official plotline is:

A CIA analyst questions his assignment after witnessing an unorthodox interrogation at a secret detention facility outside the US.

http://www.imdb.com/title/tt0804522/?ref_=nm_flmg_dr_6

I let slip that prison definitely *wasn't* a fun experience, and when he prodded me to explain myself, I spilled the beans. I told him I'd been jailed briefly the previous day, possibly to get their arrest numbers up, and had in fact just driven here from the court house, and was still pretty shaken up by the whole experience. He shouted over his shoulder to someone at Nu Metro that *this* was the sort of thing he was interested in discussing. When I mentioned that I actually found the prisoners less scary than the police, the point seemed to resonate with him in a big way. I pointed out that what was interesting was it wasn't just ordinary corruption playing out, there was collusion between the old lady and the cops, and maybe an expectation of some grease money from a desperate suburbanite hoping to be allowed to go back to work.

Side note: *The biggest shark, of course, worse than the old lady, or the cops, was* the lawyer *my friend called. He arrived and before he could introduce himself, told me he wanted a R1000 for himself, and another R1000 grease money.*

I said, "So, you're not even interested in what happened? I mean, I didn't actually damage the refrigerator."

He said, "Look, I want to get you out of here immediately. And that's what it's going to take."

I told him I wasn't paying R2000 just to get out of jail, that was almost the value of the compensation the old lady wanted. I wasn't paying anyone a thing without anyone showing the least interest in verifying my guilt or innocence. He said in that case I should be prepared to spend the night, possibly the next 48 hours in jail, and maybe even the weekend. I asked him if he was just here to make a buck or was he actually going to practise law, and try to find out what was going on.

He – the lawyer who I didn't know from a bar of soap – kept plying me for money, so in the end I sent him away, and approached another officer, and asked him what it would take to get this sorted out. That's when the whole 'we'll give you a warning to appear in court' thing was offered. Because they'd seen I was pleading poverty, and their spiel wasn't going to net them any weekend pocket money, might as well get rid of me before I caused any problems.

Then I mentioned to Hood – whose name suddenly seemed seems oddly portentous – that all his movies seem to feature troubled characters. All of them are trying to make it in the world, are gifted but also sort of in trouble with the law (or authority) in some way. A troubled hero, whether it was *Tsotsi*, the oke in *Rendition*, *Wolverine* or Ender in *Ender's Game*. He said that was quite an astute observation. See for yourself:

http://youtu.be/J0aoKGsScYs

I did the interview for Men's Health, but they dumped the text in favour of the video. They uploaded it to their site, but it's since been revamped so the original links are no longer accessible. What's interesting about the interview is Hood's comment that so many of us may not even like our own nature's, the rage that may take root in a young person's life, and lie dormant there throughout adulthood. It raises the singular question:

Did Oscar ever truly love or accept himself?

Sticking to the cinematic narrative, here's an interesting piece of insight from Barry Ronge, writing about *Jerusalema*, an action crime-buster set in South Africa, and rated 7.8/10 by IMDB:

> *Jerusalema is as audacious and skilled as an ATM bombing in the precinct of the Union Buildings, and it sets a new benchmark for our moribund film industry.*
>
> *The story of Jerusalema began when expat writer- director Ralph Ziman heard a South African friend talking about how a gang stole a building in Hillbrow.* **"How do you steal a building?"**[my emphasis] *he asked and his friend explained.*
>
> *One day a couple of expensive cars pulled up outside a shabby Hillbrow building, carrying important – looking men who brandished documents implying that they were legitimate businessmen who had formed an association to protect the rights of inner-city dwellers.*
>
> *Henceforth they would be collecting all the rents. In return they promised major improvements and undertook to deal with the expulsion of the drug dealers, pimps and hookers who made life in the building so dangerous.*
>
> **The men looked so genuine that the people were fooled**[my emphasis].
>
> *Those who had objections were told to pack up and move out. If they didn't they would be helped out, often via a 10th-floor window, straight onto the pavement.*
>
> *In the face of that rough justice, everyone signed up and, within the hour, a couple of buses arrived with new tenants who moved into the apartments from which the dealers and the whores had been ejected.*
>
> *Once all the apartments were filled, the legitimate owner of the building no longer had control.*
>
> *The "businessmen" had stolen it out from under him and, in most cases, the owners caved in and sold the building for a mere fraction of its value.*
>
> *That's how these men acquired valuable real estate for which they had paid a pittance.*
>
> *The rent money came directly to them, not via properly audited accounts, of course, and inevitably the new owners had their own profitable supply of pimps, dealers and whores, who worked the district.*
>
> *Ziman was fascinated. "I came back to South Africa and started researching," he says, "because it sounded so unlikely."* **But as he spoke to reporters, police, social workers and lawyers he realised that it was not only true but commonplace** [my emphasis] *and that's where he got the idea for both the film and its title.*
>
> *"I wanted Jerusalema to take a harsh but realistic look at Johannesburg, but I also wanted to reflect the hopes and aspirations of its citizens. When you look at Hillbrow from a distance, it does look like that shining city on a hill, the New Jerusalem that will be our salvation, but* **when you get onto its streets, you find another story**[my emphasis].

http://crimebeat.bookslive.co.za/blog/2008/09/03/cine-crime-barry-ronge-reviews-the-ground-breaking-jerusalema/

Indeed.

Ronge also has some great insights about how the legacy and narrative of St. Valentine (and the day we celebrate in his name) and how it has become corrupted. By avarice more than anything else:

*Stuck between Christmas and Easter, however, sits Saint Valentine's Day, which is observed on February 14 each year. It is not really a public holiday nor is it a religious one, **but lots of money is spent on those "sweet for the sweetest" gifts***[my emphasis]*.*

...As I trawled around on the Internet, I found this statement: "It's a fact that in America, more or less 220,000 wedding proposals take place on Valentine's Day every year. The really striking fact is that a billion Valentine's Day cards are exchanged each year in the U.S. It is the second-largest seasonal card-sending occasion after the avalanche of Christmas greeting cards," it continued.

*...That caught my attention. As thing are now, St. Valentine is money-spinner but was he ever a genuine religious leader? Has **his created image been tweaked and expanded over many centuries to a point at which he has become merely a puppet in a sentimental, vaguely religious fable***[my emphasis]*?*

The answer to that question came from the Catholic Church itself. It had looked back over the centuries and revised its liturgical calendar and they decided to remove several of the more dodgy saints whose historical origins are questionable.

St. Valentine was one of the first saintly casualties that the Catholics dumped, but instead of vanishing into the past, Valentine's memory has survived, century after century and what we know about him, is a giddy mix of folk-tale and history with Valentinus as the star.

One story states that he was imprisoned for performing weddings for Roman soldiers who were forbidden to marry people for another race. Another is that he protected Christians, who were persecuted under the Roman Empire.Yet another story says that, during his imprisonment, he healed the daughter of his jailer, Asterius. Another story states that before his execution he wrote her a letter signed "Your Valentine" as a farewell.

Inevitably, the word "Valentine" slipped into popular speech and it has been there for centuries. For example, in the 14th century, author Geoffrey Chaucer wrote the tragedy of lost love in "Troilus and Cressida" and "The Canterbury Tales" in 1380. He called them "valentines" a song of affection between two people.

Centuries later, Shakespeare used the phrase in his play "Hamlet" when the rueful Ophelia said, "To-morrow is Saint Valentine's day, all in the morning betimes and I, a maid at your window, to be your Valentine."

*It was not all kisses and roses, however, and to end down this exploration of "St. Valentine's Day", I will leave you with the memory of **"The Saint Valentine's Day Massacre" which was one of the most notorious crimes in the history of the USA***[my emphasis]*.*

It happened in Chicago in 1929 when two powerful criminal gangs who were both trying to take control of the criminal underworld and the prohibited liquor. There was the "South Side" Italian gang led by Al Capone and his opposition came from the "North Side" Irish gang led by Bugs Moran. It was one of the bloodiest gun-battle in the annals of crime.

So, take a moment to **think about today's events, the headlines and TV-news following the gangs, the violence, the politician, the poverty and the greed that is the usual newspaper fare. Then look at a cute American Easter Egg ritual**[my emphasis].

Valentine's Day is likely to make you feel romantic and sentimental. It's a time of charming gifts and blossoming romance that could easily lead to true and lasting love but for all that, it's an odd holiday.

It falls between Christmas on December 25 and Easter Sunday on April 20, and both those holidays involve a powerful sacred events for Christian followers. There was the birth of Christ, followed in later life by the tragedy of the crucifixion, through to the RESURRECTION of Jesus.

That miraculous re-birth was expressed in the image of a hollow egg, a symbol of an empty tomb, which carries its own religious message that life continues, despite sadness and loss[my emphasis].

http://www.ratheronge.co.za/News-Blog/Blog/Valentine

Full Circle (well, almost…)

Okay, we've dealt with *Jail Time*, and here's a last link that deals with what might be in store for Oscar:

http://www.ibtimes.co.uk/oscar-pistorius-still-faces-serious-jail-time-if-cleared-murdering-reeva-steenkamp-1458744

Now we get to *Injustice* both in the broad and the narrow sense of the word.

The bad news is I'd been a bad writer. It's my fault for straying straying far from the topic at hand especially in these last chapters. *Digress* isn't really the word that comes close to describing what we've been doing. Noah's ark, Bloemfontein, the Bronze Age, Mythopoeic thought, prison lingo, Gavin Hood – seriously? What's next?

It may feel like silliness, that we've been playing Legal Hobbits, jumping from toadstool to toad and back again, crossing various streams of thought – at random? – going off on tangents and then shooting off our mouths, first playing Spock, then Captain Kirk, using the powers of logic and then emotional intuition, going in search – where no media man (or woman) has gone before, in search of ~~strange new worlds~~ further reinforcement in the ~~galaxies~~ Didacts and Deducts of history, psychology and semantics. I assure you, there *is* a method behind this madness, as there is a method behind the madness of the next chapter.

The good news is we are about to cover full circle. There is a small segment we still need to sketch. It may be small, but it's a critically important one. What we we'll do now is something similar to the thing the original *Man on Wire* once did, when he sneaked up the twin towers, and then, illegally tightrope walked between them. This guy:

http://en.wikipedia.org/wiki/Philippe_Petit

In order to set up a tightrope (which was actually a cable) between the two towers, Petit first fired an arrow (yes, from a bow) which was attached to a very thin thread. Someone on the other side then collected the arrow, and pulled on the thread. Petit, the tightrope walker, then attached the thread to a thicker string, then to a cord and then finally they pulled the heavy duty cable across to make a bridge strong enough to walk on. The cable had to be pulled taught, but not so taught that the winds tugging at the towers made them too taught, and not to slack that they became wobbly, like spaghetti, and tossed the tightrope walker into the abyss.

So, that's sort've what I have been doing, but we're well passed the shooting-an-arrow-across the-abyss stage. We're also passed the passing-of-the-thread stage. We're even passed the stringing-along stage. In order to close this circle we need to get-the-cable-across and then *tighten* it.

The next chapter will be the process of writing the incident – which is essentially the *method* behind the madness. And yes, it *is* a tightrope walk. One has to maintain balance between flights of fancy, bias, imaginative musings, and logic. And reasoned intuition. In other words, we have to be realistic while we are being creative. And that requires courage, a second opinion (*Juror13*), a loyalty to facts, details and minutiae, and then that mysterious thing that is proportionate and gives the correct perspective. That's an art. Like the truth it's not simple or easy. But we're going to try.

So, we've recently touched on Saint Valentine, and like Christopher Nolan in *Inception*, I didn't do that for nothing. I planted a seed. We've planted a few together, you and I. Now I am going to bring the pendulum back, the pendulum that we've avoided for some time, and that is the whole context of Valentine's Day. 14 February. Many people, when they first heard that Oscar had shot his girlfriend early in the morning on Valentine's Day intuited (consciously or subconsciously) that there must have been some sort of lover's quarrel. Jealousy, in other words, must have been a part of the equation.

But the state hasn't intimated anything like that, and neither have I. Not really. Someone mentioned Francois Hougaard, at one point, but that's suggesting that *Reeva* may have received a late night Valentine (possibly whilst they were in bed together). Well, what about Oscar?

This morning I had a 70-something discussion over the phone, an international call between South Africa and the States, with *Juror13*. We're trying to batten down the hatches and tighten the narrative into a singular cord, and singular cable, tying all the threads together. If the reader thinks I have done a lot of work in this department, and I have, give *Juror13* a lot of credit for doing the same. During our discussion we agreed on quite a lot, but both of us were able to point out things the other had missed, and this is important. But even between the two of us we're likely to overlook something. All I am saying is there's no way we have touched on everything, but I think it's fair to say we've touched on most of it. 90% perhaps. Perhaps 95%.

Have I revealed all the things about myself, my experiences with crime and injustice in South Africa? Not at all. I failed to mention, for example, in 2012, travelling to Namibia with a friend, and being denied entry at the gate (on the way back) because my passport pulled up a flag on the computers. I discovered at the border that my official status was WANTED. For what? For a case pending in Johannesburg, Malicious Damage to Property. But I went to court? Yes, well, it was re-opened. You're WANTED sir. We're going to be arresting you, putting you in a *vangva*, you'll leave your car here, spend the night in jail in Upington, and then we'll drive you up to Johannesburg to face trial. Well, the blood drained from my face, and my knees turned to jelly. And since I was travelling with a young woman, I not only felt embarrassed, I also felt…well, not a little ashamed.

In the end I was at the border post for about 4 hours. And in the end, they simply allowed us in, because they said although my status was officially WANTED, they couldn't find the police file at the police station in Johannesburg. And so that was how it was resolved. I didn't pay a bribe, I simply waited for the police to find their file so I could be arrested and jailed.

So there's a glimpse into a recent episode of…*Injustice*. Is that a fair word to use? Have I told the full story here? Not even close. Have I given all the examples I can think of, of people close to me, family and friends that have suffered injustice. Not even close. I can tell you my sister has had 5 cars stolen, my father's car has been stolen once (and retrieved), my ex-girlfriend (my last long relationship in other words), her father was murdered on Christmas Day. She was pregnant with her first child at the time, and her husband divorced her a few months later. Remember the close girl, but not girlfriend I mentioned in Vredehoek, whose clothes weren't stolen when mine were? Her brother was murdered last year in Kwa-Zulu Natal.

My girlfriend during my jail episode (yes, the entire terrible fourty minutes) is a victim of another sort. She was in a horrible car accident where a biker tore through their vehicle at night, slicing away half her face (requiring half a dozen or more painful reconstructive surgeries) and killing her sister. I mentioned earlier that car accidents are almost commensurate to murders in South Africa. Well, the impact of those accidents are just as real too. My point is, do I have to reveal everything in order to do what is sufficient? In other words, do I need a measuring instrument to calibrate the tension of the cable, or can I use my intuition, can I sort of sense, that it is just right?

I hope you answered the later, because that is also what a judge must do in this case. They must weigh up the evidence, use logic as far one can, facts, as far one can, trends, expert opinion, science and everything else, and then…evaluate it all with intuition, with intelligence and with respect not just for the law, but for the law of precedent.

What we don't know, for example, is exactly how much time is needed for *Premeditation*. This fascinating topic is discussed here:

http://www.politifact.com/punditfact/statements/2014/mar/31/nancy-grace/nancy-grace-talks-oscar-pistorious-trial-could-pre/

Both *Juror13* and I believe there is a strong case for premeditation, both in the sense that there was a process involved in retrieving a firearm and approaching the door (that's the first process) and then secondly, in the apparently sentient process of firing four shots at a door, needing to be supported, correcting aim (trajectory) and achieving, in the end, a 75% record for those 4 shots, with each successive bullet fired (with the exception of 'b', the second shot) more 'on target' (ie closer to vital organs) than the last. But it's possible a judge may look not at the long approach to the door, but only the short period between firing perhaps the first and remaining shots. Even so, the time duration for premeditation is an interesting question. If we say 'moments' are sufficient, when do those *moments* become *mini seconds*, and then simply (mindless) reactions?

So, to reiterate, Valentine's Day probably did play a key role in why what happened when it happened. Is there any specific evidence to support this? Besides online generic connections (in other words, the phones were used, we simply don't know to whom, what for and why), by both Oscar and Reeva's handsets throughout the night (and we'll provide the specifics on that) – no. No we can't prove either Reeva or Oscar sent any Valentine's messages to anyone besides each other. Is it possible? Or is it likely? What do you think? An icon with over 300 000 twitter followers – isn't going to get some fan mail on Valentine's Day? Reeva, a beautiful girl, courting the spotlight, might not have a few guys – as they say in Afrikaans – *wat vir haar kersie hou*. It literally translates to *someone holding a candle for you*, in other words, being in love or bearing a flame of affection, often surreptitiously.

Please don't hate me for diving into semantics at this late stage of the game, but if we're talking about Valentine's Day, and a lover's quarrel, and we're trying to figure out how everything fits together, let's look at the centre of what Valentine's Day pretends to be. It's about love, right? The symbol of Valentine's Day is either a *heart* or *an arrow through the heart*, right? Right? Are you sure you're ready for this? Okay, buckle your seatbelts, here we go:

http://www.merriam-webster.com/thesaurus/heart

1

the capacity for feeling for another's unhappiness or misfortune

Synonyms bigheartedness, charity, commiseration, compassion, feeling, good-heartedness, humanity, kindheartedness, kindliness, kindness, large heartedness, mercy, pity, soft heartedness, sympathy, warmheartedness

Related Words feelings, responsiveness, sensibility, sensitivity; affection, love, regard; affinity, empat hy, rapport; altruism, benevolence, benignancy, benignity, generosity, goodwill, humaneness, humanism, humanitarianism, philanthropy

Near Antonyms callousness, coldness, disinterest, indifference, unconcern; cruelty, harshness; animosity, antipathy, dislike, hatred, hostility

Antonyms coldheartedness, hardheartedness, inhumanity, inhumanness, mercilessness, pitilessness

2

a thing or place that is of greatest importance to an activity or interest

Synonyms axis, base, capital, central, core, cynosure, epicentre, eye, focus, ground zero, heart, hub, locus, mecca, navel, nerve center, nexus, nucleus, omphalos, seat

Related Words headquarters; happy hunting ground, hive, hotbed, hot spot, playground, playland; kernel, nub, pith; deep, thick; essence, quintessence, soul; attraction, lodestone (*also* loadstone), magnet, polestar

3

strength of mind to carry on in spite of danger <never lost *heart* while she was lost in the woods>

Synonyms bottle [*British slang*],

bravery, courageousness, daring, daringness, dauntlessness, doughtiness, fearlessness, gallantry, greatheartedness, guts, gutsiness, hardihood, heart, heroism, intestinal fortitude, intrepidity, intrepidness, moxie, nerve, pecker [*chiefly British*], prowess, stoutness, valor, virtue

Related Words backbone, fiber, fortitude, grit, gumption, mettle, pluck, pluckiness, spunk, temper; determination, perseverance, resolution; endurance, stamina, stomach, tenacity; audacity, boldness, brazenness, cheek, cojones [*slang*], effrontery, gall, temerity

Near Antonyms cold feet, faintheartedness, fearfulness, mousiness, timidity, timorousness; feebleness, softness, weakness; impotence, ineffectualness; hesitation, indecision, indecisiveness, irresolution

Antonyms cowardice, cowardliness, cravenness, dastardliness, poltroonery, spinelessness

4

the central part or aspect of something under consideration <at the *heart* of the problem is the school's outmoded computer system> <avoided any small talk and got right to the *heart* of the matter>

Synonyms

bottom line, bull's-eye, centerpiece, core, essence, gist, heart, kernel, keynote, meat, meat and potatoes, net, nub, nubbin, nucleus, pith, pivot, point, root, sum

**Related
Words** course, direction, drift, tenor; body, content, substance; hypothesis, proposition, purport, subject, theme, thesis

5

the seat of one's deepest thoughts and emotions <deep down in her *heart*, she knew he was telling the truth>

Synonyms belly, blood, bone(s), bosom, breast, gut, heart, heartstrings, inner space, inside, quick, soul

Related Words conscience, mind

Juror13 has highlighted *two* distinct pair of jeans, a dark blue pair beside the bed (on the floor), and a light blue pair (outside, below the toilet window). But *Juror13* goes even further. *Juror13* asks if both those pairs belong to Reeva. It ought to be an easy question to answer. Gina Myers could/should/would know, wouldn't she? Unfortunately the truth is rarely pure and not often simple. If we could ask Gina, or Reeva's mother, we would. Unfortunately we haven't, and even if we did, we couldn't be sure whether they would answer (at this stage).

So is it possible one of those pairs of jeans weren't Reeva's? Yes. Is it probable? In my opinion no, although *Juror13* suggests the dark blue pair 'look bigger'. Point is, I am not going to factor this into the spanning of the cable, just because it's too hypothetical, too much of a long shot.

What I want to end off with here is:

- the importance of gun control. More people shoot themselves or each other with their own weapons than are shot by intruders. By a factor of something like 4:1. That's a lot. Want to be secure in your home? Don't keep a firearm at home, as counterintuitive as that may sound. Many attackers target homes specifically to steal the weapons, so by keeping a weapon you create a nasty self-fulfilling prophecy
- is paranoia justified in South Africa? Well we should differentiate between healthy Obsessive Compulsive Disorder

http://www.smh.com.au/sport/tennis/doctor-warns-against-trivialising-rafael-nadals-oncourt-routines-20140121-316w8.html

https://www.youtube.com/watch?v=KE2NjuSd7-Y

https://www.youtube.com/watch?v=oAMiaXvKd7I

- and neurosis. Barry Ronge, who I've referred to previously, has said that in South Africa s certain amount of paranoia is normal, and even healthy. So is OCD, mind you, in the sense that we use certain prescribed rituals, or actions, or behaviours to order our world. It might be locking doors, keeping certain lights on or off, making sure alarms are activated – point is, nature rewards certain behaviours, and punishes others (especially when our responses become paralysing anxiety).

- Oscar lived in a very secure security estate in Pretoria. Yes, South Africa is a dangerous country. Crime is amongst the highest in the world. That said, Pretoria ranks somewhere behind Cape Town, Port Elizabeth, Durban and Johannesburg. If Johannesburg is twice as safe as Cape Town, and Pretoria is safer than Johannesburg, then it ought to be fairly – not completely – safe.

- Oscar had no burglar bars on his windows, there was also a broken window ~~in the bathroom~~ downstairs and, yes, he admits to being afraid of crime but by the same token, sleeping with the balcony door open (and yes, ladders were lying around in the garden outside). What makes Oscar's version seem ludicrous is this idea getting up on a hot night to close the gaping hole in the wall that is the balcony door, then hearing the sound of a small 2nd storey window opening (allegedly), whilst closing this massive gaping hole, and feeling terrified. Believable?

- If you think car wrecks in South Africa aren't worth the bother of thinking about, or since there aren't reliable statistics

http://www.news24.com/SouthAfrica/News/Road-death-stats-dubious-analyst-20140109

but the Oscar case *is worth* your attention, please reconsider. Your chances of coming to grief through your own actions, behind the wheel of a car – in South Africa – are perilously high. And even in terms of the Oscar trial we know Oscar's own brother has killed a woman:

http://www.telegraph.co.uk/news/worldnews/oscar-pistorius/10071680/Carl-Pistorius-cleared-over-death-of-female-motorcyclist.html

and more recently (like, yesterday – last night in fact – based on the time of writing (2 August 2014), almost killed *himself*

http://citizen.co.za/223409/carl-pistorius-danger-crash/

and in 2009 *A woman died at the scene of the accident after walking in front of Anneke Kruger's oncoming car. Kruger works for In/sight, the company which manages* [Oscar]*Pistorius's business interests.*

http://www.news24.com/SouthAfrica/News/Pistorius-threatens-photographer-20090310

- are the police in South Africa trustworthy? In the Oscar trial we've seen some excellent police officers, Mangena and Van Staden (the photographer) come to mind, along with Mike Van Aardt. But, at the same time, we know someone sold photos of the crime scene to Sky news, and we also know Hilton Botha isn't one of South Africa's finest, otherwise he would have been called back to testify for the state, not so? Under-reported by the media of course, as the world breathalyses on all-things Oscar, is this: *Her father told Beeld newspaper* [July 22 2014]*the investigation into her murder had come to a standstill after investigating officer Captain Mike van Aardt was transferred to the Oscar Pistorius case last year.*

http://www.news24.com/SouthAfrica/News/Inquest-ordered-into-Anikas-murder-20140722

The Anika Smit murder took place in 2010. She was raped, strangled, and both hands sawed off presumably to remove DNA evidence under her fingernails. Her boyfriend was the prime suspect, but charges have since been withdrawn and the case has come to a standstill. Justice deferred is justice denied.

Coming back to the way the police ~~mismanaged~~ handled the crime scene at 286 Bushwillow Crescent, we know one of his watches were stolen, and Oscar was allowed to keep his personal phone for two weeks after the incident. How was that possible if there *wasn't* collusion with the police?

So, can the police be trusted? Well, we have to trust them, because they have authority over us, mere citizens. Even if the police flout the law, we must obey it. Because this could happen to you:

http://www.iol.co.za/news/crime-courts/police-throttled-him-until-he-collapsed-1.1728859#.U9uinhCSxOg

If South Africa's police HQ can be robbed, can we really assure ourselves that there is a credible system of law and order in this country?

http://www.news24.com/SouthAfrica/News/Double-robbery-at-Interpol-HQ-in-Pretoria-20140730

http://www.news24.com/SouthAfrica/News/Police-mum-on-robbery-at-Interpol-HQ-in-Pretoria-20140730

Meanwhile, there are also good cops, and they are fighting their own war:

http://www.iol.co.za/news/crime-courts/146-off-duty-cops-killed-in-3-years-1.1729416?utm_medium=twitter&utm_source=dlvr.it#.U9ynnhCSxOg

- Can the state be trusted with the state's case? It looks that way. Nel looks like a solid bloke, Masipa looks like a solid lady. But there are also two assessors. And there's a very powerful family in Pretoria able to pull strings. I have said it before, that if criminals are the bane of society, if corrupt policemen are further flies in society's ointment, then lawyers can be even worse. Justice, whether it is done, ultimately or not, is ultimately in their hands. Are they sharks, or *sheisters*?

http://www.urbandictionary.com/define.php?term=sheister

In both the case of the old lady bearing false witness (not once, but on several occasions) and the incident at the police station (the illegal arrest) I contacted an attorney based in Pretoria, paid a deposit, and asked him two prosecute both parties. Guess what happened? This individual has since been disbarred.

On 25 July 2011 I wrote the following email to…let's refer to him as BB:

A few years ago I paid you two deposits of R2000 each in order for you to pursue two separate cases. I would like feedback on these cases, and if you cannot provide any meaningful result/information, you will need to please explain what has happened. I would like to offer you a chance to explain your actions before I report you to the applicable law society.

BB's response:

Hi Nick,

I can only offer my apologies. This is not how I wanted things to turn out, but I have been suspended by the Law Society in December 2010 and they have all my files. I was under the impression that they would let everyone know so that the clients' won't be prejudiced, but it appears that they didn't. You can contact Estelle Veldsman at the Law Society of the Northern Provinces to get your files.

Regards,
BB

There is a lot more I can add, from other *sheister* lawyers but then there are a number of very good lawyers too, some are friends of mine, some are friends of my father. Point is, in the stories I've illustrated, the lawyers at the finishing line of many of these trials did not only frustrate my attempts to remedy my situation (in other words, my injustice) but actually made *a mockery* of my attempts to do so.

If we take BB as an example, he offered legal services, failed to perform them, and stole my money at the same time he abused my trust. Does that inspire confidence in the law? Is that a case of the law being done and 'seen' to be done? Absolutely not.

Which is why I don't have a helluva lot of faith in South Africa, and many of its systems. I said as much here:

http://www.nickvanderleek.com/2009/07/view-from-my-bicycle-column_27.html

So just how dangerous is South Africa? Is living here like being a trapped animal? For me, it is. We have certain freedoms in terms of space, and fresh air, and sunshine, but we've also given up many many personal freedoms such as the freedom to be pedestrians, the freedom to send our children to school by bicycle, the freedom to enjoy public transport, the sense of security that comes from a crime being committed and then prosecuted. If a crime is committed, the last people South Africans call, in fact, is the police. My brother was attacked at his residence a few months ago and he made three phone calls. To my father, to a security company and to the police. He saw the intruders outside when he made these calls.

My father arrived on the scene first, with a huge dog, and the animal did what it thought was its duty.

The security company arrived next, and despite pleas from one of the attackers, the security guard did not come to the attacker's aid.

As far as I know, the police never responded to the call.

Before I end of this section, and before we get to the incident itself, let's look at what happens when you 'take on Oscar Pistorius'. Let's look at how one is treated and whether one can expect 'justice' or 'injustice' within these circumstances. Here's the excerpt from ENCA.co.za. [Note, <u>underlined emphasis</u> by the author]:

MW: Can you talk me through the events of what happened on the night of the incident?

CTM: On the 12th of September 2009, I attended a party at Oscar's house. He was dating a friend of mine and it was the second time I had met him. I, along with two other friends, arrived late as we had been at our part-time student jobs. The party was held out in his garden and I sat with my girlfriends. During the night, <u>Oscar and Melissa had a fight</u>. This led to <u>Oscar asking all of Melissa's friends to leave (using vulgar language)</u> which included myself. I had left my handbag in the garden where we all had been sitting and needed to get back into his property to fetch it (we had all gone outside with Melissa). As I approached his large outside doors, <u>Oscar was furiously trying to close them. He started to punch the door and that is when one of the top panels fell and hit my left leg</u>. Six weeks prior to the party my plaster cast had just come off after having reconstructive surgery on my left ankle. After this happened I went to tell Oscar that he had hurt me, to which he replied <u>"well go call your f**king lawyer"</u>.

MW: What did you think of OP's behaviour?

CTM: I thought it was <u>aggressive and unreasonable</u>.

MW: Did this surprise you? Had he shown any previous volatile behaviour while he was dating Melissa?

CTM: Yes it did. Not that I knew of.

MW: Why did you choose to go to the police and open a case?

CTM: After the incident at Oscar's house I arrived home and was <u>hysterically crying</u>. Like any loving parents would do, my parents wanted to protect me and my mom and felt it was best to let the police deal with the matter and for them to decide what should be done. The police saw the cut on my leg and they thought it would be best to open a case of assault against Oscar.

MW: He claims you were drunk. Were you?

CTM: I was most certainly not drunk! The police who interviewed me after the incident never asked to test me for alcohol.

MW: There were also suggestions from his camp that you were chasing the money and the fame?

CTM: That is incorrect. <u>All I wanted was an apology from Oscar</u> and the settlement of the legal fees. I have never made a public appearance or even approached the media about it.

MW: What kind of treatment were you subjected to after the incident?

CTM: <u>I was utterly harassed</u>. I was harassed by the media as well as the public. I received hate mail on a daily basis. People who didn't know me from a bar of soap were calling me the most horrific names. It became so difficult at a stage that I needed a bodyguard when I went out in public due to all the hate rants.

MW: Did you expect the matter to drag out for as long as it did?

CTM: No, definitely not. I would never have thought that I would still be dealing with all of this to this day.

MW: How was it ultimately resolved and how do you feel about it now?

CTM: Oscar eventually dropped his case against me, but I didn't drop mine against him. It has ultimately been resolved through a settlement in December 2013. Some days I wish I had never gone through with it all, but <u>I stood up for myself, which was extremely difficult, especially when you feel like the whole country is against you</u>. But I'm proud of the fact that I never backed down and I learned that you should always stand up for what is right, even when you stand alone.

MW: Would you say what the settlement was and why you agreed to it?

CTM: Oscar settled the legal fees but <u>I did not receive an apology</u>. <u>I agreed to it because I was so tired of it weighing me down</u>, I wanted to put this incident behind me.

MW: What was your reaction when you heard about Reeva being shot?

CTM: I was shocked and once I learned more about it, I was heartbroken for all of those who had lost Reeva.

MW: Does this murder case surprise you considering OP's behaviour in the past?

CTM: I don't wish to answer.

MW: How did OP's family behave towards you during this process?

CTM: I don't wish to answer.

http://ewn.co.za/2014/02/12/EWN-Exclusive-Taylor-Memmory-speaks-on-Oscar-Pistorius

Earlier in this narrative I made a shocking revelation. Well, it might shock some. I said if I could leave South Africa, I would. Well, in 2010 I did travel to Australia to do exactly that. To check out the scene. Unfortunately the boat has since sailed, one can only apply for citizenship to Australia up to the age of 40, and I am now just over 40. Also, Australia (and New Zealand) are hellishly expensive. They are also nanny states, and there is something tough, and resilient, and heroic about our common struggles here.

Certainly, there's never a dull moment with our news coverage, and our bevy of interesting politicians and countrymen, and with the Oscar Pistorius trial dominating the world's airwaves, the print media, online and social media, we're reminded that *a lot* is happening here. So if anything, as long as you manage to stay alive, you're rewarded with the nugget that your life here won't be boring. (Hey, being bored is like being dead). The wildlife and the landscapes in this country are unbeatable. So it's not a case that for me personally, I hate being here. But I do feel a continuous nagging sense of anxiety, about crime, about the difficulty of trusting the authorities here (municipal, police, political, judicial). I don't hate being here, yes, but if offered the choice, I would live somewhere else. Canada. New Zealand. Scotland. Or Australia.

I hope the Oscar Pistorius trial shines a massive spotlight on this country, and shows the dirt and crime. I think it has, but I also think it is nowhere near enough. There's a lot more that isn't working, our court systems are dysfunctional and hugely backlogged in general. Our prisons are overcrowded. I think there is a culture of corruption in this country that needs to be addressed. It's a lot more widespread than South Africans know or realise. There's widespread collusion at almost every conceivable level. In terms of the law, it will be great, for a start, if cameras can be placed in many more courtrooms (and police stations) and the public and media can get more and more involved in seeing justice done.

Since I can't leave South Africa right now, other than making the occasional foray to Namibia, or London (despite the discontinuous threat of imprisonment when one approaches passport control), or Iceland (wherever my freelancing spirit takes me) I will make the best of it. It's not that hard to do. There is plenty to love about this county. And we do have the freedom to travel elsewhere so when one needs a break, take that break. But I do maintain now what I said five years ago in this blog post:

As for me, I'd leave if I could. I love the food, the weather, the environment. The problem is <u>the people</u> - the criminal element I mean. There are thousands more just like me, trapped in a country, filled with mixed feelings of enjoyment and dread.

http://www.nickvanderleek.com/2009/03/just-how-dangerous-is-south-africa.html

I'm serious. Why wouldn't you leave if our prospects elsewhere might be better, and brighter? If better, more judicious systems still remain elsewhere, why shouldn't we – we who hold law and order in high regard, we who have the means, and good lives left to live – flee to safer havens? Hence, I shared this particular article on Facebook today, crying: "Take me with you!"

http://www.news24.com/SouthAfrica/News/South-Africans-thriving-in-US-20140802

It's important to maintain the right perspective, and a sense of humour, given our not simple or easy circumstances here in South Africa. I realise it is a small minority, perhaps 100 000, perhaps 500 000, corrupt leaders, and criminals and opportunists, who do enough to ruin the faith of everyone else. It's a few hoodlums hijacking the joy of living for all their fellow citizens. Yes, we are the 99%, the 50 million others who care about an equitable society, but as things stand right now, do most of us trust the mechanisms that operate throughout this land? How can you, when you can't even rely on the lights staying on, or water flowing out of the taps? How can you when the president is seemingly above the law (and immune to the Public Prosecutor).

Is a tiny minority of selfish, malevolent South Africans spoiling it for the rest of us? Perhaps that is naïve. Perhaps if 25% of my countrymen are unemployed, the number of evil men roaming the streets is a lot higher. I hope not. I'd like to believe we are better than that.

*http://mentalfloss.com/article/12794/50-prison-slang-words-make-you-sound-tough-guy

Author's Final Note:

The next, the fifth eBook in this series is *Restitutio*. In it we'll look at how the IAAF ought to handle the plight of disabled athletes fairly – and honestly – going forward. We'll get the views from Dr Ross Tucker. We'll listen to what some of those that knew Reeva personally have to say about her.

If it's not obvious by now, all five books have been a tribute – of some sort – to Reeva Steenkamp. Her image is on every cover, and her initials, R and S. But *Restitutio* aims to do a far better job at finding something affirming out of this colossal myopia, than the four preceding narratives combined.

We'll begin the process of turning this whole narrative around, and investigate how we can turn a negative – the loss of an entire life – into a positive. Is it even possible? It may be. If it is, we can find out by answering – as innocent as children – a few simple questions, and then attempting to find answers. One of the questions we'll be asking is an apparently elementary one:

How can we learn from our mistakes?

But right next to this question are a few more that are less easy to answer. Why are we so afraid of being wrong? What is the nature of transcendence (away from the Oscar Trial), in our personal lives. And in *our* world. One of the ways we'll address these questions is by seeing what we can learn from Kathryn Schulz.

Schulz is the author of Being Wrong, Adventures in the margin of error. Schulz writes that *looking for counterevidence – as I have – often requires time, energy, learning, liberty, and sufficient social capital –* that's you *– to weather the suspicion and derision of defenders of the status quo.*

It's especially tough to find counterevidence in a society that is up to its eyeballs in collusion. As ours is. But, it's not impossible. And the benefits, the revelations, the RESURRECTIONs, the liberties and the joys that flow out of all these newfound freedoms are immense. And worthwhile.

I'm happy to say, yes, it's time to turn this exhausting, negative narrative into something affirming. I think Reeva would like that. I like the idea of a bursary, in her name, which goes to a female student interested in studying law. Perhaps, if we – her supporters – can come together collectively, we can put something together. Perhaps we can achieve something genuine, an authentic *restitutio ad integrum*.

But before we get there, something remains to be done. Yes, we're finally here. After ducking and diving throughout the course of the entire narrative that *Revelations* is, we have ultimately come to face the music. The music of the door. The challenge for us in the next section is to not get lost in the myopia

http://www.allaboutvision.com/conditions/myopia.htm

of the incident. In other words, what Juror13 and I will attempt to do in the next, the last chapter, is try see the wood for the trees, and also, to see the trees, and their leaves, and feel – intuit – how the winds of fate really blew that night, through the mysterious woods that are Love and Loss. Only once we can do that, and do that with courage, and through collaboration, holding hands and taking a long look at the cold, hard truth, can we begin to lift our sails and swing our prows towards dreams of Restitutio.

The Method – and the Madness

Insanity – mental illness of such a severe nature that a person cannot distinguish fantasy from reality, cannot conduct her/his affairs due to psychosis, or is subject to uncontrollable impulsive behaviour.

[**Disclaimer:** the entire scenario below (including the *Notes*, *Juror 13 Annexure* ~~and the Script~~) is presented in the present tense, in the form of an obviously fictionalised narrative, followed by in-depth analysis. These scenarios and comments follow the schedule as the actual events of 13 and 14 February 2013 *may* have unfolded. It is not meant as a definitive treatise, merely a *thought experiment*.

While certain events may or may not have taken place, the author will use a certain level of license to assert that a certain action *could have* taken place. However, to strengthen the narrative, words such as 'seem', 'may have' and 'perhaps' will for the most part be left out of this section.

Appended to this section, besides the bail affidavit and plea, is a second, third and fourth section which includes *Notes*, showing how and where certain events are drawn from, and a *Juror 13 Annexure* evaluated by the American analyst, *Juror13*. The *Juror 13 Annexure* provides an alternative of 'Extended Version' in a sense, with more in-depth analysis of some of the pertinent questions and answers raised by *Revelations*.

Note: All *Juror13* commentary below is highlighted in **bold**.

Note: *Italicised sections refer to Oscar's own words* from his *affidavit*, *plea statement* and *testimony-in-chief*.

~~Last, and possibly least important, a *Scripted* version is provided which may provide an emotional reality to the scene, or not. The reader must decide whether the latter rings true, and if not, why not.~~

Suggestions re ~~to enhance~~ the 'Script' can be emailed to nickvanderleek@gmail.com or tweeted to @HiRezLife. **Thank you for reading.**]

Clinical Version of 'The Incident'

On the afternoon of February 13, just hours before the shooting, Pistorius attended the 10th birthday party of Firzt, the estate agency he was buying the house from. One of the staff attendees, Valerie Berkow-Kaye, [subsequently] tweeted:

"He delighted all of us with his interesting childhood stories and was most charming and personable. It is clearly a very tragic accident."[1]

Or was it?

When Oscar pulls up onto the driveway, in his white BMW, just after 6pm on a muggy Wednesday evening in February 2013, he's in an irritable mood[2]. A business meeting earlier in the day hasn't gone well[3], and a meeting with a physio to treat his injured shoulder has been tedious because the doctor ran out of needles. He's also been to see a dentist and must return to the same dentist the next morning.

Most of all he's let down because a party he's attended with his realtor, in effect celebrating a massive new investment, he's had to attend without Reeva[4].

Also, it's been a struggle trying to get his girlfriend Reeva involved in his plans, and as things are coming to a head, as deadlines are advancing and urgency is setting in, she's getting even more slippery, because she doesn't want to spend the night. She won't commit.

He notices her mini Cooper parked in the driveway. It's just past 6pm. Peak hour traffic is almost over and Reeva's intending to leave soon. It's been a blistering hot day (33 degrees Celsius), yes, one of those energy sapping days.[5]

He arrives to a locked door and the dogs running round the outside of the garden.

On the 13th of February 2013 Reeva would have gone out with her friends and I with my friends. Reeva then called me and asked that we rather spend the evening at home.

I agreed and we were content to have a quiet dinner together at home.

Actually that's not quite correct. On many occasions on the 13th Oscar had asked Reeva, again and again[6], to please stay over. Not exactly begging her, but perhaps making her feel obligated in a sense, and possibly she would have felt guilty if she'd insisted on attending her function with Nimue, or simply going home.

Reeva had slept over on the 12th, so what was the big deal about not sleeping over on the 13th? Quite a few things. Contracts were being discussed, details were being confirmed, and the news for Oscar wasn't good. Capacity Relations didn't feel Oscar was good for her brand, and telling him this was likely to ignite an emotional brushfire with him. Reeva knew this.

She wanted to avoid a confrontation,

15:46 RS: Angel I'm going to go home at like 6pm[7].

That's why she sent a message to Oscar rather than directly over the phone, when he would try to talk her down.

She also spoke to her mother that day[8].

I [Juror13] take this to mean she is going to <u>her</u> home. At this time she was still at Oscar's house, per tower pinging. Oscar calls her 8 minutes later while he is with Justin Divaris and Samantha Gryvenstein at Justin's dealership in Johannesburg... probably to convince her to stay at his house and he will come home.

She had obligations to her career, commitments she means to keep, but wants to console him if she can. And he needed consoling.

At 15:54:27 – yes, 8 minutes after her message - Oscar calls her again and speaks to her for two minutes **(she's still at his house)**.

Whatever they discuss and decide, it's sufficient for Reeva to change her plans at the last minute. She cancels her engagement with an important client she represents – Nimue – but only <u>45 minutes</u> after Oscar's last call[9] to her. It's likely that Reeva struggled to make a call on this. Duty or loyalty? Duty to a man, or loyalty to a brand? Even though she changed her plans (ie not to attend the Nimue function), at that time she *still intended* sleeping in Johannesburg. Oscar tries to create the impression that she contacted 'a friend' Gina Myers early on[10], telling her her intention is to stay the night, but this only takes place after 10pm, very late in the evening to finally settle on one's Valentine's Eve plans, not so? And what are those plans? To stay home and do nothing. Well, to argue.
https://www.youtube.com/watch?v=cMMdyuXfFUg

By about 22h00 on 13 February 2013 we were in our bedroom. She was doing her yoga exercises and I was in bed watching television.

My prosthetic legs were off. We were deeply in love and I could not be happier. I know she felt the same way. She had given me a present for Valentine's Day but asked me only to open it the next day. After Reeva finished her yoga exercises she got into bed and we both fell asleep.

Easy cowboy, slowdown. Let's go back to 6pm standing at the front door[11]. The door is locked (nice and secure), the dogs are on duty running around outside (nice and secure) and Reeva's also on duty, in the kitchen, preparing a meal. It's all exactly as you might expect.

"I chatted to her for a short time. I went upstairs then, I wanted to get out...of the clothes I'd been in, for the day."[12]

And then, stepping inside… What happened next?

Even in Oscar's own version to Barry Roux very little happened. It's very disassociated. He finds Reeva in the kitchen cooking. There's a brief interaction, and then, he's upstairs taking a shower and changing into pajamas for the next hour.

Hold on. Taking a *shower*?[13]

No, no. Running a bath.

And was he on his iPad[14], possibly checking emails, possibly surfing porn, possibly answering early Valentine's Day fan mail? He tells Barry Roux he was on it all day, possibly even in the bath (but he can't remember that last part for certain).

What time did you eat?[15]

Uhh…I started dinner, we started dinner shortly after seven, my Lady.

Another slip, Oscar? Did *you* start cooking dinner at seven or did the two of you start *eating* dinner at seven? Or neither? [16]

"We started dinner shortly after seven…uh seven pm (really, not am?)…

Roux: is this why your iPad shows now activity between 19:10 and 20:00?

that sounds about right my Lady…that, that would be correct, my Lady."[17]

He doesn't sound too sure of himself, though. What if, by seven you *weren't* cooking or *eating* what *could* you have been doing instead?

Arguing.[18]

About what?

Oscar admits to discussing contracts with Reeva that day[18] (in the early evening), because he was helping her with the details.

After they ate, they sat at the dining room table and chatted about Oscar's day and Reeva's new work contract[19].

Reeva's work from that day was on the table and <u>she asked Oscar to go through her modeling contract that she was about to sign</u>. He went through it and made some changes for her that he felt were in HER best interest.

And then the downstairs portion is over.[20]

It's all very thin, Oscar's testimony of what took place between 6pm and 8pm. In fact the total explanation time is about 1 minute, although it feels much longer.[21]

I agree with *Juror13* that Oscar does badly even in this harmless section of the evening.

Oscar really fumbles here. He starts to say again that Reeva was in the kitchen (almost as if this part is rehearsed), but he says he was also talking on his iPad... then he says he was surfing the net... he was looking at cars[22] that he wanted to get around to that day to get a look at...

His sentences were very broken and honestly didn't make a lot of sense...probably [because] he is ... not telling the whole truth of that day...his nervousness and fumbling is very telling...

They'd argued for the first two hours, and then reconciled. But there was still a brittle tension between the two. They'd argued, they'd surrendered but it was a fragile peace.

Cos right now I know u aren't happy and I am certainly very unhappy and sad.

Oscar couldn't get over the fact that he was about to move into an empty house

And be travelling alone, for months at a time – again

And that Reeva was putting her career above one of the greatest icons in the world – the nerve!

Reeva was getting nervous at the huge amount of pressure involved in being Oscar's girlfriend.

Towing the line with her agency.

Towing the line with him (or trying to)

And walking the razor edges of positive public opinion and celebrity apocalypse.

We are living in a double standard relationship where you can be mad about how I deal with stuff when you are very quick to act cold and offish when you're unhappy

286 Bushwillow Crescent even quite early on the night of 13 February wasn't a happy place for either of them, but they tried to put it behind them.

Tried, but failed.

Testimony is disassociated, very little quotes from what was actually said, which implies most of what was said can't be repeated, because it would make him look bad.

Because it wars probably the same refrain again:

I get snapped at!

Stop chewing gum.

Do this don't do that.

You don't want to hear stuff; cut me off.

I'm also the girl that gets sidestepped when you are in a shit mood.

Your endorsements; your reputation; your impressions; blowing shit out of proportion and fucking up another special day for me.

And for him?

I wanted to show her, why I (Oscar), cannot go to functions.

I wanted to show her, why I (Oscar), have to sleep.

I wanted to show her, why I (Oscar), cannot go to events.

Why I (Oscar) am on a strict diet[23]

Those must have been things that they argued about, or things she (Reeva) couldn't understand.

Specific routine, specific diets, specific rest and recovery periods – must Reeva fit in with *all* that? And deal with his moods[24]

I do everything to make you happy and you do everything to throw tantrums

We are living in a double standard relationship where you can be mad about how I deal with stuff when you are very quick to act cold and offish when you're unhappy.

I am not some other bitch you may know trying to kill your vibe.

I'm sorry that you think that little of me.

I'm scared of you sometimes and how you snap at me

And of how you will react to me.

Oscar's on his iPad. With Peet[25].

Trying to sort out her shit.

Contracts, air tickets, Peet, focused on the iPad…this is the real source of the night's tension.

Is she on board or not?

Is she coming?

They want an answer?

And Reeva is feeling the pressure. And all she wants to do is go home. But it's too late for that now.

So they'd argued for the past hour – about her not joining Oscar in Manchester.

And after 8pm[26]?

Reeva was on her phone [and] on social media[27], [according to Oscar] occasionally showing him pictures of cars and interior decorating, things that she liked.

He very specifically added "things that she liked".

Again – Oscar's trying to steer our inferences to her willingness to move in with him. She'll decorate[28].

What we do know for certain was that after a period of intense arguing, both of them went back to their own devices for a while.

Since he and his cousin were continually texting back and forth, he figured he'd just call him at that point.

20:25:07 – Oscar - Outgoing call to 3964 (Graham, cousin) – 1,757 seconds (29 min) – tower closest to Oscar's. This was the last voice call made prior to the shooting.

29 minutes! That is one whopper of a call slap bang in the centre of Oscar's romantic evening together!

While Oscar is on the phone, Reeva got out of bed and was doing yoga stretches on the floor. He had the phone on speaker. Every now and again Reeva would lean up and give him a kiss.

I don't think so. I don't think they are talking about redecorating either. They may have reconciled, but it's an uneasy truce, and both were still feeling shaken, and prickly. Both were feeling guilty and invalidated, especially Oscar, who has designs on marrying Reeva, but even greater designs on using her to leverage his career…but she doesn't want to be involved! (The nerve of this chick!)

And Reeva knew she would have followed her intuition; she's wishing she'd gone home at six after all. But now it's too late. The steamy humidity that night also does nothing to cool things down between the overheated pair.

Juror13 reinforces this impression: **Now, if Oscar and Reeva had been arguing about contracts just an hour or two earlier, would she be lovey dovey and kissing him. I highly doubt it. I think Oscar greatly embellished when he said that Reeva was kissing him. She very well may have been in the other room doing her yoga, blowing off steam.**

The important point here is that even in Oscar's own testimony, they were simply *not together*.

Then, at around 9pm or 10 pm they settled in for the night. Oscar testified: When asked when he fell asleep he first says just after 9pm. Then he says between 9pm and 10pm.

Since Oscar was often up at 5am, 9pm or 10pm sounds right (and that would be an 8 hour sleep)[27]. Perhaps she was in bed with him, perhaps she was downstairs working, or sleeping elsewhere. There is a short but distinct choke and tremble in Oscar's voice during his testimony, where he says both of them went upstairs[29].

Finally, sometime after 10pm Reeva finally communicates her fatal decision, a decision that will ultimately cost her life. It's tired and humourless, and ultimately, she will *not* see them or anyone else besides Oscar tomorrow, or ever again. Her sleep, in a few hours will permanent.

Hi guys, I'm too tired. It's too far to drive. I'm sleeping at Oscar's tonight. See you tomorrow[30].

Reeva's not happy, and not in the mood to cuddle. She may be feeling pushed around, and thus very reluctant to go upstairs, or so she may have chosen, initially, not to join Oscar upstairs to begin with (she may have elected to sleep downstairs in the lounge, on the sofa). In any event Oscar's description of watching television together in bed and looking at car's online feels artificial. Nevertheless, it's possible both of them tried to go to sleep at around 10pm. Tried, but failed[31].

While they lay in bed together, he couldn't sleep, was anxious, and this failure to sleep on his part, was an additional irritant adding to the interminable tension that was welling up that Valentine's eve. They may be lying in bed together, still nursing a tense silence, with Oscar breaking it now and again to raise a complaint about how unreliable, how untrustworthy she was. How unhappy he is to be travelling abroad by himself. She'll respond, calmly, and soothingly and try to console him but he won't stop, and so eventually, in a huff she gets up and goes downstairs. Hungry, she eats alone in the cold light of his kitchen.

She looks up at the clock. It's moving on to 2am. She puts a plate in the basin. This is to be her last supper.

Then, wordlessly she goes back to bed. She pads softly upstairs and finds Oscar awake, working on his iPad. He says nothing to her. She slips into bed beside him, and lies there, blinking at the wall. How to resolve this impossible situation with this impossible man[32].

Then a critical connection at a critical time:

01:48:48am Feb 14 – Oscar – GPRS[33] – 309 seconds (5 min) – tower closest to Oscar's

Reeva, lying beside Oscar[33a] turns around in bed, and sees what he is doing on his iPad.

Oscar then says "My Lady, that's the moment that everything changed".

Everything did change in a moment. But there will be two moments, two points of no return. **This was the first.**

I'm sorry that u think that little of me

Every 5 seconds I hear how you dated another chick.

I get snapped at

Stop chewing gum. Do this don't do that. You don't want to hear stuff cut me off.

Your endorsements your reputation your impression of someone innocent blown out of proportion.

You f***ed up a special day for me.

I'm terribly disappointed.

In how the day ended and how you left me

Estelle van der Merwe is awake.[34] She hears something along these lines, mostly from Reeva, who now feels distraught, betrayed and hysterical.

Van der Merwe, who lived just under 100 metres from Pistorius' Pretoria house, said she was woken just before 2am on St Valentine's Day by the row. *This* was the row. And it kicks off with a GPRS connection initiating at **01:48:48am**[35]. It lasts 5 minutes.

At 1:56am the argument that is to last for over an hour and end sometime around 3:15[35a] with 4 shots through a door, begins.

It is prompted by jealousy, yes[36]. And anger. Reeva is appalled and having made her feelings clear, is now adamant that she wants to leave. Most people would under similar circumstances. For an hour Oscar and Reeva joust verbally. But Oscar's reaction is what truly terrifies her. Becomes *unhinged*.

Reeva moves to take her things.

Oscar throws aside the duvet, and puts on his prosthetic legs so he can stop her.

She's packed and ready to go, and about to get dressed.

Even though he's disabled, with his legs on he's bigger and stronger than her. And he won't let her leave. She throws the duvet at him, tries to dive past him. But he's too quick. There's something about his demeanour that is beyond ordinary emotions, it's almost mercenary, and it scares the crap out of her.

She tries to put on a pair of jeans, but he pulls it out of her hands and throws it on the floor. The edge lands on the lip of the duvet, which is lying on the floor.

He tells her she won't be going anywhere, *put your shit down,* and *just go to sleep. We'll sort it out in the morning.*

He has to do damage control, not just with Reeva emotionally, but to make sure this doesn't get out into the media.

OSCAR THE CHEAT

No, he can't have that.

ABUSIVE OSCAR CHEATS ON HIS VALENTINE

No, at all costs, that has to be prevented. But it's not looking good.

The bottom-line is that *Oscar won't let Reeva go*.

Reeva runs downstairs, to get away from him. He follows her, but she's able to evade him. Perhaps she manages to open the door and go outside. But she needs her keys, and her phone.

She enters the house again, dodges Oscar, runs upstairs and locks him out [during the course of the entire night the alarm is deactivated].

He insists that she let him in. Enraged, he begins hammering on the bedroom door. Reeva panics, grabs a pair of jeans (perhaps she places her car keys in it) and throws it out the bathroom window. Oscar is still banging on the door, and then there's a BANG!

She's startled by this. She knows Oscar has guns in the house and he's just used one! He's also got a gun in the fucking bedroom!

But she can see he's going to break through that door eventually. It will be better if she lets him in, than if he breaks his way through. But once she lets him inside she'll have one chance to get around him. He's out of control!

It's now a few minutes past 3am. She's defeated. She can't run away. He stands on the other side of the bedroom door, so she can't get to her car. But she has her phone.

But if she's vulnerable, he's vulnerable too. Maybe she has a card to play too. Maybe she can *trick* him[38].

What does Oscar fear more than anything – being found out, for his sins, by the media.

And without his legs he's like Superman carrying a chain of Kryptonite around his neck, right?

And Reeva's fit and strong, she boxes to keep fit, she hits a punching bag to stay in shape…

So, knowing the gloves are off now, it's all or nothing, she warns him:

"Oscar if you don't stop this now, I'm calling the police. I'm calling the police, do you hear me! If I do that your career is over! I don't want to-."

That's when he breaks down the door. They scuffle. She screams. She pushes him. He falls over like a ton of bricks. She's got to get away, but she can only do that if he's lost his legs.

She grabs the foot end of his legs. She pulls off the first one quite easily and tosses it aside. But when she goes for the second he kicks her smartly – a glancing blow with his rubber toe (covered in a sock) in the face; on the nose. Humiliated, he curses her. She struggles to get hold of the second leg, and he kicks her again, but he's useless on one leg. Her nose begins to bleed[37].

All she has to do is get a headstart, then she'll be away. But she also knows he's a Paralympian. And if she makes a run for it she won't have much time, he's going to do everything he can to stop her.

But she can't get past him to freedom! He's on his stumps but blocking the door. The look on his face says it all.

I'm going to kill you!

She screams. She can't get past him, through the bedroom door, and is horrified to see Oscar running on his stumps towards her a look of sheer malice on his face. She pushes him over again, and runs screaming to the toilet, closing the door and locking it.

I felt trapped.

Oscar reaches the door moments later, his stumps bruised, hurting. He curses. He's out of breath. He bangs on the door with his fists. Hits it with his shoulder. Hanging in the ether now is her earlier threat. To call the police.

To end him.

This is the slow burn eating away the last minutes of two lives.

"Get the fuck out of my house!" he screams, hurt that she's gotten the better of him, hurt that she's seen him hobbling like a dwarf. He feels humiliated, embarrassed and angry.

"Get the fuck out of my house!" he screams again. He has to get to her, get to that phone! He does what he did to the first door; he rushes to fetch a bat. But he wants something more solid.

There's no time.

Got to get to her!

Got to get through that door!

I have to stop her!

He chooses the cricket bat. No time to put on his legs.

He returns, turns on the lights, and whallops the door.

But he's different man on his stumps. Not Superman. Not the Bladerunner. Not even a man. He falls. Another searing pain from his stumps. He's heartbroken, enraged, panicked and chronically fatigued from lack of sleep.

Inside the small dark space, each BLAM of the bat on the door is deafening. Reeva's felt safe until that moment, but now she screams, her screams growing in intensity with each blow.

From her side she sees the wood crack; she can see light through the other side. In the slit of wood she can make out Oscar[37a], the legless halfman lurching in the bright light of the bathroom. It's monstrous!

"Get the fuck out of my house!"

She screams as loud as she can.

Just give me the fucking phone!

Just let me go!

She screams that he had better let her go now, or she's calling the police. This time she's going to do it. And if the police come his career is over. Stop now, let me go or I'm calling the police. I'm NOT bullshitting you Oscar.

The shit just got real...

STOP NOW

OR I'M CALLING...

And this was the second point of no return.

Oscar, beating on the door, hesitates. He hears the sound, *like a window opening*, as Reeva 'opens' her smartphone. Oscar sees the faint light of her phone shining from the direction of the bathroom. He wants to...needs to extinguish that light!

SHIT! FUCK!

He feels a sense of terror rushing over him.

There was no time to think.

He rushes to the bed, on his stumps, the pain stinging through his bones. He snatches at the holster, pulls the silver Taurus Parabellum from its holster, and ambulates as fast as he can back to the toilet. Reeva's still screaming. The moment he has line of sight, he supports himself against the bathroom wall with his left shoulder, and *fires at the phone*[38a/39].

The recoil knocks him over. His face close to the floor, he tries to regain his position against wall. Then the shock of it hits him. The noise in the enclosed space. The red hot fire of his stumps.

He's just shot a person. How to cover *that shit* up?

He pauses just one moment more. Takes stock.

In a second time can stand still.

It does. Two lives stand at a precipice. One already lost, the other beginning to gush blood.

A whirlpool of dreams…a candle, snuffed out.

He hears Reeva fall. Hears the phone drop. Hears her scream in pain. It sounds like she's fallen on the magazine rack.

your impression of someone innocent

blown out of proportion

and f***ed up a special day for me.

He suddenly sees the terror of it, the horror of it, and the absolute simplicity of it. This was *never* going to work out. It's sure as hell not working out now. He must take her life, so that he can resume his. A simple trade.

He'll take her life so that he can have his back. The whole evening is a mess. She was never going to love him. And no chance in hell after tonight. Now he has a chance to clean it up. His way. Shut her up. *Get rid of her*. It will be so easy. He has the media, the cops eating out of his hands… All he has to do is make up a stor –

Reeva screams and he fires again[40].

But it's a miss.

In an instant he fires two more shots[41], following the sound of her screaming and the faint visual he has of her through a crack in the door.

It's 03:14.59[42]. His ears are ringing.

But instantly he is thinking of covering it up.

So he rushes to the balcony, and shouts loudly, "HELP HELP HELP[43]."

Oscar then puts on his prosthesis…

I thought she was a burglar.

I heard a sound…a door, no a window opening...

He grabs the cricket bat and runs back to the door. He clobbers it three times before the panel smashes through on the other side. He grabs the key, lets himself in.

What a mess!

He uses the toilet to try to drain the blood from her body[43a]. As he does so a bullet casing drops into the bowl. He's got to get her out of there. He can't have photos of this in the newspapers. He's got to clean it up, get her to a hospital.

Hospital! He has to make it look like he's rescuing her and…and mess up the scene.

He's got to phone someone. Make it seem as though he's calling for help.

Stander …Divaris…

SHIT! What about her phone? Did she get through? He lunges at it. He can't make it out but it looks like she didn't get through.

That's when he notices she's still alive. Barely breathing.

What a fucking mess you've made!

He puts his fingers in her mouth, and yes, he can feel she is breathing. He squeezes his fingers firmly, blocking her airway. There's a weak shudder, as the last of her life ebbs away.

Reeva's time of death is approximately 03:17.

At 03:19 he calls Stander. The Estate manager. They're good friends and he can take care of things.

For good measure he calls security, then cancels the call.

When security calls back, Oscar's annoyed. He doesn't want anyone in the house, so he says – to Pieter Baba[44], "Everything's fine."

He finds some towels and mops up some of the blood[45]. He rushes back to the bedroom to fetch his and her other handsets and drops them on the bathroom mat. The police can seize those.

According to call logs he calls Netcare 911, talks to them for a minute. We can't say for sure what he said to them, but it's certain they didn't tell him to move the body, and he didn't give them information that resulted in the dispatch of the ambulance. To date – besides the digital timestamp, there is no record of this call.

He runs downstairs, unlocks and starts his car. He leaves the front door open so that Stander can get in without him having to come out. He needs to fuck up the crime scene some more.

He carries her bag to the chair, takes out her toiletries and puts them in the bathroom. He hears something outside. No time to sort out the jeans…

He picks Reeva up and carries her downstairs. She's already dead, but a lot of blood is still draining out of her body. An arterial spurt, on the walls along the stairway, is not due to her heart pumping, but the pressure of Oscar holding her, trying to balance, and squeezing her broken body.

Baba, Stander and his daughter are horrified by what they see. Oscar shouts how relieved he is to see them. Begs them to help him take her to hospital.

"Haven't you called the ambulance?" "They said there's no time, I must take her to the hospital."

Carice, seeing part of Reeva's arm danging on sinews and shattered bone, and blood still seeping out of it, begs Oscar to put Reeva down. He does. Tells her she's breathing, he's keeping her airway open. She asks him to fetch something to stop the blood loss, but he won't leave her body. She fetches it herself. He fetches a few black bags, suggests transporting her in Johan Stander's car…[46]

When Stipp arrives[47], havoing detoured to the gatehouse security to make sure it's safe, arrives to find no ambulance is on its way. Oscar doesn't seem to have called one, neither has Johan Stander or his daughter. It appears Stander is outside, on the phone to someone when Stipp arrives. Stipps ETA is +- 03:25[47a]

"He looked sincere to me[48],*" Stipp said of observing Pistorius minutes after he'd fatally shot his girlfriend. "He was crying. There were tears on his face."*

"At the bottom of the stairs ... there was a lady lying on her back on the floor," Stipp said of his first observations.

"I went near her and as I bent down, I also noticed a man on the left kneeling by her side. He had his left hand on her right groin, and his right hand, the second and third fingers in her mouth."

Stipp found Reeva's corneas were turning milky, a process which takes at least 5 minutes.

[Interestingly Barry Roux, Oscar himself and Stander all seem allied in thinkly masked contempt for Doctor Stipp. One has to wonder, *why*? Did Stipp foil their best laid plans?[49]]

She'd died upstairs, while Oscar was portraying her as still alive, and in need of help and rescue not that he did much to attend to her himself, besides putting his fingers in mouth, presumably to prevent her either from talking or breathing, and/or provide a sincere-seeming *pretence* of aid[50].

Via http://forums.digitalspy.co.uk/showthread.php?p=71844537:

At 3:27:14 *Dr. Stipp phones security* -**Per the phone logs, he did call security at this time but I believe they determined that it was an accidental call.**

At 3:28 Stander calls Netcare & hands the phone to Dr. Stipp. Stipp is supposed to explain to the ambulance how to get to the estate, but Stander has been living there for around 4 years.

Mrs **Stander** says: I hope this doesn't get out to media.

At 03:55 Oscar calls[51] Justin Divaris.

At 03:59 Stander calls Carl Pistorius on Oscar's behalf (interestingly the friend is called before the brother).

At 4:17am Mr. Stander phones Dr. Stipp to say Oscar's lawyer may be in touch, not the police? In his evidence Stipp he found it strange no one from the police contacted him, despite giving his details to Stander

07:28 Hagen Engler posts a story on Reeva in the Daily Maverick.

08:03: Beeld's breaking news tweet 'officially' announces the incident to the media

Later that morning, 14 February 2013, Cecil Myers visits the morgue in Bronhorstspruit and identifies Reeva's bullet riddled corpse.

Notes:

1. **Source:** http://www.telegraph.co.uk/news/worldnews/oscar-pistorius/10946964/The-luxury-home-where-Oscar-Pistorius-planned-a-life-with-Reeva-Steenkamp.html
2. **Why *irritable*?** Because a *shitty thing* came up in conversation earlier that day, the 13th. Shitty enough for Reeva to suggest Oscar rather spend that night with his siblings, and shitty enough for her to say words to the effect of *at least you have your health, and talents, and supportive people around you.*
Juror13 and I have speculated that the shitty thing was Reeva's revelation to Oscar that she would not be giving up her career anytime soon, thus would not be imminently part of Oscar's career or travel plans. In other words, the shitty thing was a shitty thing for Oscar, not necessarily for Reeva, but Reeva did feel she ought to play a part in consoling him.
Reeva's announcement that she would be putting her career first (at a time when she was really emerging as a model, and actress) was a major setback for him. Remember he was moving to a new home in Johannesburg, ostensibly to be closer to *her*, and had been pleading with her all day that she stay over.
Besides the emotional undertow, on that same Wednesday Oscar testified to receiving treatment for an injured shoulder, and dental treatment (unfinished), and besides these, had made two long calls to his estranged father in short succession. It was also on this day that his agent would try to finalise contracts and air tickets for the pair of them to go to Manchester together, but things weren't looking good on either front. Contract-wise or Reeva joining him on any of those overseas trips.
When he arrived at 6pm she had *not yet decided* to spend the night. Oscar, by his own account, said Wednesday had been a taxing day – for both of them – and as a result both felt too tired to go out (the plan was separately) with friends. Reeva, in her final message to Gina Myers, reinforces this weariness, saying *I'm too tired* further implying that staying overnight with Oscar was a change to an original plan Gina and her father may have been aware of.

So it is *unreasonable* to speculate in this way, that Oscar's mood and mindset was less than sanguine when we arrived home?

3. When advocate **Barry Roux asks Oscar about 'the shitty thing'** Oscar references a business meeting. Whether this is true or not, what we *do* know is something shitty was in the air on the 13th, which provided those first undercurrents of tension before the broiling sun had even set. Oscar also later describes the 13th as 'a taxing day for both of us'. His shoulder hurts, his teeth need treatment and Reeva was ill, suffering from a cold just days before the incident.

4. **No mention is made of this party in court testimony**, perhaps for this very reason – if Reeva is moving in with him, if they're starting a life together, why is she at Capacity Relations discussing her career and commitments with them? Why's she not with him?

5. Weather Report:
http://www.wunderground.com/history/airport/FAPR/2013/2/13/DailyHistory.html?req_city=Pretoria&req_state=&req_statename=South+Africa

6. In Oscar's testimony-in-chief he says that **Reeva's plan that day** was to return to Johannesburg:
https://www.youtube.com/watch?v=cMMdyuXfFUg **32:39-32:52**

7. **Did Oscar call Reeva again and again?** According to Juror13 and cellphone records from Moller, yes:
15:41:54 – Reeva - Incoming voice call from 4949 (Oscar) – 93 seconds – tower closest to Oscar's house
15:46 RS [via whatsapp, ie an almost immediate response, but made via message, not via voice]: Angel I'm going to go home at like 6pm. Please stay and do whatever it was you were gonna do.
15:54:27 – Reeva - Incoming voice call from 0020 (Oscar) – 113 seconds (2 min) – tower closest to Oscar's house (she's still at his house).

8. Here's how Reeva's mother remembers Reeva's version of the relationship:
*I called to ask her if this was a new special friend. She said **she didn't want the public speculation that would come from them being seen together. She wanted to keep a low profile until she was sure it was going to be serious***. A few weeks later, in early December last year, she told me **she had decided to give Oscar all her attention, all her time. She was going to invest in the relationship, she'd made up her mind he was important to her.'**

9. **16: 45 Reeva emails Nimue Skin Technology SA. She is an ambassador for them and apologises that she won't be attending the announcement of a new jewellery line. (source: Nick van der Leek, *Resurrection*). So at this point, has she decided not to go to this event and ... have dinner with Oscar at his house instead?**

10. Tells a friend/Gina 'then' = **early in the evening** (?) that she was going to spend the night at Oscar's. Note the uncertainty and stuttering in his voice between **33:55 – 34:09** at this link:
https://www.youtube.com/watch?v=cMMdyuXfFUg

11. According to Oscar he knocked on the front door just after 6pm, and **Reeva was cooking.**
https://www.youtube.com/watch?v=cMMdyuXfFUg **34:38-34:42**
But why would she have to open the door for him, and also go out grocery shopping if he needed *her* to unlock the door?
Based on the calls at 15:41 and 15:54 it sounds like Oscar was in the vicinity and that *he* went grocery shopping.
Also, why would Reeva already be in the kitchen, preparing a meal . That's not an inference, Oscar says: 'I arrived home and Reeva was preparing dinner in the kitchen.' Really? In the kitchen? And she was dutifully doing this, *before* Oscar arrived, and as early as 6pm?
If it's true – and it may be – Reeva would have emailed Nimue at 16:45 then rushed out to buy groceries (in peak hour traffic) and made it back just before 6pm, in time to start preparing dinner before he arrived.
Some estates do have shopping centres situated nearby, but on Valentine's eve, at 5pm, it's likely the shops and tellers even inside or associated with these estates were busier than usual.
Yes, Reeva may have suggested cooking for him initially, but we know she also had a change of heart that persisted throughout the day and until late in the afternoon. Her intention was to leave that night at 6pm (and that would preclude cooking), and sleep in Johannesburg.
Oscar may have twisted her arm and said *he* would cook for *her*. This would also explain his arriving relatively late (ie a grocery shopping foray). If, on the hand, what Oscar says is true, Reeva would have left the complex after 4pm for one last foray, in order to arrive back by 6pm. Did she? The security estate cameras would show this? But do they? Yes they do:
Did Reeva really leave and come back? And did cameras catch that? The answer is yes and yes. See link to attached pictures.

Here is a summary of the beginning of Baba's testimony:
Baba saw Reeva at 6pm that night when she arrived at the gate. She was alone inside of her car. He spoke with her. They did not phone Oscar's house that night when she arrived because Reeva had already been there earlier that day. They opened the gate and let her in. Oscar arrived a few minutes after Reeva. Baba greeted Oscar and Oscar was on his cell phone [talking to his estranged father Henke ---

[**Correction November 2014:** This is an error, the number actually refers to Jenna Edkins. See 35 for more details.]

In addition, Reeva's cell phone was pinging from a different tower during this communication:

17:44:54 – Reeva - Outgoing call to 0020 (Oscar) – 144 seconds – **she had moved, different tower now.**

Why is it important that Oscar shows Reeva cooking dinner when he gets home? Why does dinner matter? Because Oscar needs – at all costs – to ward off speculations around:
a) An argument
b) Reeva wanting to leave
c) Reeva's feelings/commitment to him not being absolutely 100%
   Her cooking dinner suggests Walton Family-level Wellness.
   http://en.wikipedia.org/wiki/The_Waltons#Story

12. After the flurry of urgent messages throughout the afternoon asking Reeva to stay (and her plan was to leave at 6pm) **Oscar** tells us when he arrives, he simply **chats with her for a short time**, as married couples do, and **then cooly saunters upstairs**. Because *everything's fine*, right?
    https://www.youtube.com/watch?v=cMMdyuXfFUg **35:00-35:15**
    Really? He didn't ask her then and their about her contract? He didn't ask her then and there why why she wanted to go home, why she'd missed the Firzt party, whether she was joining him in Manchester after all (he needed a decision then and there), whether Capacity Relations had said they could tweet about being together on Valeentine's Day, whether – having spent a fortune on a house – she would continue to insist on living on her own in her apartment? Was she in or was she out? Was she committed? What was the problem?

13. **Shower/bath?** *At night I go to the loo without prosthesis but I don't walk around at home without prosthesis,* Pistorius claimed. *I bath rather than shower because I can't stand for long. I sit in the shower.*
    http://www.enca.com/oscar-trial-pistorius-was-completely-sane-when-he-shot-reeva

14. Was he on his iPad? https://www.youtube.com/watch?v=cMMdyuXfFUg **35:57- 36:44**

15. **Who cooked dinner?** https://www.youtube.com/watch?v=cMMdyuXfFUg **38:30-38-40** *"I started dinner…we started dinner…"*

16. Barry Roux suggests that the period from 19:10 to 20:00 **there is no activity of Oscar's iPad** is because they were having dinner. It could also be because they were arguing about their contracts. A lot of contracts were up in the air, or on the table that day. Not least of which a house purchase, whether Reeva would be joining him overseas (no, she wouldn't, as per her contract/instructions with Capacity Relations) and Oscar's contract with Manchester (which he asked be extended to include Reeva, and include a business air ticket for her). But she won't be joining him overseas, and so he tries to bargain with her. She wants to go home, she doesn't want a confrontation, so he tries to bargain with her.
    https://www.youtube.com/watch?v=cMMdyuXfFUg **38:50-39:00**

17. When Barry Roux points out the 'gap' in the iPad's online activity between 7pm and 8pm, and that **one can infer from that that they were having dinner**, Oscar says,

"We started dinner shortly after seven…uh seven pm (not am?)*…that sounds about right my Lady…that, that would be correct, my Lady."*

Juror13 also picks up a weird vibe here: **Nice "leading" questions here… apparently SA is a little more liberal with this [than the USA].**

In *RECIDIVIST ACTS* I covered 911 call analysis and how extraneous information is a clear giveaway when an accused person is guilty. Here Oscar does't say "Yes" or "No" or "That's right." He says it *sounds about right* and *that would be correct*. We're talking about the night someone *got shot to death*. Something sounding *about right* is far too casual! Why say *that would be correct* when you can simply say *yes*?

Why? Let's try to answer that.

Is it in order to disassociate from a possibly untrue version? And let's recall, the time Reeva ate is CRITICAL to piecing together a timeline of the incident. Is it likely she at at 1am if she'd also eaten at 7pm? This is a model serious about her career, serious about what she eats. Is she really comfort eating at 1am so the extent that large amounts of food still remained in her gut hours after digestion and death? No *that would be correct…*doesn't ring true.

18. Arguing could be about Oscar helpfully making **changes to Reeva's contract** (which we may assume was from Capacity Relations, a company she met at 14:15 that day according to Simphiwe Majola). Interestingly Majola only confirms that they discussed Reeva's Valentine's Day speech, not confirmation about a contract. However, Reeva had been working hard that day, so it looks like, with Tropika Island of Treasure and a slew of other appearances and magazine spots, her modelling contract was not only in play, but in need of ~~upgrading~~ updating.
Oscar volunteers in court, evidence that he was involving himself in Reeva's contract (remember, Capacity Relations felt he was not going to be an asset for her brand) in things that could be binding to ~~Oscar~~ Reeva in a negative way. Could this have added fuel to an argumentative fire? Of course it could.

19. https://www.youtube.com/watch?v=cMMdyuXfFUg **39:01 - 40:03** *After dinner we chatted about my day…and Reeva's contract…* Not during dinner? If not during dinner what did you chat about during dinner? Isn't it true that there was *no dinner*, there was just bickering about contracts? What's interesting is **Oscar devotes no more than 1 minute talking about dinner and Reeva's contract**. There's no a single quote to exactly what was said, and it's the contents of the exchange is even more brief if one considers, within that minute, Oscar repeated a third of his story as he was admonished for speaking too quickly. So 40 seconds maximum to describe eating dinner, what was said over dinner, and their 'discussion' about contracts. At the end of all this Oscar talks about it being a 'taxing' day, and while they were usually downstairs, they decided at this relatively early point in the evening to go upstairs. And…*do nothing.*

7:29pm – Peet Van Zyl is emailing the director of the Manchester event to get a ticket for Reeva. This is [supposedly] during their dinner, and when Oscar claims they are discussing HER contracts. Is this the conflict/the real meat of their argument that ties in to what Oscar needed consoling about earlier? – her contracts vs. his contracts + travelling abroad = somebody is going to have to make a sacrifice. It's not going to be Oscar.

20. https://www.youtube.com/watch?v=cMMdyuXfFUg **40:04-40:15**
21. The total testimony time used to elucidate this 2 hour foundation is very short. In fact it's just over a minute. Say what? Just over a minute to describe critical issues such as Reeva's last supper (except it probably *wasn't* at 7pm) and their bickering over contracts. Even though the Youtube clip covering this section begins at **34:40** and ends at **40:04**, don't be fooled, the testimony is way less than 5 minutes. Firstly:
    a) Because it includes two tedious sections where Oscar repeats his testimony (after being admonished first by Masipa, then Roux, for talking too fast and too softly), and
    b) Secondly because a large section **36:42 – 38:32** is *deadtime* with Roux fumbling through files and looking (unsuccessfully) for Exhibit WW (Oscar's iPad activity).
22. There's an interesting **psychological component** to fictionalising a story, and having one (and one's lost beloved) looking at vehicles together. **What is a vehicle**? It is a means of expression, a medium for getting one (or a couple) from one place to another. It is a thing that can transport a couple into a different world.
    But the whole bail affidavit is fictional:
    The balcony door is a metaphor for the bathroom door.
    The fan a metaphor for Reeva (whom he must place, and move and control accordingly)
    The LED light the light of the phone.
    The sound of the window...well...we'll get there.
23. https://www.youtube.com/watch?v=yJ_hUzn5vaY **[24:05** Nel: *then, I've carefully noted* **Mr Pistorius calculated reasons to take Reeva**, *I think to Manchester* [Oscar looks up, chuckling visibly in the background at **24:40**]
24. The moodiest I've ever heard Oscar is during a BBC radio interview. For the entirety of it Oscar sounds subdued, even hungover. A small portion of Oscar sounding *gatvol* on air is provided at this link:
    http://www.telegraph.co.uk/sport/olympics/paralympic-sport/8744690/Oscar-Pistorius-storms-out-of-BBC-interview-after-insulting-question.html
    Cecil Myers described Oscar as *"impatient and very* moody". The impression we get from Arnu Fourie vacating his room, because Oscar was screaming on his phone all the time, is more "moodiness" and "anger". Overall Nel leaves an impression of a *quick-tempered gun-obsessive who was controlling and mood. Reeva uses the word 'tantrums'. What's a tantrum:*
    - Outburst
    - Fit of temper
    - Emotional paroxysm

25. https://www.youtube.com/watch?v=yJ_hUzn5vaY **[15:49 – 16:30]** Nel: *did you discuss the incident with Mr Pistorius*? Peet van Zyl clearly panicked, takes 40 seconds so say yes, no, I don't know. There is so much extraneous info here, including this admission: *a couple of hours before I heard the call* (that Reeva was dead) *I was sending an email* **working on planning these trips for them together**... (Through the audio it is clear as day that Van Zyl is dry-mouthed, highly anxious and seems to be gulping). Why? Because he is fully aware that both he and Oscar were pressuring Reeva that night.

26. **20:04:17 – Reeva's last GPRS activity – 41,029 seconds (over 11 hours) – tower closest to Oscar's. This application remained opened throughout the incident and in to the next day. No details of what this application was, or its contents, were openly discussed in court. The Judge however does have access to this information.**

27. http://www.telegraph.co.uk/news/worldnews/oscar-pistorius/10946964/The-luxury-home-where-Oscar-Pistorius-planned-a-life-with-Reeva-Steenkamp.html

28. If Reeva was **going to move in** with Oscar anytime soon, she would have told her Gina and her mother, but all her mother knew was that it was *very early to be fighting a lot*.

29. Oscar's voice trembles as he mentions Reeva joining him upstairs at https://www.youtube.com/watch?v=cMMdyuXfFUg **40:40 – 40:52**
My intuition tells me that getting her to agree to stay the night was a huge deal, a huge deal for him that she stay, and a huge deal for her, because she was starting to feel bullied and caged in.

30. **Tone suggests too stressed for usual cheerful signoff that was typical of Reeva's messages to people close to her.**

Besides the evidence of her death. This is the last digital evidence Reeva leaves us, as far as I'm aware. Even so, she's right in a sense, *we do see tomorrow*, we are seeing her tomorrow, because since February 14 2013 we've all been seeing glimpses (photos and video of Reeva again and again...

At the time of writing 8 August 2014 (near midnight), I have in my hand a *You* magazine dated 7 August 2014, with 6 pages dedicated to photos of Reeva promoting the Legacy Lifestyle (though of course *You* discreetly calls it a shoot for a 'luxury lifestyle group'). It looks like the magazine have been holding onto this until the last possible moment. Here's the 'classic mode' Reeva wanted to be, this is how she planned to 'reinvent' herself, and yes it's a far cry from the sexy bikini babe in FHM. This is a woman of substance and style, and class. It's easy to see Oscar's shooting, tattoos and boyish bravado doesn't *quite* fit with this kind of branding – it's too brash, too unsophisticated.

There's also a strange irony in these images. They promise a wealth and extravagance, they're alluring, and it's step far beyond where Reeva's life was at the time, but it was a big step towards it. There's also an implicit irony that while Oscar had material wealth, oodles of it, and a dynasty of uncles backing him all the way, Reeva had no such privileges. And yet here she was, a genuine person with a real sense of self, and something rich, and true, and filled with treasure, shining out of her. The world, in February 2013, was just about catching a glimpse of it...

Here's a link to some of those beautiful images:

http://www.nickvanderleek.com/2014/08/you-magazine-finally-comes-to-party-in.html

Incidentally immediately after the article on Reeva is a three page article titled (wait for it) *12 Questions at the heart of the Matter*. So yes, the tabloid media *do* eventually analyse the Oscar case, on the very last days of the trial...hence the questions burning holes in people's pockets.

31. But it was no ordinary night and I suspect if they lay in bed **they slept little if at all**. Reeva certainly didn't sleep. According to Oscar's testimony he may have slept (he also had an early start the previous morning) but Reeva was awake throughout.

32. Oscar and Reeva may have explicitly **decided to go to bed at 10pm**, but it's certain that neither of them slept through from 10pm to 3am. How do we know?
Well there are a few reasons:
   a) Late night fan mail for both Oscar and Reeva to attend to (or ignore)
   b) Late night snipes on how they were or won't going to be working together.
   c) It was hot and humid
   d) Reeva, above all, an intuitive, intelligent, possibly even precognitive soul, may have felt in her gut, that things weren't kosher with Oscar, a sinking feeling...
   e) The alarm system would need to be deactivated and reactivated if Reeva was *not* downstairs
   f) We know Reeva was downstairs eating sometime between 11pm and 1am which reinforces the impression that she may have been downstairs all along (certainly for most of the evening)
   g) based on the objective evidence we know Estelle van der Merwe heard intermittent voices 'that sounded like an argument' for 'about an hour' Finally, there is damage to the bedroom door as well, which suggests either a tussle to get out, or to get in – perhaps to get her keys, perhaps an initial attempt to get out and when that failed, she ran to the toilet. But what we may have is a possible struggle at *two* doorways, not one.

33. **We don't know if this was an automatic connection made by his phone to update an app or if it was an intentional connection made by Oscar – texting?**

    No more phone activity on either phone until the shooting.

33a. Perhaps it was that she went upstairs right around 1:48 or so, and walked in on Oscar chatting with somebody else or doing something on that iPad that she didn't like. We saw the photo in evidence of the <u>right side pillow on the bed in an upright position</u>, indicating that somebody was sitting up in bed.

See top two images at this link:

http://www.nickvanderleek.com/2014/08/juror-13-notes.html

The loud arguing begins (1:56am).

34. **Insomnia** almost certainly made things worse:
    What's possible is that whether or not Reeva was sharing his bed, neither of them could sleep.

    Since Mrs. van der Merwe's bedroom is on the other side of the house, I tend to think that they may have been in the upstairs lounge area outside of Oscar's bedroom and fought over there (with a window open). Reeva may have huffed out of the bedroom and Oscar went after her and they ended up in the lounge OR one of the guest bedrooms – the one that had the used toothbrush in it. I'm pretty sure that room faced the other side of the house.

    But what we get from Oscar's own version is this:

    During the early hours of the morning, I brought two fans in from the balcony.

    It's clear from photos that the fans are placed at the corner of her bed over his prosthetics, to ventilate his prosthetics as one would smelly shoes.

    I had shortly before spoken to Reeva, who was in bed beside me.

    > In other words, in Oscar's version Reeva was awake even when Oscar was sleeping. During his testimony in chief, he notes that when he wakes up, Reeva is already awake (yes, at 3am) and says to him, "Can't you sleep, Baba."

    > Juror13 also highlights the following:

    > Once Reeva had returned to the bedroom (having eaten downstairs) wouldn't Oscar have had to get up to close the bedroom door behind Reeva and lock it **as he does every night? He also put the cricket bat between his sunglass display cabinet and the door. He says the bat fits that space fairly perfectly. The lock mechanism on his door is not very strong. So he uses this bat for extra security up against the door.**

35. It might be that he has a sudden urge for porn, yes, but since it's almost 2 hours into Valentine's Day, it's more likely this **activity** – perhaps **the most critical of the entire timeline** – is due to a late night romantic missive from Erin Joy Shear*

http://lifeissavage.com/2013/05/22/who-is-this-cape-town-blonde-being-questioned-in-oscar-pistorius-case-pic/

Let's face it, porn may cause a number of responses in a woman – disgust, humor, affection.

But getting caught out in a late night Valentine rendezvous while your significant other, who you've been harassing the whole day, is lying next to you? That will definitely be the absolute last straw – for anyone.

You want to move in with me, you want me to join you on your trips, you want me to make sacrifices, my life and my career….while you're cheating on me!

That would be the tone. And there's no coming back from that that night, or for a few days.

The downside to neither of them communicating their plans on social media was that the world didn't know they were spending the night together. Which is why a late night message is not only entirely probable, but more than likely what triggered the last battle between Oscar and Reeva at Bushwillow Crescent.

"Reeva was still awake, she was obviously not sleeping." (How the hell can he make this claim that she was obviously not sleeping when he testified that it was pitch dark, he never saw her, and had only just woken up??) He again fumbled a bit here and then said Reeva rolled over to him and said "can't you sleep my baba". He said no he can't.

[*Update: Jenna Edkins is a more likely candidate than Erin Shear. Oscar contacted Jenna just before 6pm on the 13th of February when he was returning home to Silver Woods…and they spoke for nine minutes. Reeva had passed through the boom gates minutes earlier, and was already at Oscar's home, waiting for him to arrive.

http://www.citypress.co.za/news/police-missed-oscars-chat-ex-hours-shooting-reeva/

I knew he had been seeing his ex, Jenna Edkins – pictures of the two of them together had been posted on her Instagram account just a few weeks earlier. In fact he had been seeing her on and off throughout his relationship with my daughter [Samantha]. – Excerpt from Oscar: An Accident Waiting to Happen

http://www.africanman.co.za/?p=2715

The phone on which Pistorius called Edkins was one of two handsets, and was apparently removed from the crime scene for almost two weeks before it was handed over to the authorities.

By the time it was given in, its entire call history had allegedly been wiped*.

As a result, Edkins was never questioned by the authorities and therefore did not provide a statement.

The apparent addition to Pistorius' story is set to be published in *Behind the Door* – a book about the trial by two leading journalists on the case, Barry Bateman of *Eyewitness News* and Mandy Wiener.

According to Bateman, the prosecution has so far declined to comment on how the evidence was missed.

http://www.independent.co.uk/news/people/oscar-pistorius-made-nine-minute-phone-call-to-exgirlfriend-jenna-edkins-before-he-killed-reeva-steenkamp-new-report-claims-9770353.html

*Who wiped Oscar's phone? Juror13 references reports that a user calling himself 'Titanium Hulk' accessed the phone remotely. 'Titanium Hulk' is an avatar used by Carl Pistorius, Oscar's brother. Further, South African Police found this collage

https://juror13lw.files.wordpress.com/2014/10/jenna-and-op1.png?w=300&h=228

[given by Edkins to Oscar for his birthday] in Oscar's upstairs TV lounge.

https://juror13lw.wordpress.com/2014/10/02/babyshoes-and-titanium-hulk/

Remember: On January 27 2013, just 2 and half weeks before Reeva was killed, at 4:17pm she sent Oscar a Whatsapp that starts: "You have picked on me excessively...I was not flirting with anyone today... I feel sick that you suggested it and that you made a scene ... We are living in a double standards relationship. Every five seconds I hear how you dated another chick. I do everything to make you happy and not to rock the boat with you... You do everything to throw tantrums..."

Oscar responded at 5:01 that he wanted to "sort this out."

http://www.timeslive.co.za/local/2014/03/24/reeva-was-sometimes-scared-of-oscar-whatsapp-messages

...**Update Ends]**

35a. Mrs. VDM heard the arguing starting at 1:56.

36. Between 2am and 3am:

> *Estelle van der Merwe, who lived just under 100 metres from Pistorius' Pretoria house, said she was woken just before 2am on St Valentine's Day by the row, which went on for around an hour before she heard shots fired.* – via The Telegraph's Aislinn Laing
>
> https://www.youtube.com/watch?v=ISnGmwCc9eQ
>
> https://www.youtube.com/watch?v=qkBEJptxIV4
>
> At the second link above, note what Van der Merwe says in Afrikaans at **1:00**:

"Ek het baie beweging [gehoor], op en af...en dit was nie 'n man se stem nie..."

Translation: "I [heard] a lot of up and down movement [pitch] ...and it wasn't a man's voice."

Also notice Oldwage and Roux pulling faces and looking pretty animated in the background whilst van der Merwe is speaking.

As the argument continued and got more heated, closer to 2:50, Reeva goes back in to the bedroom to get her things to leave, and locks the door behind her. Oscar whacks at it with something [a baseball bat?]**, cracking the door.**

http://2.bp.blogspot.com/-ACRW-i5SSgs/U-YfMybgyhI/AAAAAAAdRo/S-6qPvV10rg/s1600/Fullscreen+capture+20140809+031547+PM.jpg

It also seems as though he shoots at the door with an air gun.

http://www.nickvanderleek.com/2014/08/wtf-another-battered-door-and-is-that.html

Reeva is scared. Already screaming... but she's more afraid of what will happen if she doesn't let him in [the bedroom door].

This would also explain the cacophony of bangs, screams and noises leading up to the shooting in the bathroom. The argument is so chaotic it makes it almost impossible for ear witnesses to make sense of, or to establish a cogent timeline for the gunshots. Impossible? No. *Almost* impossible.

37. How do we explain the **blood spatter on the bedroom wall**? Well, it's possible Reeva's nose was bleeding. The blood through her nasal cavity may seem to have flowed due to the head wound, but it might also have been inflicted just prior. She had no blood in her airways, but we know Oscar had his fingers in her airways. We also have this image:

http://i.ytimg.com/vi/ApE65nCQYdA/hqdefault.jpg

37a. http://2.bp.blogspot.com/-5fDtRvcEqM8/U-YZnLcF44I/AAAAAAAdRA/kCnkaw8a5VM/s1600/pistorius-door.jpg

38. Reeva's weathered violent men before, with her mother, with **a door as an effective barrier** keeping the intruders away. But this time it wouldn't be enough.

Reeva tries to reason, to bargain with Oscar through the door. She tells Oscar he can't force her to stay, tells him that she's terrified. That he's out of control. Tells him she won't tell the media because it's also her brand, her reputation on the line. But she wants to leave. He has to let her go!

Is it here that Reeva throws her jeans out the window, or has she done so already?

Or did Oscar throw Reeva's jeans out the window somewhere during the long hour long argument…to prevent her from getting dressed. The latter seems more likely. Are there car keys in the jeans? Where were *they*? But what we do know beyond a shadow of a doubt, is Reeva has her *phone* with her.

38a. Shots were likely right around 3:15, as Dr. Stipp got through to Baba to report the shots at 3:15:51.

38b. He can hear the phone. He can hear her. He can probably see her too through a crack – already made – in the door. Holding the wall with one hand, the firearm in the other hand, he fires at her hip, and to her right, where it would be if she were standing and waiting for her call to connect. And he hits his intended target.

39. **Bullet A.** Michelle Burger testified about a long pause after the first shot (1-3 seconds)
40. **Bullet B.** *4.5 The discharging of my firearm was precipitated by a noise in the toilet, which I, in my fearful state, knowing that I was on my stumps, unable to run away or properly defend my self physically, believed to be the intruder/s coming out of the toilet to attack Reeva and me.*
41. **Bullet C** to her arm (which effectively amputates it) and **D** to the top of her head, and the tips of two fingers, as Reeva takes a defensive position.

The defensive posture alone illustrates that the shooting could not have occurred without Reeva screaming, as she had time to respond to the first shot, and attempt to defend herself. This pause, also reinforces the case for a premeditated adjustment of aim, before firing the last, fatal gunshots.

Juror13: One important point that I originally missed with Burger's testimony (so it's not in my blog) but picked up on from discussions on Websleuths, is that during cross-examination, Burger told Oldwage that the toilet room window looked slightly illuminated. She could see full light on in the bathroom, but as we know from testimony, the toilet room light was broken. The toilet room should have been pitch black. Yet, Burger did see what she thought was some light in that small toilet room window. The only way for that to be possible is either the door was slightly open, or there were cracks in the door letting some light in!

If that's the case... that could substantiate the bat hitting the door at 3am, and making some cracks, but not losing any panels. And then we know Oscar shot through those panels closer to 3:15am, and tore the panels out afterwards.

Check out the pictures of the window from outside at night time, to see what I mean about the lighting.

42. Time the bullets were fired is between 03:14 and 03:17 according to the state, the defence says 3:19. Oscar calls Stander at 03:18/19

    When Oscar called at **3:19 a.m.**, he was asleep (Really? Carice wasn't.). Oscar said, "Johan, please, please come to my house. I shot Reeva. I thought she was an intruder." Stander and his daughter Carice got in their car and drove over.

http://www.talkleft.com/story/2014/5/5/41932/90596/crimenews/Oscar-Pistorius-Trial-Resumes-Estate-Manager-Testifies

43. Dr Johan Stipp, his wife and Oscar corroborate that a man **shouted help three times, after gunshots** were fired. This makes perfect sense.

    Juror13 has offered another possibility. She says Oscar may not have gone to the balcony to shout *at all*, but shouted it from the bathroom window; hence Dr Stipp was able to hear it but Estelle van der Merwe wan't. **Juror13** speculates that the fan was in the way...

    I am not sure if I agree with **Juror13** on this one. If Oscar's modus operandi was indeed to immediately cover up the crime, his first priority was to break down that door, and to do that he'd need his legs. His legs were right beside the balcony door. There is also – to my mind – clear furrow through the centre of the duvet which resembles a path. Further, Nel spoke of blood spatter on the duvet. This implies that Oscar may have made *several* trips to this point (over the duvet) including, one would imagine, after he dragged Reeva out of the toilet, soiled his prosthetic legs and then went to fetch *his* phone. Unless of course he went from the toilet door, to fetch his legs and phone, and en route, shouted 'Help' three times.

    Also, Michelle Burger said she heard a man shouting 'Help' three times.

    43a. I'm not sure on this – seems a little bit too over the top. I know we've discussed the point that there doesn't seem to be as much blood as one would think from this type of shooting. But I think a lot of it from her head naturally drained in to the bowl on its own as she lay slumped over the toilet for minutes possibly? Also, there were quite a few bloody towels in the bathroom that could have absorbed more.

    http://www.nickvanderleek.com/2014/08/not-bloody-enough.html

44. *Roux says OP made a* **call to security cell number at 03.21.33.** *Baba: That was time OP called me but he was crying too much.*
    http://sports.nationalpost.com/2014/03/06/weeping-oscar-pistorius-said-prayer-tried-to-help-girlfriend-breathe-after-shooting-witness-testifies-in-murder-trial/

45. **The amount of blood on the crime scene**, given Reeva's injuries (especially the near amputated arm), is actually very little, bearing in mind it is a tiled surface with nowhere for the blood to drain to or be soaked up in.

    As a retired head-mechanic, the **Narcissistic PD hypothesis** has been going through my mind for quite some time.

    The behaviour, verbal and non-verbal, fits the clinical profile.

    Watching the de-compensation, however, is not a pretty sight. Hence, I do get the sense that **Oscar's PTS 'suffering' is genuine** although **it does not fall under the umbrella of heart-felt remorse.** – Robyn Burger

46. Note Carice misspelt by eNCA here:

Clarice Stander, said Pistorius, asked the athlete if he had any plastic bags or tape or something she could use to stop the bleeding from the wounds.

Pistorius said he directed her to a utility room, but testified that he could not remember whether he or Clarice had fetched the plastic bags that were later found around Steenkamp's body.

It was after these events that Stipp arrived, said Pistorius. Stipp entered the house and **Pistorius described the doctor as being appeared "overwhelmed" and "unsure" of what he was doing.**

He said Stipp walked outside and **Pistorius shouted to him to come back and help**.

Thereafter, Pistorius recalled that paramedics arrived and asked for space to work, prompting Pistorius to step back.

Breaking down in tears again, **Pistorius said he realised Steenkamp had died in his arms**. He said he stepped back and a female paramedic approached him and told him that "Reeva has passed".

47. Via the Digitalspy online forum: Oscar asks Stander to take Reeva in his car to Hospital, Oscar has brought, Reeva downstairs, Stander says no, I'll call ambulance, Security and Dr Stipp(neighbour) arrive Stipp asks if ambulance has been called, it hasn't , Stander calls ambulance, passes phone to Stipp to explain injuries, he can't help her so he leaves before police and ambulance arrived. Then on way out he sees Mrs Stander, who says 'hope this doesn't get out to media'. !!!!

If Oscar had already called Netcare after calling Standers which is in his statement, but his statement is vague, no times ------why did Stander have to call them again?

Oscar asked Mr. Stander to **take his car and transport the deceased to the hospital**. Carice recounted her father said he was not going to take Reeva, they would rather wait for an ambulance & medical people who would give assistance.

Carice informed the officer she was the one who went to get plastic bags to try & stop the bleeding. She asked Oscar to get something else to stop the bleeding, the officer was not sure if she or Oscar went on his own to the 1st floor. Where they had gone for extra towels, together they tried to stop the bleeding.

According to Carice that's when her father called the paramedics.

Similar to the restaurant shooting Oscar remained silent while someone else explained what happened.

http://forums.digitalspy.co.uk/showthread.php?p=71844537

47a. Stander had arrived at 3:22-3:23. It's likely that Stander and his daughter were both surprised to see Stipp, but not as surprised as Oscar was. Stipps arrival at 03:35 is ten minutes after he heard the shots, plenty of time to get dressed, make a detour to the gatehouse and reach Oscar's house (which is only a few hundred metres away from his own).

48. http://www.news24.com/SouthAfrica/Oscar_Pistorius/Live/LIVE-UPDATES-Pistorius-on-trial-day-5-part-2-20140307 **14:21-14:28**:

   Baba: Stander didn't even greet me, he ran directly to the house.

   PB: No one opened the door for us. Mrs Stander opened the door and went in. Mr Stander stood at the door.

   PB: we followed him. As we arrived Pistorius came down the stairs with Reeva. I was so shocked that I couldn't even think for a few moments."

   PB: I was so shocked because OP told me everything was fine and I arrived to find him carrying Reeva down.

   Stander told me to call the police and ambulance, says PB.

49. Will Stander mop up his home while Oscar takes Reeva to hospital, or will Stander be playing taxi?
50. This pretence, this cover-up, this 'mockery' took seconds after Bullet A was fired and has been maintained, at various levels throughout the trial. In some cases, yes, there is real regret. There is real sorrow. But it is not regret for Reeva's lost life, but his own. And not sorrow for her, but himself.
51. **03:55:02 – Outgoing call to 8888 (Justin Devaris) – 123 seconds**

Another GPRS for 83 seconds
04:01:38 – Outgoing call to 7775 (Deco – Heinrich Pistorius) – 54 seconds
2 more GPRS connections
04:09:03 – Outgoing call to 6940 (Peet Van Zyl) – 11 seconds
04:09:42 – Outgoing call to 6940 (Peet Van Zyl) – 13 seconds
04:10:21 – Outgoing call to 6940 (Peet Van Zyl) – 3 seconds
04:11:25 – Incoming call from 6940 (Peet Van Zyl) – 49 seconds

   A few more GPRS connections

Then after this time, all incoming calls were diverted to the voice mailbox center. No outgoing calls were made. The phone was pinging to the tower closest to Oscar's up until 8:00am and then it left the location

   Final Note: Oscar couldn't have been *in* bed when he heard Reeva in the bathroom, because the duvet is *under* the jeans. Unless they were thrown there subsequently, by Oscar or a policeman tampering with the scene. But the duvet and the jeans look like they landed just as they fell…

   Additional Background:

   http://www.iol.co.za/news/crime-courts/oscar-tells-his-side-of-fateful-night-1.1655690#.U98_fRCSxOg

   http://forums.digitalspy.co.uk/showthread.php?p=71844537

http://www.websleuths.com/forums/showthread.php?238286-Oscar-Pistorius-Defense/page41

http://www.websleuths.com/forums/showthread.php?240029-Trial-Discussion-Thread-17&p=10408745#post10408745

http://www.latimes.com/world/africa/la-fg-pistorius-trial-20140804-story.html#page=1

http://www.biznews.com/health-biznews-com/2014/05/oscar-pistorius-performance-may-prove-mental-state/

http://www.biznews.com/oscar-pistorius-trial/2014/06/oscar-really-stumps-shot-reeva/

And now that we are at the end of a life, let's step back and have a look at where it all started. Pause. Reflect. Because it can so easily go wrong, and for Oscar, it has.

http://www.nickvanderleek.com/2014/08/oscar-early-days.html

The best we can do is look at it carefully, and then put it away. We can do that when we've learned the lessons of this narrative.

I think we have learnt a few, haven't we? For in these lessons lie the vital essence that is *REVELATION*. Apply them, remember them and the result can only be a *well-lived life*. Better, perhaps, than we may have lived otherwise. And we receive this gift of a better life by taking notice of someone else. Someone young and beautiful who had her life stolen from her. Someone who lost her life, someone who would have been just 31 years old this month.

Juror13 Annexure

Timeline

He says he's finishing off at (with) Ryan. This is his real estate agent. Oscar testified that he had to meet up with him to do some paperwork. What he did not say in testimony is that he actually attended a birthday party for Firzt Realty. Even though he was needing to be consoled just a few hours earlier, he was apparently happy-go-lucky at this party...
*An estate agent who attended a party with Pistorius on the **evening** of Feb 13 — hours before the shooting said he was **"delightful, charming and happy".***
Valerie Berkow-Kaye said: "We were all mesmerised by such a smiley, delightful person. He certainly wasn't planning a murder on Wednesday afternoon."

15:41:54 – Reeva - Incoming voice call from 4949 (Oscar) – 93 seconds – tower closest to Oscar's house

15:46 RS: Angel **I'm going to go home at like 6pm. Please stay and do whatever it was you were gonna do.**

I take this to mean she is going to <u>her</u> home. At this time she was still at Oscar's house, per tower pinging. Oscar calls her 8 minutes later while he is with Justin and Samantha G at Justin's dealership in Johannesburg... probably to convince her to stay at his house and he will come home.

15:54:27 – Reeva - Incoming voice call from 0020 (Oscar) – 113 seconds (2 min) – tower closest to Oscar's house (she's still at his house).

Takes her 45 minutes to cancel.

16: 45 Reeva emails Nimue Skin Technology SA. She is an ambassador for them and apologises that she won't be attending the announcement of a new jewellery line. (source: Nick van der Leek, Resurrection). So at this point, she has decided not to go to this event and apparently has decided to have dinner with Oscar at his house instead?

On the 13th of February, 2013, Justin invited the applicant (Oscar) to stay over in Johannesburg for a boys' dinner. The applicant had spoken to Reeva and decided to go to Pretoria and spend the night with the deceased. (source:
http://transcripts.cnn.com/TRANSCRIPTS/1302/22/sp.03.html)

On the 13th of February 2013, Samantha messaged Reeva to watch a movie with her in Johannesburg and <u>she said she would come back to her and later meet Oscar.</u> **The applicant (Oscar) who called Reeva suggested they stay home in Pretoria**. (source: http://transcripts.cnn.com/TRANSCRIPTS/1302/22/sp.03.html)

In testimony, Oscar claimed that Reeva suggested they stay in at his place in Pretoria to have dinner. Conflicting statements here.

17:12:57 – Reeva - Incoming voice call from 0020 (Oscar) – 63 seconds – tower closest to Oscar's house

Reeva has some more GPRS activity

17:30:46 – Oscar - GPRS – 254 seconds (4+ min) – Midrand Gardens tower

As Oscar made more GPRS connections during this time frame, the towers indicated that he was moving closer towards his home.

17:44:54 – Reeva - Outgoing call to 0020 (Oscar) – 144 seconds (2.5 min) – she had moved from his house, now pinging from a different tower. Where was she going? Oscar testified that she went out to get groceries for their dinner.

17:56:51 – Oscar - Incoming call from 7775 ~~(Henke/Dad)~~ – 307 seconds (5 min) – Mustek George Rd tower

[**Correction November 2014**: In fact this was a call to Heinrich = Carl Pistorius, Oscar's brother, and not his father. It was possibly to confirm that he would not be joining his family for dinner as per Reeva's suggestion....]

http://www.iol.co.za/news/crime-courts/oscar-s-frantic-calls-after-shooting-reeva-1.1665841#.VGWzHPmUfTo

~~Why are Oscar and his Dad communicating? I thought they were estranged.~~ I find this interesting, considering that earlier in the day *Reeva was suggesting that Oscar spend time with his family due to what he needed consoling over*.

18:07:22 – Oscar - Outgoing call to 5937 (possibly Alex P, his friend?) – 522 seconds (8 minutes) – Volpatron CelC NGA tower

Baba testified that Oscar was on a cell call when he was driving through the main gate. He arrived home around 18:15 (6:15pm).

18:47:59 – Oscar - Outgoing call to 7775 (~~Henke/Dad~~ Heinrich/Carl) – 56 seconds – tower closest to Oscar's

Why is he calling him again? At this point (6:47pm), according to his testimony, he was home and upstairs while Reeva was downstairs cooking. He never mentioned making a phone call to his ~~Dad~~ brother during testimony.

Oscar arrived home shortly after 6pm. He parked his car in the driveway and went to the front door and it was locked and the dogs were running around the house. He started to say "the door was locked..." and the Judge cut him off and asked him to slow down. He then starts up again and says Reeva was cooking dinner in the kitchen. For some reason he abandoned that previous sentence. Oscar chatted with Reeva for a short time then went upstairs to shower and change. He changed in to his pajamas. He started to say that he went downstairs at 7pm then Roux jumps in and asks him if he had access to his iPad that evening.

Oscar says yes he had access to his iPad all day. Roux says no, he means only that night. Oscar really fumbles here. He starts to say again that Reeva was in the kitchen (almost as if this part is rehearsed), but he says he was also talking on his iPad… then he says he was surfing the net… he was looking at cars that he wanted to get around to that day to get a look at…

Then the iPad is upstairs with him while he is drawing his bath. He may have even used it while he was in the bath. He took off his suit on the bed and he used it there again. It was really hard to understand exactly what he was doing with it. His sentences were very broken and honestly didn't make a lot of sense. (probably for two reasons – he knows that the court is going to see the porn from the iPad records, and he is also not telling the whole truth of that day – his nervousness and fumbling is very telling)

Oscar says he stopped using it when he went down for dinner. Oscar and Reeva started dinner shortly after 7pm. Roux tells him due to website activity he can see an open period from about 7:10pm to 8:00pm, so is that the time that they were having dinner and Oscar says that sounds about right. (nice "leading" questions here… apparently SA is a little more liberal with this)

They'd argued for the past hour – about her not joining Oscar in Manchester.

Interesting that Oscar did not call Peet but it's likely if Peet was emailing, Oscar may have contacted PVZ by email (subsequent correspondence could easily be erased later, by both parties)

7:29pm – Peet Van Zyl is emailing the director of the Manchester event to get a ticket for Reeva. This is during their dinner, and when Oscar claims they are discussing HER contracts. Is this the conflict/the real meat of their argument that ties in to what Oscar needed consoling about earlier? – her contracts vs. his contracts + traveling abroad = somebody is going to have to make a sacrifice.

Per Van Zyl in testimony, the reason that Oscar wanted to take Reeva on his trips was: "I actually want Miss Steenkamp to see what my world is about... so she can understand why I can't go to events or functions with her... events I can't go to due to my own sponsor commitments"

20:04:00 – Reeva - GPRS – 17 seconds – tower closest to Oscar's. This is the text message from Reeva to Gina and Cecil saying that she is too tired to drive, going to spend the night at Oscar's. Tone suggests too stressed for usual cheerful signoff that was typical of Reeva's messages to people close to her.

Oscar testified that Reeva texted her friend implying it was in afternoon, early evening to let her know she was staying. Inference is that she intended to stay with him all along. Another inconsistency. She only decided at 8pm to stay, she had intended to leave at 6. Possible they argued for 2 hours, then reconciled.

20:04:17 – Reeva's last GPRS activity – 41,029 seconds (**over 11 hours**) – tower closest to Oscar's. This application remained opened throughout the incident and in to the next day. No details of what this application was, or its contents, were openly discussed in court. The Judge however does have access to this information.

Back to Oscar's testimony… He says that typically they watch TV downstairs after dinner but they **both had a taxing day** and so they decided to go upstairs. Again, a red flag to me that all was not the norm that night. They are off their usual schedule.

He helped her with the plates. Reeva asked him if he wanted anything else to drink, a coffee or a tea, and he said yes. This was a really odd tidbit that he threw in here. Why even mention this detail? It feels very well placed to me. Oscar went upstairs and Reeva joined him a few minutes later.

Around 8pm, Oscar opened the balcony doors in his bedroom because it was a very humid evening. Let's stop here. They are back upstairs at 8pm? He just testified that dinner started after 7pm, maybe 7:10pm and that consisted of both eating and review/discussion about contracts. That's a fairly brief time to be going over important stuff like that.

He goes on to say that contractors had been working on his house for some time. His air conditioning was not working and it was one of the things on their list. He has two fans; a silver tripod fan and a small plastic fan. He placed the back leg of the tripod fan out on the balcony and the other two legs just inside the sliding door. The small fan was placed in between the legs of the tripod fan below it. (So he never went out on the balcony as was stated in his bail affidavit)

He closed the doors up to the edge of the fans. There are insects outside so he was trying to minimize the open space for them to fly in. He drew the curtains so that they were draped around the side of the standing fan, again to try to seal off as much open air as possible. They are black-out curtains. When they are drawn, it's virtually pitch-black even during the day.

At this time, one of the lights in the room was on. Reeva came in to the room. He took his drink and put it on the bedside table (there's that coffee cup again that is so important to mention!)

Reeva was on her phone on social media, occasionally showing him pictures of cars and interior decorating, things that she liked. He very specifically added "things that she liked". The iPads are going to come up in cross-examination.

Since he and his cousin were continually texting back and forth, he figured he'd just call him at that point.

20:25:07 – Oscar - Outgoing call to 3964 (Graham, cousin) – 1,757 seconds (29 min) – tower closest to Oscar's. This was the last voice call made prior to the shooting. Graham and Oscar both testified that they chatted about cars, etc.

His cousin's name is Graham. He was coming out for a business engagement. They were chatting about cars, a mutual interest.

While Oscar is on the phone, Reeva got out of bed and was doing yoga stretches on the floor. He had the phone on speaker. Every now and again Reeva would lean up and give him a kiss.

Now, if Oscar and Reeva had been arguing about contracts just an hour or two earlier, would she be lovey dovey and kissing him. I highly doubt it. Graham did not testify, all we have to go off of is his bail affidavit and Oscar's testimony. I think Oscar greatly embellished when he said that Reeva was kissing him. She very well may have been in the other room doing her yoga, blowing off steam.

There was a brittle tension between the two. They'd argued, they'd surrendered but it was a fragile peace. Testimony is disassociated, very little quotes from what was actually said, which implies most of what was said he can't repeat, because it would make him look bad.

He says he talked to his cousin for a half hour. When the hung up, Reeva got up and walked to the bathroom.

Then, at around 9pm or 10 pm they settled in for the night.

Oscar testified: When asked when he fell asleep he first says just after 9pm. Then he says between 9pm and 10pm.

Since Oscar was often up at 5am, 9pm or 10pm sounds right (that would be an 8 hour sleep). But it was no ordinary night and I suspect while thjey lay in bed, he couldn't sleep, was anxious, and this failure to sleep on his part, was an additional irritant adding to the interminable tension that was welling up that Valentine's eve.

He closed the bedroom door behind Reeva and locked it as he does every night. He also put the cricket between his sunglass display cabinet and the door. He says the bat fits that space fairly perfectly. The lock mechanism on his door is not very strong. So he uses this bat for extra security up against the door.

The house has an alarm system. It does not have door monitors but it has outside sensors. The sensors are battery operated, not wired. When his house was painted in 2010, they had taken all of the eyes off of the outside walls. His house was currently in the process of being re-painted and he was having troubles with the sensors. He goes on to explain how if you take one of the sensors off the wall before you activate it, it doesn't have a memory to remember what was in its scope the previous time it was activated. It was another confusing explanation that felt very forced. (WAY OVERKILL on the alarm description – he is explaining away something that wasn't even asked of him… providing an excuse before he even needs to)

But nevertheless, he did put his alarm on every night and activated it with the remote on his house keys. He pushed the button every night.

So if we take a tally… the air conditioning is broken so he must use fans on the balcony, the bedroom door locks are not good so he has to wedge a cricket bat in at night, his alarm system is unreliable yet he still activates it every night but it probably won't work. There are a lot of coincidences brewing and for somebody who has a paid live-in helper, I find it odd that so many things are not functioning properly.

He then takes his legs off at the bottom of the bed to give them some air. He put them next to the bed and climbed in to the bed, and Reeva got in to bed as well. The TV was on and he was texting with his cousin in Port Elizabeth. (the problem here is that later in cross examination he testified that he placed his legs on the right side of the bed that is closest to the door... yet here he is supposedly sleeping on the left and he stated that he took his legs off and got in to bed – that implies they were on the left side – inconsistent!)

[Nel --- use graphic to show Oscar's various versions for how he moved, and then the state's version]

While Reeva was in the bathroom she called Oscar to come brush his teeth. This really struck me as odd. I don't know anybody who tells a grown man to come brush his teeth. He walked to the bathroom without his legs on and brushed his teeth. (according to later witness testimony, Oscar does not walk on tile floor on his stumps due to pain and instability – therefore logic states that he would have brushed his teeth before taking his legs off).

While he was doing that, she went back to the bedroom. When he went back in the bedroom, she was in bed and he walked to the closest side of the bed (the left side) and got in.

He explains that earlier in the evening when he got home, he put his gun under the bed next to the attached pedestal (nightstand). When he got in to bed that night, he got in on the left side, the same side where his gun was. He didn't usually sleep on the left but because of his shoulder injury he couldn't sleep on his right side. He had been sleeping on the left side for a few weeks.

Shortly after, he started falling asleep. It was very warm in the room. Reeva was sitting up with her back against the headboard. (I believe he added this in because the pillows on the bed show the right side pillow in an upward position – implying that somebody had been up all night, not sleeping) He was lying with his head on her stomach watching TV. She would show him photos every now and again. He was getting increasingly tired. He asked her if she would bring in the fans, close the curtains and lock the door when she was getting ready to sleep, and she said she would.

Roux stops him there and wants to talk about Valentine's Day, which would be the next day. He asks Oscar if there was a gift for him.

Well, there was:

He was going to open it but Reeva told him that he wasn't allowed to open it until the next day. He goes on to say that on August 8th of last year, on Reeva's birthday, he opened it. It was a photo frame that had 4 photos of the two of them. **It was pointed out on Twitter today that Reeva's birthday is actually August 19th, not August 8th.**

I think Oscar misunderstood the question because he then talked about **what he got Reeva**. He says in pretty much this exact order... he bought her a bracelet from a designer that she really liked earlier in the year. He hadn't made any plans for Reeva for Valentine's Day. He had a dentist appointment the next morning. Reeva wasn't supposed to stay at his house on the 13th. So the plan was to meet her in Johannesburg at this jewelry store. The bracelet had a couple of charms on it. There were two bracelets he bought her. They had an agreement that they would not make a big deal out of Valentine's

Day. They were just going to have dinner. That was a nice evening for them to just be alone at home.

My opinion here again is that his answer made no sense at all and he was greatly fumbling all over the place. It felt like he couldn't remember his script or was making shit up, and was just blurting out words. What does a dentist appointment have to do with anything? The question was whether or not there was a gift.

Why is the bracelet still at the jewelry store? Why did he say he bought it earlier in the year when it's only February… that would have just been a few weeks ago. Why did he suddenly say there were two bracelets? I'm really scratching my head to understand his answer. The only way I can process this is that it's not genuine.

Roux then refocuses him and asks him specifically if she bought him something. He says there was a wrapped present with a card that said Ozzy on the kitchen counter when he got home that night.

01:48:48am Feb 14 – Oscar - GPRS – 309 seconds (5 min) – tower closest to Oscar's

We don't know if this was an automatic connection made by his phone to update an app or if it was an intentional connection made by Oscar – texting?

No more phone activity on either phone until the shooting.

Some notes from the bail hearing

On the 13th of February 2013, at 10 past 8:00 that evening, the applicant and Graham exchanged various messages on what's up. The applicant phoned the deponent at about 25 past 8:00 and they spoke mostly about cars as they shared a common interest.

Graham wanted to bring his new VW up to Pretoria and Oscar suggested that he shouldn't as there was a high risk of hijacking to this type of vehicle at one of the nearby complexes. The applicant told Graham he bought a new house in Johannesburg (source: http://transcripts.cnn.com/TRANSCRIPTS/1302/22/sp.03.html)

Back to that night… he is in bed without his prosthetics. Roux asks him what he was wearing. He says he was wearing basketball shorts and a grey vest (t-shirt). He then says to climb in to bed he took off his grey t-shirt and put it on top of his prosthetic legs (the grey shirt was found on the floor of the right side of the bed). So he only slept in his shorts.

"Reeva was still awake, she was obviously not sleeping." (How the hell can he make this claim that she was obviously not sleeping when he testified that it was pitch dark, he never saw her, and had only just woken up??) He again fumbled a bit here and then said Reeva rolled over to him and said "can't you sleep my baba". He said no he can't.

Oscar then says "My Lady, that's the moment that everything changed".

Everything did change in a moment.

He immediately thought he needed to arm himself to protect **he** and Reeva.

Stopping the phone call was for his own good, and hers, in his estimation.

SIDE NOTE - He (Botha) checked all the phones and discovered that no calls had been made. (source: http://transcripts.cnn.com/TRANSCRIPTS/1302/22/sp.03.html)

I believe that this is why Oscar left his other unused phone (the 4949 number) in that bathroom, and also why he picked up Reeva's phone to check it. He expected the cops to check the phones right there on the scene to see if there was any incriminating evidence. He knew there wouldn't be. Reeva was not able to call the cops (he prevented her from doing that) and the phone that he had been using (the 0020 number) was taken by someone close to him. It was not turned over to the police until 11 days later, after the bail hearing. I think Oscar believed that the police wouldn't look any further than a quick check of his phones that day. Based on him calling Stander so quickly, and call his lawyer/family/agent/manager so quickly, he thought it would all be dismissed without further interrogation.

It was an accident, case closed.

In his bail statement he actually states that he cannot fathom (paraphrasing) how the police could charge him with murder. That statement alone shows his state of mind.

The Old Man in <u>The Words</u>: "*You think you can just steal a [wo]man's life and expect there to be no price to pay ...?*"

Annexures For Further Reading:

http://www.oscarpistorius.com/downloads/Oscar-Pistorius-Heads-of-Argument.pdf

http://www.independent.co.uk/news/world/africa/oscar-pistorius-trial-athletes-bail-hearing-affidavit-in-full-9249107.html

http://www.cnn.com/interactive/2014/03/world/document-pistorius-plea-statement/

http://oscarpistorius.com/downloads/Oscar-Pistorius-Heads-of-Argument.pdf

http://www.scribd.com/doc/236123916/Oscar-Pistorius-trial-State-s-heads-of-argument

http://www.oscarpistorius.com/downloads/jn-divaris-statement.pdf

About the Author

<u>Nick van der Leek</u> *is a storyteller, photographer and editor with an unconventional background. Instead of journalism he studied law, economics and brand management. His writing career started online, as a blogger in South Korea and a citizen journalist for Seoul-based Ohmynews International. After cutting his teeth in Rosebank, Johannesburg in AVUSA (now Times Media)newsroom, he became a full-time writer and photographer, and today he is one of South Africa's most diverse and successful freelancers.*

Although he has a penchant for research and analysis his passion is creating, analysing and leveraging narratives. He is currently working on a biographical narrative, as well as a post-apocalyptic novel set in Scotland. Besides these he is a passionate sportsman. In another life he climbed Kilimanjaro and completed the Ironman. These days his pursuits are more modest: trying to run 10km in under 50 minutes.

In preparing this narrative Nick van der Leek has also prepared a script (a dramatic story) in order to provide an emotional reality and cinematic quality of the incident. However some readers and reviewers – including Juror13 – felt it felt too fictional, too contrived and departed possibly too far from the facts.

For those readers interested in reading this Script, and equally, fine-tuning it, please email the author at nickvanderleek@gmail.com. *If you simply wish to read it enter the words:*

<u>Revelations Script Request</u>

Otherwise enter:

<u>Revelations Script fine-tune</u>

If and when the Script is 'perfect' (and also meets Juror13's standards of excellence) it may be appended to this eBook and all contributors will be credited.

Thanks for reading. Please do review this work on Amazon as this helps with rankings and marketability. Please also tweet your views, comments and insights from this narrative. Follow the author on twitter: @HiRezLife

Additional content is available at www.AfricanMAN.co.za

Find out more about the author here: http://www.nickvanderleek.com/2004_07_01_archive.html

Lastly, look out for announcements on twitter, for the 5th ~~and probably last~~ in this series, *RESTITUTIO*, coming 10 September!

www.ingramcontent.com/pod-product-compliance
Lightning Source LLC
Chambersburg PA
CBHW051801170526
45167CB00005B/1837